IMAGES
of Rail

NASHVILLE'S STREETCARS AND INTERURBAN RAILWAYS

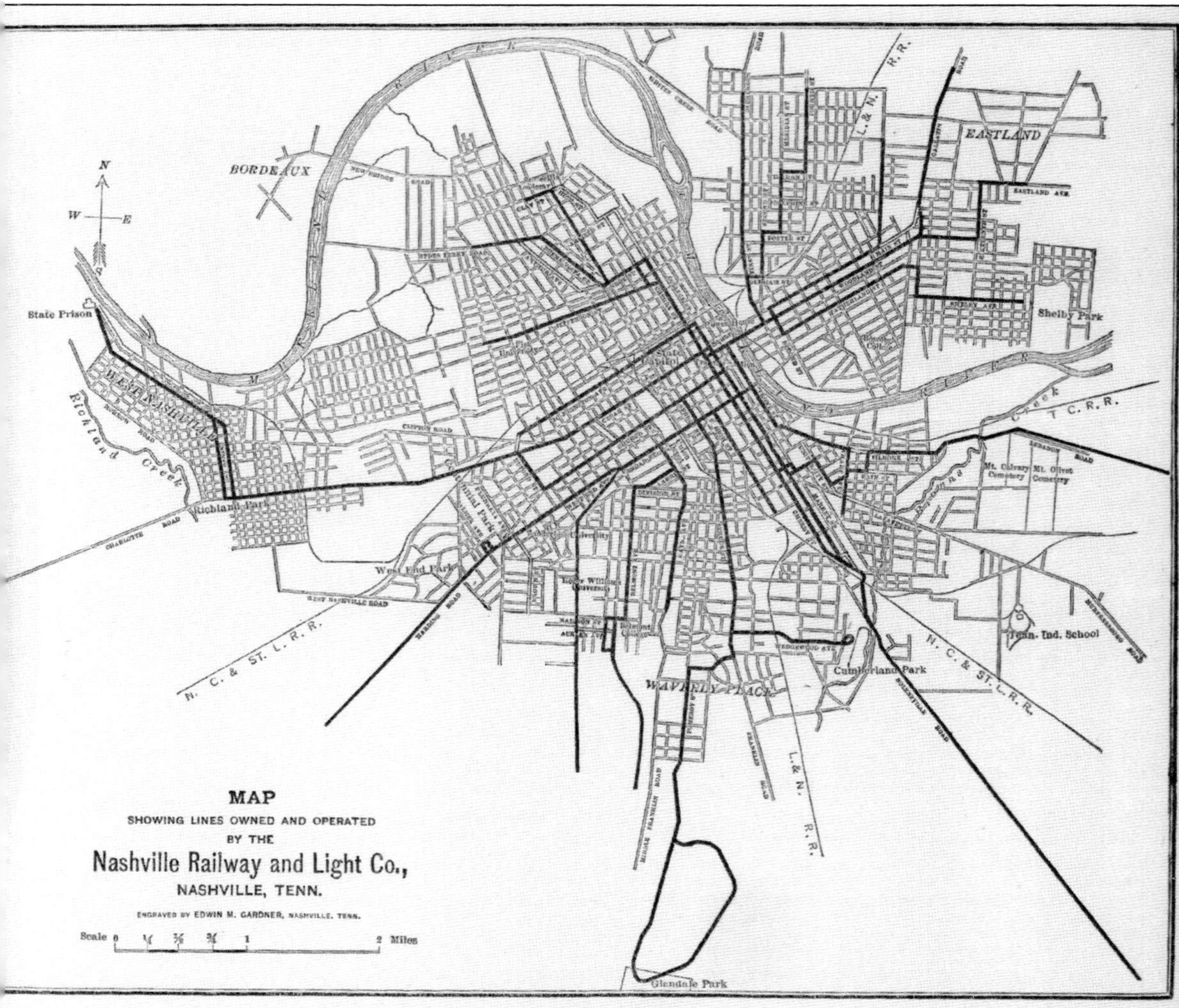

This map depicts Nashville's street railway system at its zenith in 1912, when all service was provided by the Nashville Railway & Light Company (NR&L). The various branches diverged from the downtown Transfer Station, serving virtually all areas of the city and linking major employers, universities, stores, the state fairgrounds, and even the NR&L-owned Glendale Park and Zoo. (Nashville Public Library, Special Collections.)

On the Cover: On October 29, 1926, Nashville citizens crowd Eighth Avenue in downtown Nashville to get a closer look at 15 streetcars on public display. The event, sponsored by NR&L, was the Pageant of Transportation Progress, celebrating 60 years of streetcar service in the city and inaugurating 10 new "Noiseless" electric cars delivered days earlier. The cars in this view comprised many types of equipment dating from the first mule-drawn car, at left, through the various generations of cars. This view looks south towards Broadway from Church Street. Nashville's Hume-Fogg High School and US Customs House are visible in the distance. (Nashville Public Library, Special Collections.)

IMAGES
of Rail

Nashville's Streetcars and Interurban Railways

Ralcon Wagner

ARCADIA
PUBLISHING

ISBN 978-1-4671-1686-2

Published by Arcadia Publishing
Charleston, South Carolina

Printed in the United States of America

Library of Congress Control Number: 2016932934

For all general information, please contact Arcadia Publishing:
Telephone 843-853-2070
Fax 843-853-0044
E-mail sales@arcadiapublishing.com
For customer service and orders:
Toll-Free 1-888-313-2665

Visit us on the Internet at www.arcadiapublishing.com

To Rita, my wife and best friend, without whose inspiration and encouragement this book could not have been written.

Contents

ACKNOWLEDGMENTS

For any project like this to be successful, there is always a group of dedicated and talented people with a passion for keeping history alive who are instrumental in helping to put all the pieces together. I gratefully acknowledge the many great folks who helped to bring this history to print.

First and foremost, my gratitude goes out to the professional staff at the Nashville Public Library, my initial contact for getting the photographs and information needed. This includes the staff of the Metro Nashville Archives: Ken Fieth, Drew Mahan, Kelly Sirko, and Leanne Garland. Also, equally important, was the support from Andrea Blackman, Elizabeth Odle, and Tracey Howerton of the Special Collections Division. The staff of the Tennessee State Library and Archives and Ann Toplovich of the Tennessee Historical Society were also very helpful.

Special thanks to Bryan Turner for providing additional photography and technical assistance and to Arthur Ezell for providing input and materials and for sharing his memories of riding Nashville's streetcars.

I wish to express my thanks and gratitude to Henry Clougherty, Katie McAlpin-Owens, Ginny Rasmussen, and Lydia Rollins of Arcadia Publishing for their continued encouragement and patience from the beginning.

Last but not least, I would like to recognize two scholars of local public transit history. James D. Le Croy, whose eye for detail on the technical aspects has been vital to the accuracy of this tome, supplied important images, maps, and other documents and spent hours assisting me with proofing and fact-checking the captions. And, very importantly, author and historian David H. Steinberg shared his decades' worth of research and knowledge on Nashville streetcars and interurban railways, which were the catalyst for this book from the start. Without his vision and incentive to preserve historical documents destined for the trash bin, this history would have been lost forever. David wanted to write this book!

Introduction

When attempting to sum up the 75 years of Nashville's rich streetcar history in a few pages, it is difficult to know where to begin. To adequately cover the detailed history of the myriad of street railways incorporated to serve the city is not practical within these confines. What follows is a condensed version of a bigger story, illustrated using a compilation of rare photographs, many published here for the first time.

Nashville, from its founding in 1779 through the early Victorian years, was small enough that citizens could easily walk any place they needed to go. If one was not affluent enough to own or hire horse transportation, walking on foot was the only alternative. This did not present a major problem while the young city was relatively compact. By the 1860s, with some 20,000 residents, Nashville had become large enough that some kind of public transportation facilities were being seriously contemplated. In 1865, with the Civil War over, the South had taken a tremendous pounding, but Nashville had grown explosively, not having been destroyed by war.

On May 29, 1866, just a little over a year after Appomattox, Memphis, Tennessee, became the first city in the state to show off its initial horsecar line. Nashville, the state's capital city, wasted no time in following suit. The South Nashville Street Railroad Company, the initial mule-powered streetcar line, opened on August 25, 1866. During the inaugural trip, members of the press and a number of street railway executives and other dignitaries in attendance were pleased with what they saw. The new route served the Fairfield section at Green and Decatur Streets, which served City Hospital and cemeteries in the vicinity. Less than three months later, Nashville's second streetcar company, previously chartered in 1860, the McGavock & Mount Vernon Horse Railroad Company, made its debut on November 18, 1866. The company would ultimately become Nashville's largest animal-powered street railway, serving north, south, and west neighborhoods.

During this period in the late 19th century, the method by which streetcars were powered would change from animals to steam. Initially, Nashville's streetcars were drawn by mules or horses, while three lines adopted steam "dummy" locomotives to haul their cars. A steam dummy line or dummy engine was a steam locomotive enclosed in a wooden structure made to resemble a passenger coach. Supposedly, these were less objectionable to skittish horses and pedestrians in an urban setting, despite their smoke and noise. The use of dummy locomotives allowed streetcars to travel longer distances faster than animal-powered cars. Nashville was served by three steam dummy lines. The first of these was the Overland Railway Company, chartered on March 11, 1887, to operate between downtown and Woodstock Park, south of town, later renamed Glendale Park. The city's second steam dummy line and the fourth streetcar route to reach Edgefield (now known as East Nashville) was the Main Street & Lischey Avenue Street Railroad Company, opened in 1887. The third and final steam dummy undertaking was the Nashville & West Nashville Railroad Company. This line was to connect downtown with the city's west side. Over the next 25 years, numerous other street railway companies were incorporated to provide service to various districts of the city.

On April 30, 1889, the McGavock & Mount Vernon Horse Street Railroad became the first street railway in the city to convert to electric power, making Nashville one of the first cities in the country to introduce electricity for public transportation. There was great fanfare across Nashville when the Broad Street line to West Side Park commenced operation using the new and cleaner power. Soon, trolley wire was strung over all the street railway routes, and the mule-powered and dummy line streetcars across the city were quickly replaced with cars powered by electricity. In just a few years, all of the city's streetcar systems were powered solely by this new technology. In early 1890, the newly created United Electric Railway purchased and combined many smaller street railways across Nashville, creating a 52-mile, 18-line system. Many smaller companies were absorbed by larger ones by the turn of the 20th century.

Years later, another conglomerate, the Nashville Railway Company, was created for the sole purpose of totally combining all existing companies in the city. In 1903, a group of local investors purchased the firm, renaming it the Nashville Railway & Light Company. A year earlier, the new Nashville Transfer Station was constructed on the west side of the Public Square. The new facility included waiting rooms, public telephones, restrooms, and refreshment stands. With the unification of all the street railway companies, other improvements were made by the NR&L. In 1906, a new shop and carbarn complex were opened one block north of the Transfer Station. The sprawling complex contained 15 tracks and occupied half a city block. The progressive NR&L was now operating in the golden traction years, but the private automobile, with its offspring the motorbus and the new jitney craze that had enveloped the country, began to wreak havoc on the vested street railway concern. In addition to Nashville's modern streetcar network, the city was also served by two interurban railway lines as well, the only city in Tennessee to have this distinction. The Nashville-Gallatin and Nashville-Franklin interurban lines ran in opposite directions. Both interurban railways utilized Nashville's street railway system from the city limits to the downtown Transfer Station.

For decades, the Nashville Railway & Light Company had a major presence in downtown Nashville. In addition to the Transfer Station, carbarns, and maintenance shops near the Public Square, the NR&L's offices were housed on the first floor of the stately 1882 Watkins Institute Building on Church Street at Sixth Avenue. With its ornate Gothic tower looming tall over adjacent buildings, the structure was one of the most unique on the street. Customers could pay their electric bill, purchase streetcar tokens, and shop for the latest in electrical appliances at one location. In early 1922, NR&L's controlling interests were vested in the new Tennessee Electric Power Company (TEPCO), headed by the Clarks of Philadelphia. TEPCO was the largest private-sector electrical power monopoly in Tennessee's early-20th-century history, formed in 1922 when the Tennessee Power Company, Chattanooga Railway & Light, and the Chattanooga & Tennessee River Power Company consolidated. On December 26, 1926, the Nashville Railway & Light Company introduced five motor coach routes through its subsidiary Tennessee Transportation Company.

Five years later, in early 1931, both the NR&L and Tennessee Transportation Company were legally transferred to the Chattanooga-based TEPCO, and Nashville's transit system was rebranded as the Tennessee Electric Power Company. This network remained intact until 1940. The creation of the Tennessee Valley Authority and subsequent dismantling of TEPCO signaled the demise of streetcar service on transit routes in Nashville by new franchise owner Nashville Coach Company. By 1941, all the streetcars and the interurban railways were finished, bringing down the final curtain on this colorful 75-year chapter of Nashville's public transportation history.

One

Horsecars and Dummy Lines

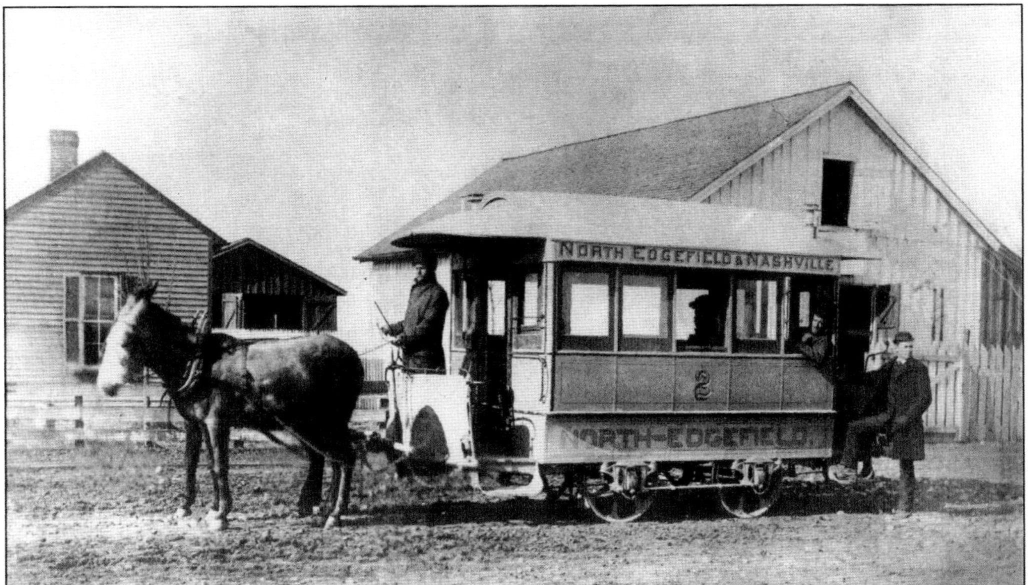

The earliest streetcars were powered by mules or horses and began regularly hauling passengers through Nashville's unpaved streets in 1866. Animal-powered cars hauling passengers over tracks embedded in dirt streets was a vast improvement over conventional horse-drawn wagons or stagecoaches. The improved technology afforded a more comfortable ride for passengers. This scene from the 1890s shows a streetcar that operated between Nashville's Public Square and Edgefield, on the opposite side of the Cumberland River. All of the city's streetcars operated in a similar fashion during the late 19th century. (Tennessee State Library and Archives.)

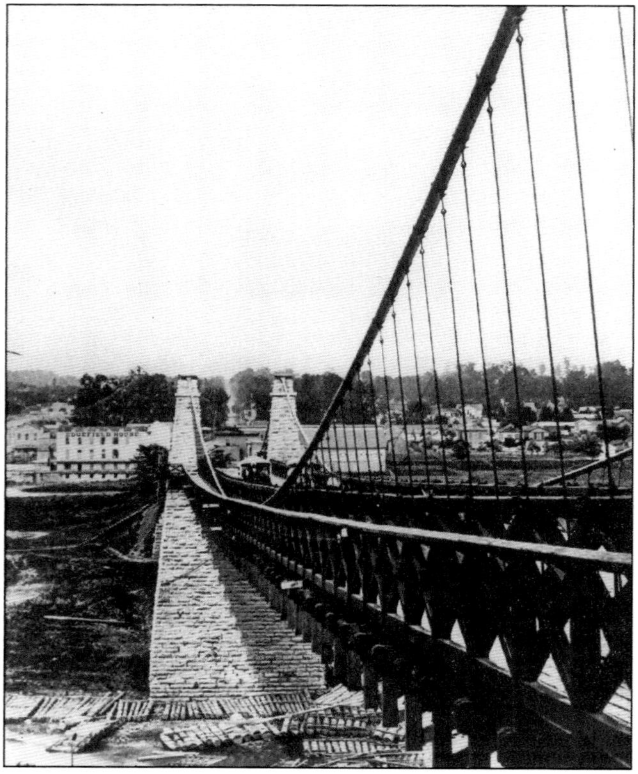

A mule-drawn streetcar from Edgefield trundles across the suspension bridge over the Cumberland River en route to Nashville's Public Square. This scene, facing east, was recorded during the mid-1880s, shortly after streetcars were allowed access to the bridge. (David H. Steinberg collection.)

In a similar view taken around the same time, the double-track Nashville & Edgefield streetcar right-of-way can be seen crossing the bridge from the west bank. For nearly 60 years, the city's streetcars continued to cross the river at this point, first on the suspension bridge, and after 1885, over a steel truss structure that ultimately replaced it. (David H. Steinberg collection.)

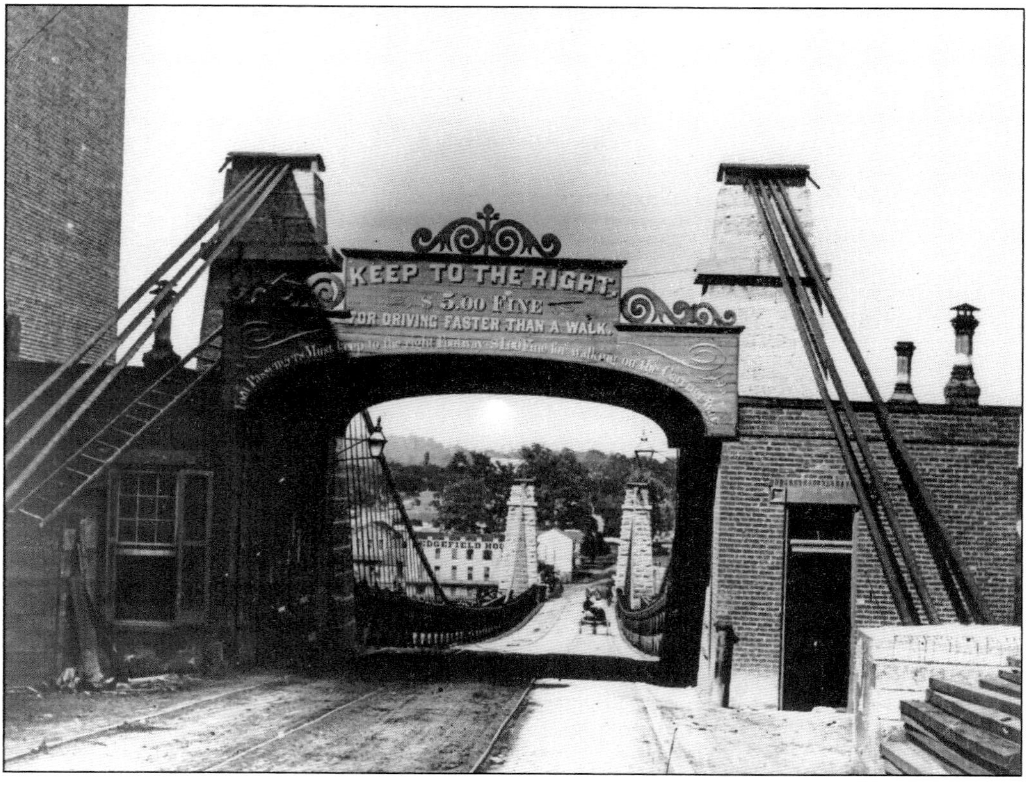

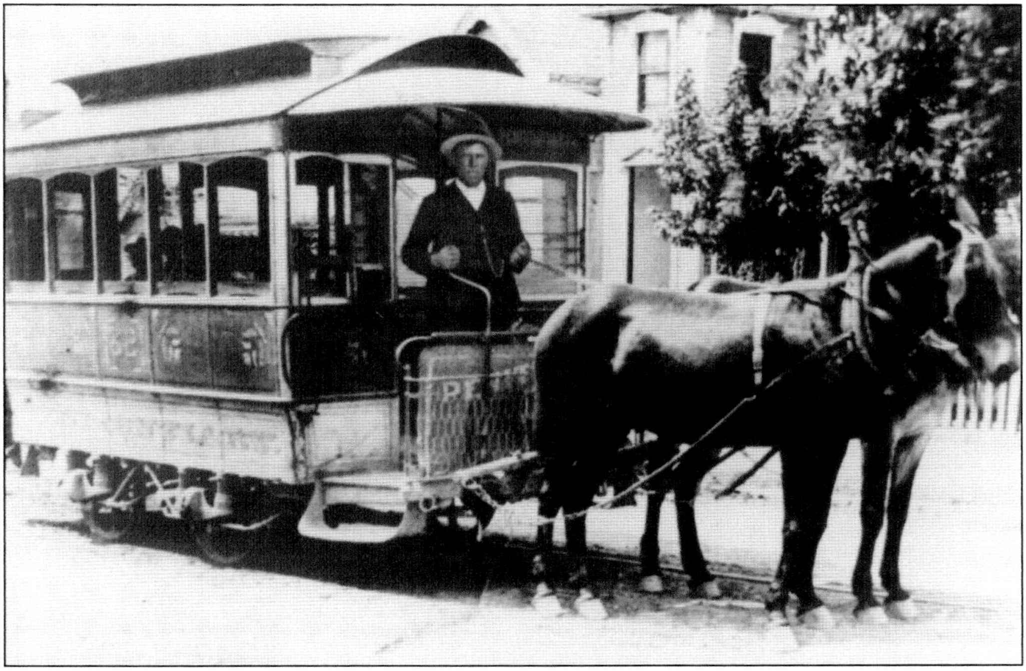

A pair of mules prepare to pull a streetcar to the Tennessee State Penitentiary, located on Church Street at the time, in the mid-1890s. In just a few more years, the state's largest prison would relocate to West Nashville; the larger facility would be served by a new and electrified streetcar line. There are no clues as to what street railway company this car belonged to. (Mel Baird collection.)

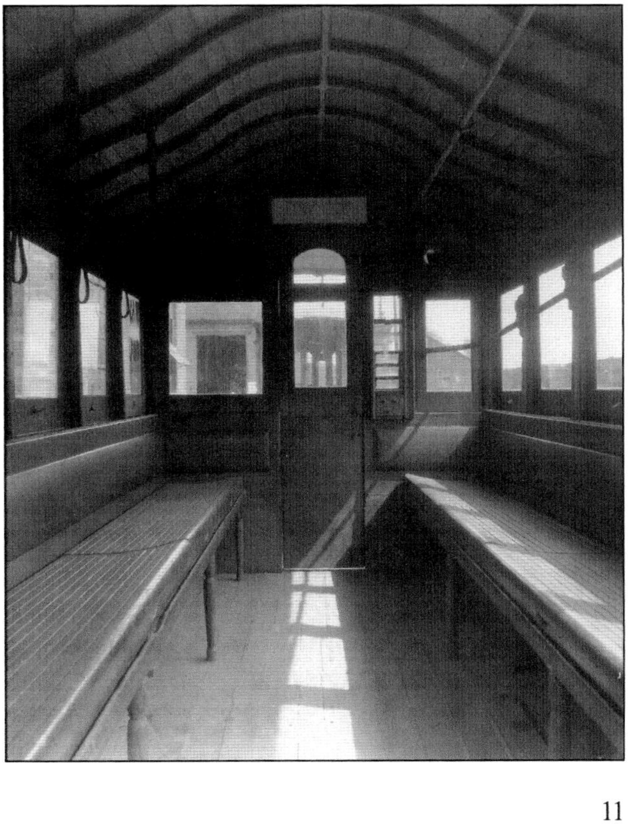

The interior of horsecars was spartan, offering little more than benches and protection from the elements. This rare view of Nashville Railway & Light car No. 102 gives an idea of what streetcar travel was like during the late 19th century. The animal-powered cars were in operation from the 1860s through the 1890s, when the entire system was electrified. Although the car dates from 1876, this photograph was taken in 1926 at the carbarn. Just three months later, the car would be placed in service for one last trip during the Pageant of Street Railway Progress, leading the parade as the oldest example of streetcar equipment. This car appears on the cover and also in chapter five. (Metro Nashville Archives, MTA Collection.)

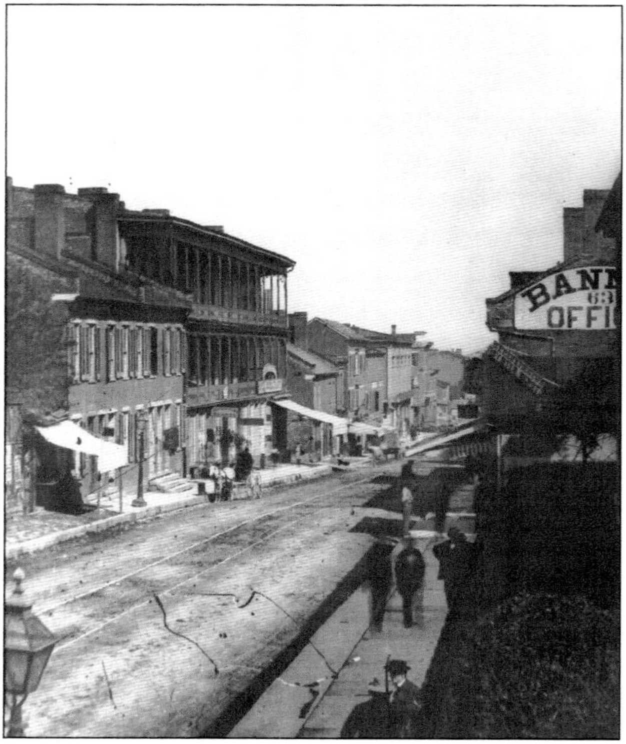

During the latter half of the 19th century, mule- or horse-drawn streetcars were the cleanest and most efficient form of public transportation in American cities. In this view looking north on Cherry Street (later renamed Fourth Avenue), the streetcar track runs down the middle of the dirt street while horses with wagons trudge up the otherwise empty thoroughfare during the late 1880s. (David H. Steinberg collection.)

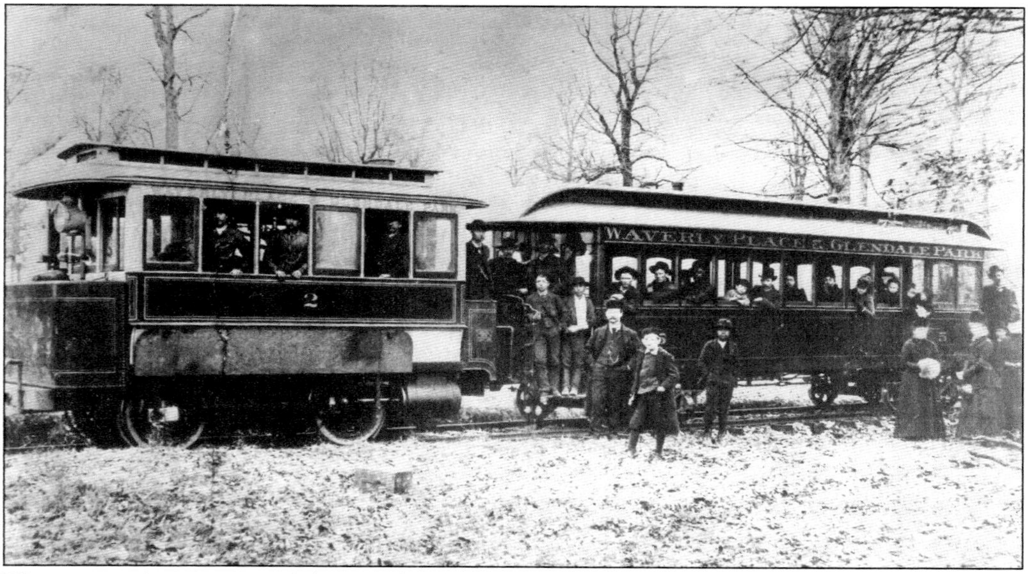

The crew and passengers of the Overland Dummy Railway pose in 1887, the year after the track opened between downtown and Glendale Park. The Overland was the first of three steam dummy lines to operate in the city. The trains typically consisted of a dummy locomotive and one or two trailing coaches. A dummy locomotive was a steam engine enclosed in a wooden structure made to resemble a coach. Supposedly, this "disguise" made the trains less objectionable in urban settings and not as likely to frighten skittish horses. Many residents regarded the smoky and noisy contraptions a nuisance. As a result, the dummy trains were short-lived, being replaced by cleaner and quieter electric cars within a few years. (Mel Baird collection.)

Two

Electrification and Expansion

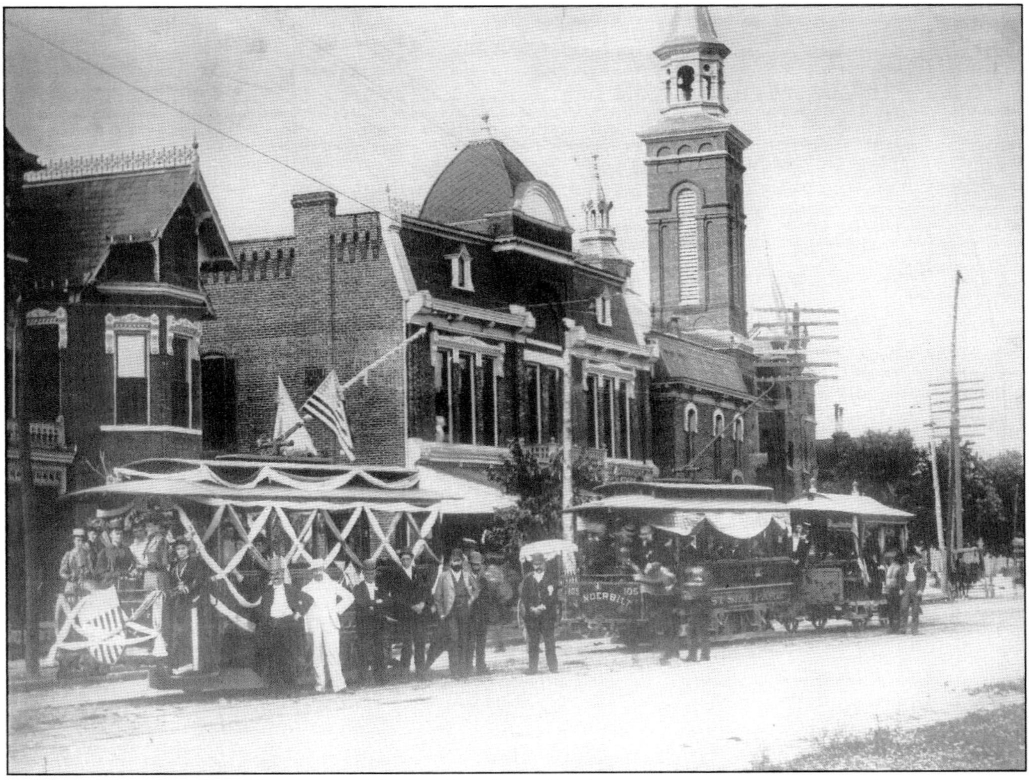

It was a great day of celebration in Nashville when the first electric streetcars went into operation with the McGavock & Mount Vernon Street Railway on April 30, 1889. On this initial day, car No. 104 is decorated with bunting and American flags as proud dignitaries and guests pose for the photographer. To the right, No. 105 boards passengers for the trip downtown. This car will pull a non-powered streetcar, formerly a horsecar. The historic West End Methodist Church provides a suitable backdrop for the occasion on Broadway near Fifteenth Avenue. During this inaugural run, the cars traveled between downtown and West Side Park, which would later be renamed Centennial Park. (David H. Steinberg collection.)

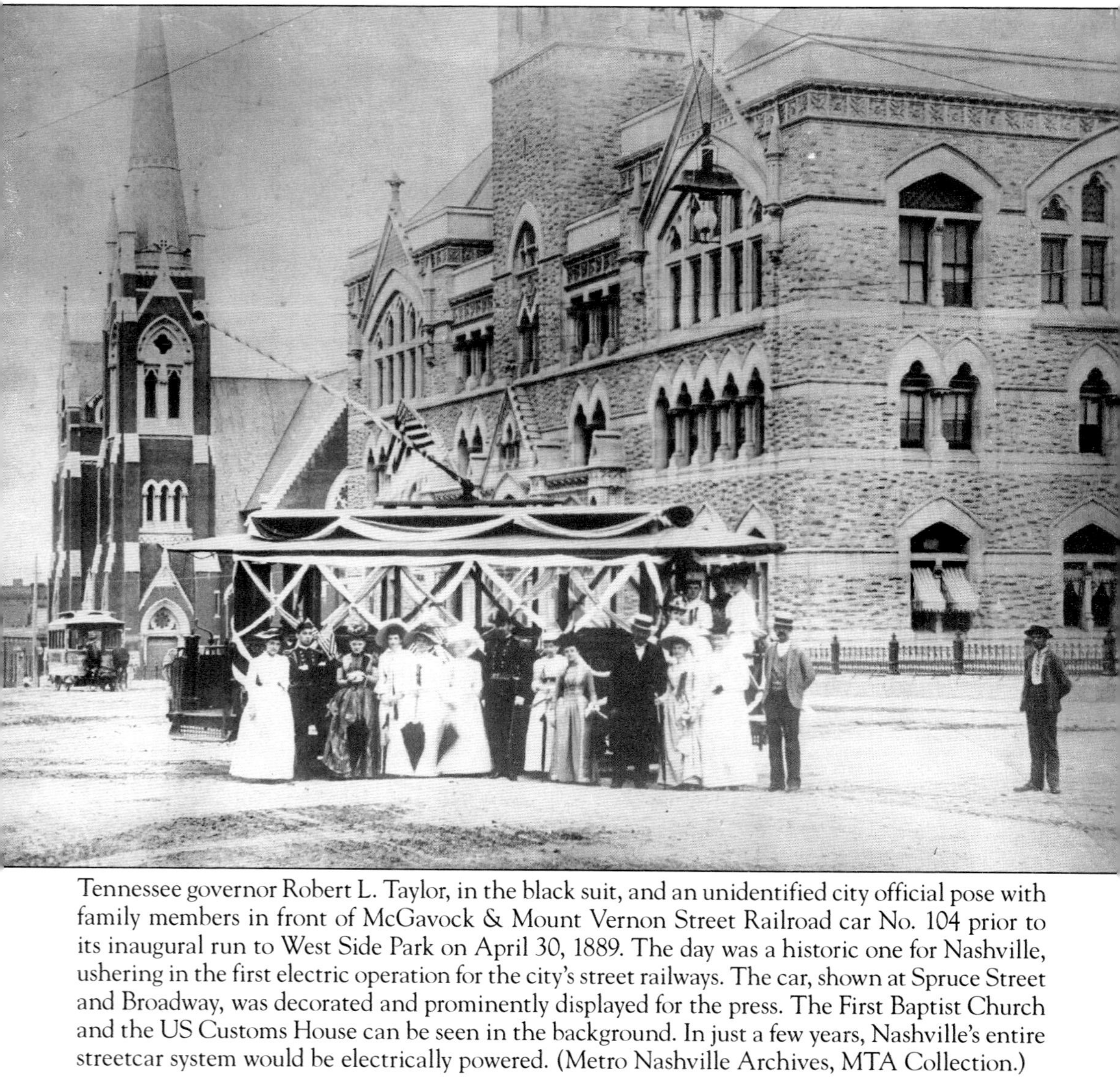

Tennessee governor Robert L. Taylor, in the black suit, and an unidentified city official pose with family members in front of McGavock & Mount Vernon Street Railroad car No. 104 prior to its inaugural run to West Side Park on April 30, 1889. The day was a historic one for Nashville, ushering in the first electric operation for the city's street railways. The car, shown at Spruce Street and Broadway, was decorated and prominently displayed for the press. The First Baptist Church and the US Customs House can be seen in the background. In just a few years, Nashville's entire streetcar system would be electrically powered. (Metro Nashville Archives, MTA Collection.)

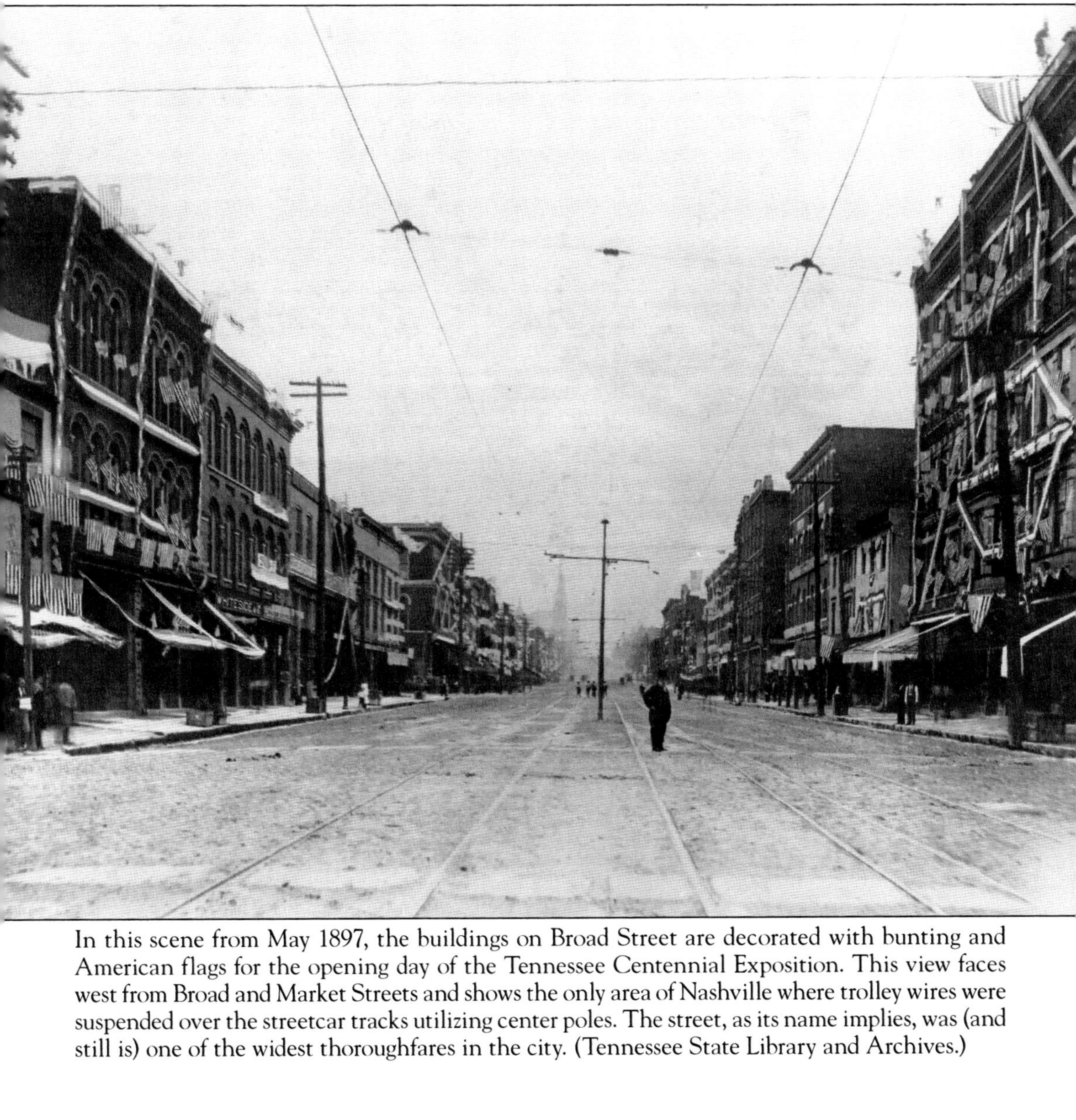

In this scene from May 1897, the buildings on Broad Street are decorated with bunting and American flags for the opening day of the Tennessee Centennial Exposition. This view faces west from Broad and Market Streets and shows the only area of Nashville where trolley wires were suspended over the streetcar tracks utilizing center poles. The street, as its name implies, was (and still is) one of the widest thoroughfares in the city. (Tennessee State Library and Archives.)

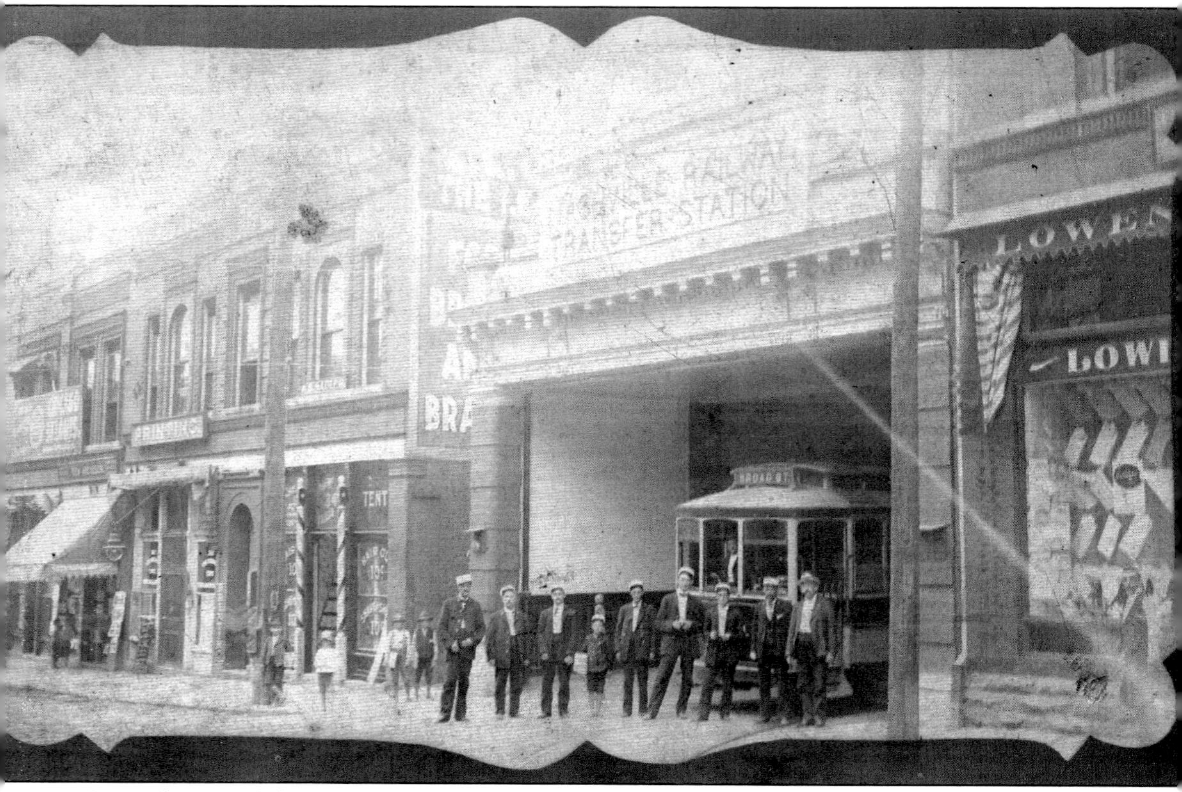

Since the consolidation of Nashville's streetcar lines in the late 1890s, all of the lines converged on a central hub near the Public Square. In 1902, the Nashville Railway opened a new Transfer Station, conveniently located on the west side of the square. The new facility extended from College to Cherry Street and contained several amenities, including a large waiting room, a refreshment stand, and public restrooms. For many years, this state-of-the-art facility was considered one of the finest in the country. In a photograph likely taken just after the opening of the Transfer Station in 1902, several streetcar conductors pose in front of a Broad Street car shortly before its departure. This is one of the few early photographs of the Transfer Station before its enlargement and reconfiguration to two tracks in 1907. (Nashville Public Library, Special Collections.)

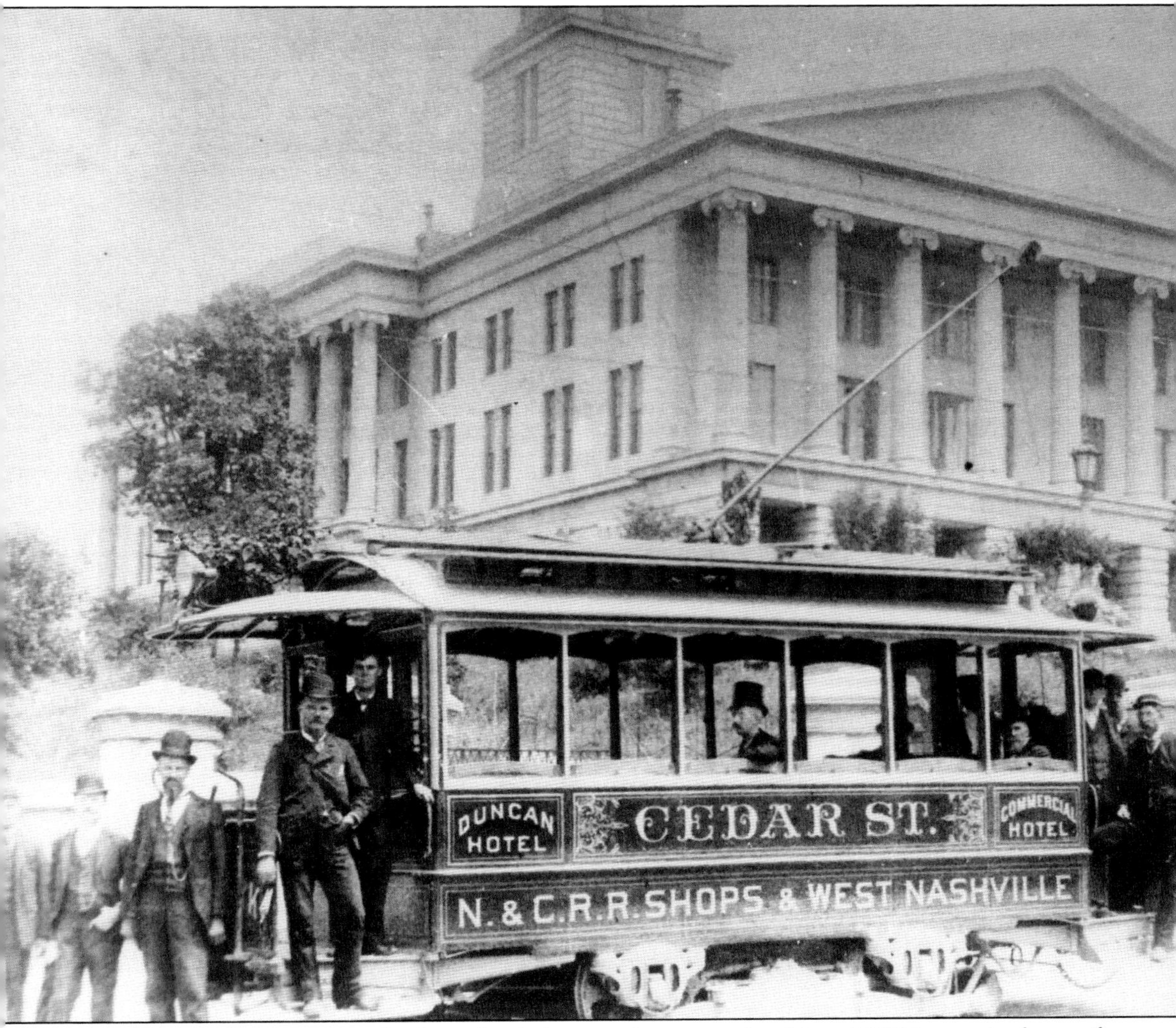

The crew and passengers of a four-wheeled car strike a pose in this c. 1900 image in front of the Tennessee State Capitol. In the days before rotating destination signs, the cars had popular attractions permanently painted on the side panels, which included hotels and major employers along the line. The "N.&C.R.R. Shops" referred to the Nashville, Chattanooga & St. Louis Railway Shops on the city's west side, a major employer at the time. (Nashville Public Library, Special Collections.)

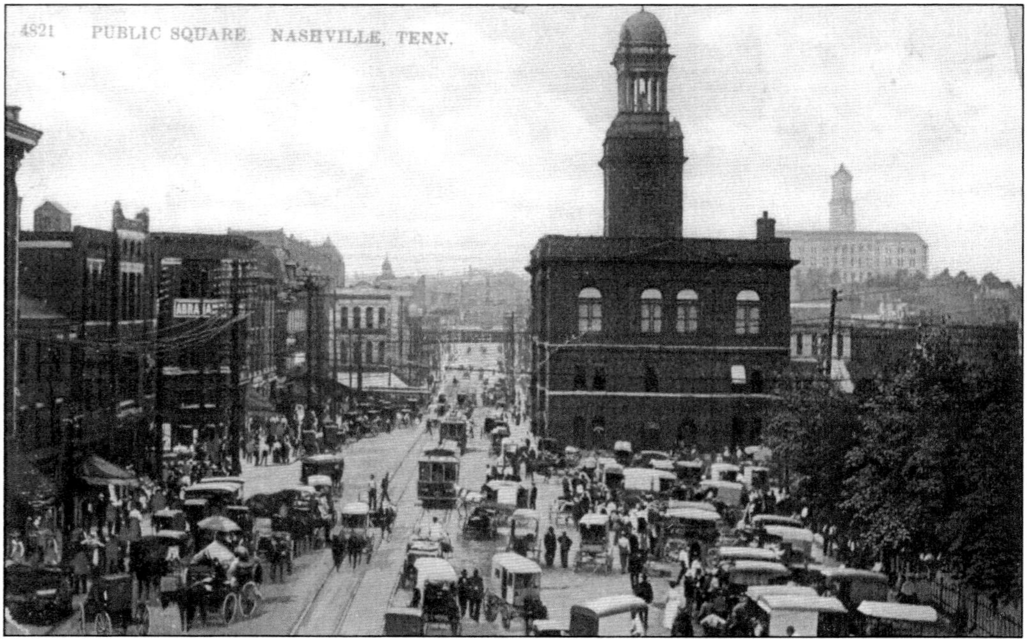

This scene illustrates how street congestion was problematic even in 1908, as streetcars and horse-drawn wagons share the streets around Nashville's Public Square. In this view, facing west down Deaderick Street, two streetcars are passing city hall as a third car in the distance travels down Third Avenue. The Tennessee State Capitol is visible in the background. (Metro Nashville Archives, Ridley Wills II Collection.)

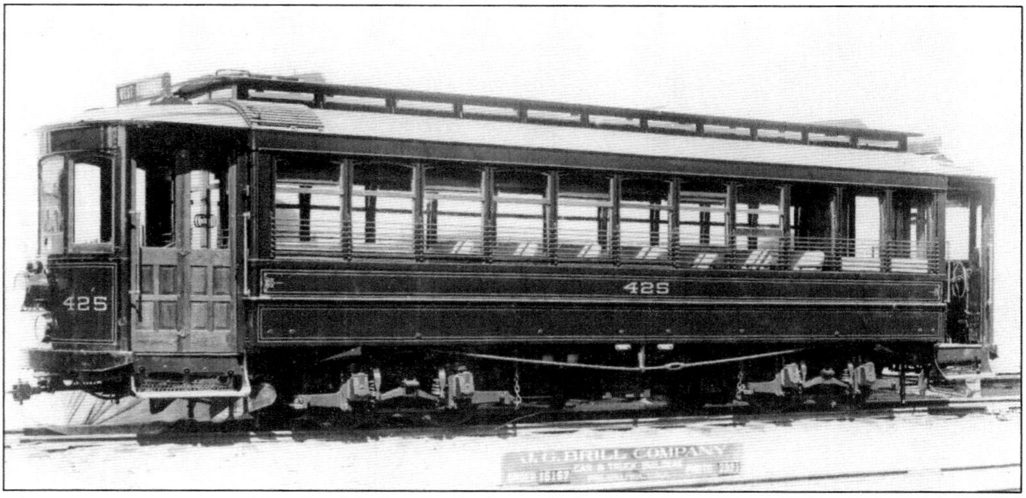

The streetcars operated by the Nashville Railway & Light Company and its predecessors were built by several manufacturers from around the country. One of the largest and most reputable was the J.G. Brill Company of Philadelphia. During the golden years of Nashville's street railways, several varieties of cars were ordered from Brill: the larger "double-truck" (eight-wheel) models and the smaller "single-truck" (four-wheel) cars that operated on lines with lighter ridership. This is a builder's photograph of No. 425 prior to delivery in 1906, one of several cars ordered by the NR&L that year. (David H. Steinberg collection.)

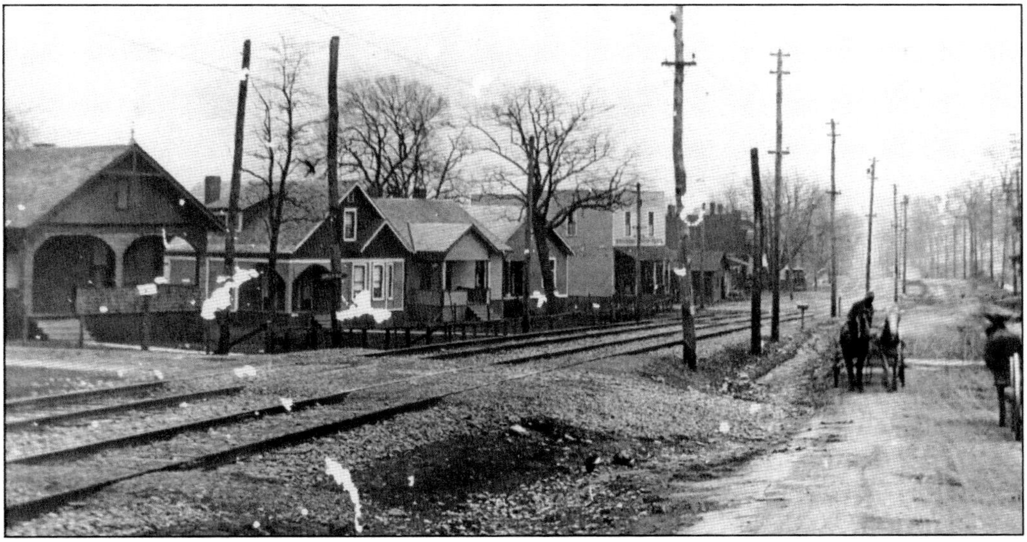

While nearly all of Nashville's streetcar tracks ran down the middle of streets, several lines traveled on private right-of-ways once outside the city. This 1910 view facing south shows the double-track Radnor Line running parallel to Nolensville Road in the community of Flat Rock. A few years later, the tracks were extended another mile to serve the Louisville & Nashville Railroad's new Radnor Yard. The two-story business in the distance is the Whitsett Grocery store. Flat Rock was renamed Woodbine in 1939. (Tennessee State Library and Archives.)

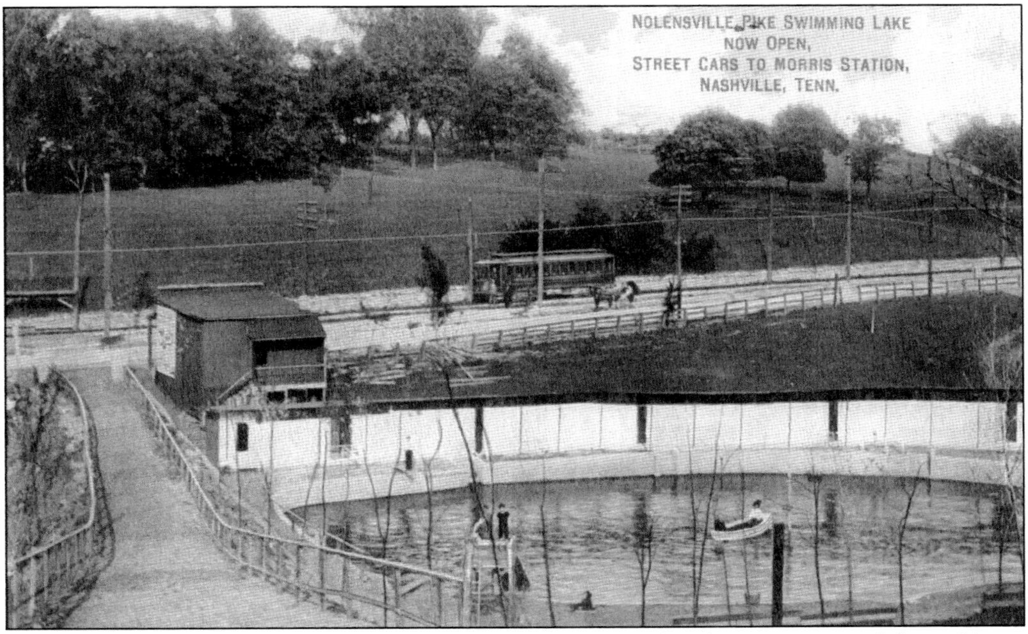

To celebrate the opening of the Nolensville Pike Swimming Lake, the owners staged this publicity photograph recorded around 1910. The attraction was nearly three miles south of Nashville's Public Square, just beyond the Tennessee State Fairgrounds on Nolensville Pike. As with many venues of the day, it was conveniently located adjacent to the streetcar line about halfway between the city limits and the community of Flat Rock. At this location, the streetcars ran adjacent to—rather than down the middle of—Nolensville Pike, as in the previous image. A conductor stands next to his car as a horse and buggy pass by. (Metro Nashville Archives, Ridley Wills II Collection.)

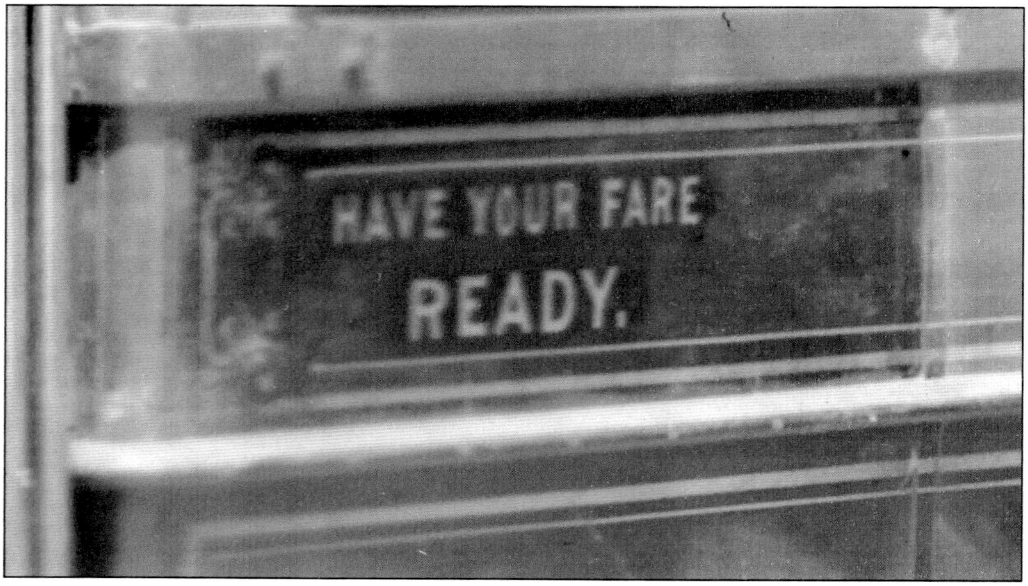

Maintaining schedules and keeping the cars running punctually was critical to running a dependable service for the Nashville Railway & Light Company managers. Signs such as the one shown here helped to facilitate loading during rush hours. (Author's collection.)

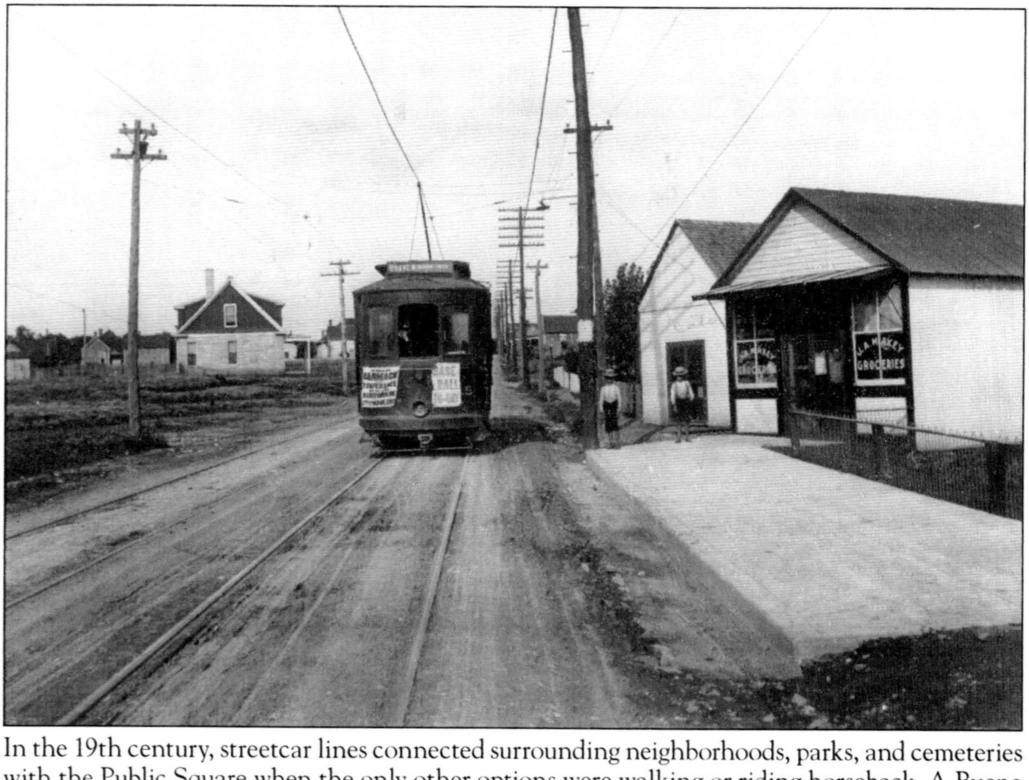

In the 19th century, streetcar lines connected surrounding neighborhoods, parks, and cemeteries with the Public Square when the only other options were walking or riding horseback. A Buena Vista Street Line car is shown passing the James A. Maxey store near Ninth Avenue and Buchanan Street on Nashville's north side in 1907. Notice the small section of sidewalk on the otherwise bare dirt street. (Tennessee State Library and Archives.)

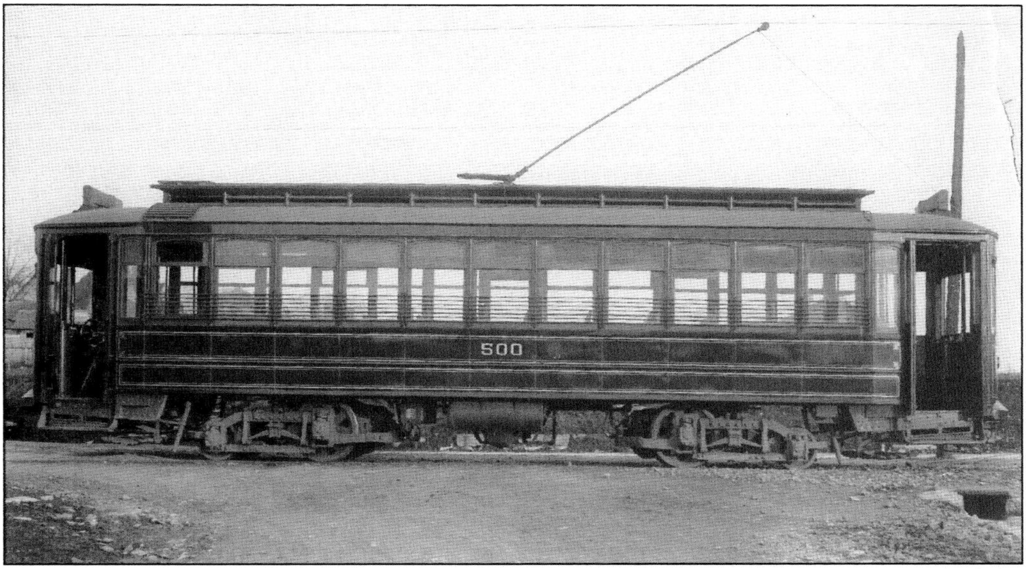

Nashville Railway & Light Company No. 500, built by the Brill Company, was typical of the equipment that operated on the system between 1905 and 1940. The cars could be operated in either direction, so they did not require turning at the end of each run. (Metro Nashville Archives, MTA Collection.)

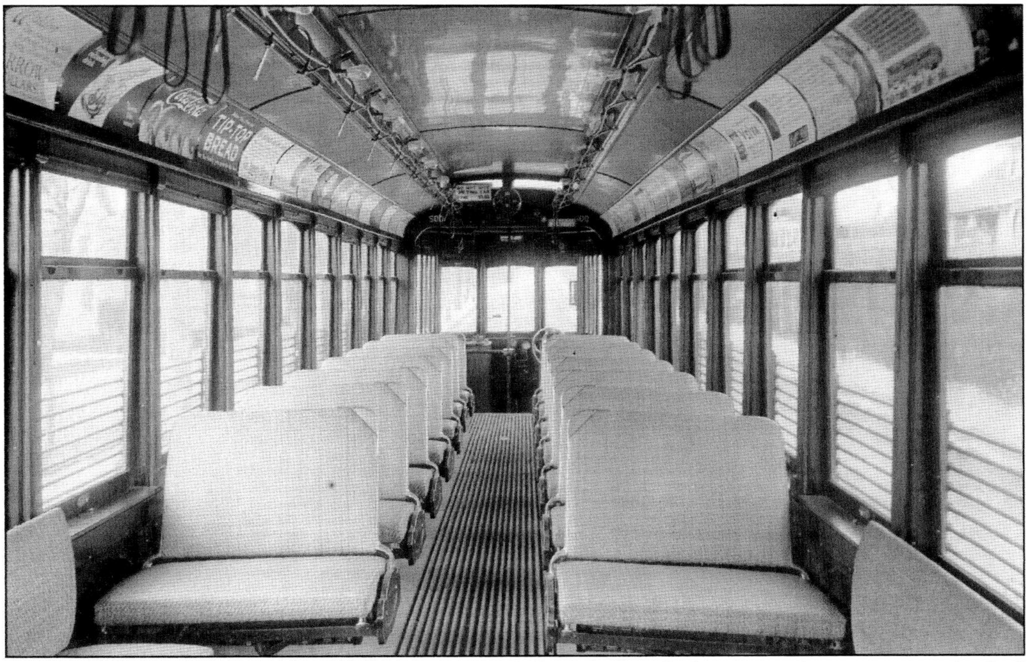

This interior view of car No. 500 provides a good illustration of what a "modern" streetcar looked like during the 1910s and 1920s. It was designed to offer riders the ultimate in comfort during their journey. All windows opened, providing cross ventilation in an era before air-conditioning. The skylights in the clerestory roof provided additional ventilation and lighting, adding an open feeling. After dark, the car was lit by more than 20 incandescent bulbs. The seats were upholstered with rattan, a large improvement over wood benches. A sign at the front advises passengers that the fine for spitting is $5—a hefty sum at the time. (Metro Nashville Archives, MTA Collection.)

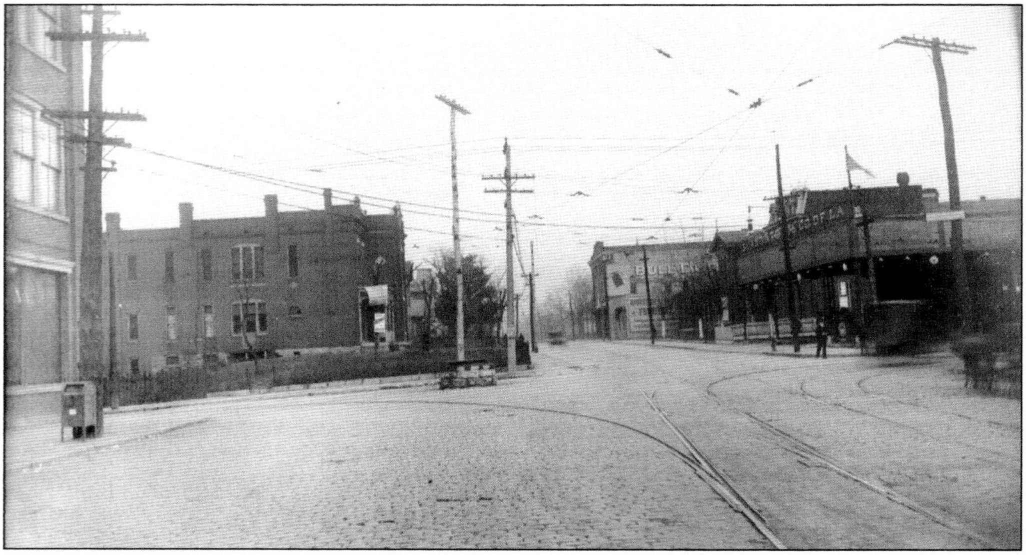

This scene, recorded in East Nashville around 1918, faces east on Woodland Street where Second Street intersects. Three different lines of the Nashville Railway & Light Company diverge here. The track swinging to the left is the Main Street line; going straight is the Woodland-Gallatin line. The tracks turning to the right are the Shelby Avenue line. Going west, in the opposite direction, the tracks cross the Cumberland River via the Woodland Street Bridge, accessing the Public Square and the Transfer Station. (Tennessee State Library and Archives.)

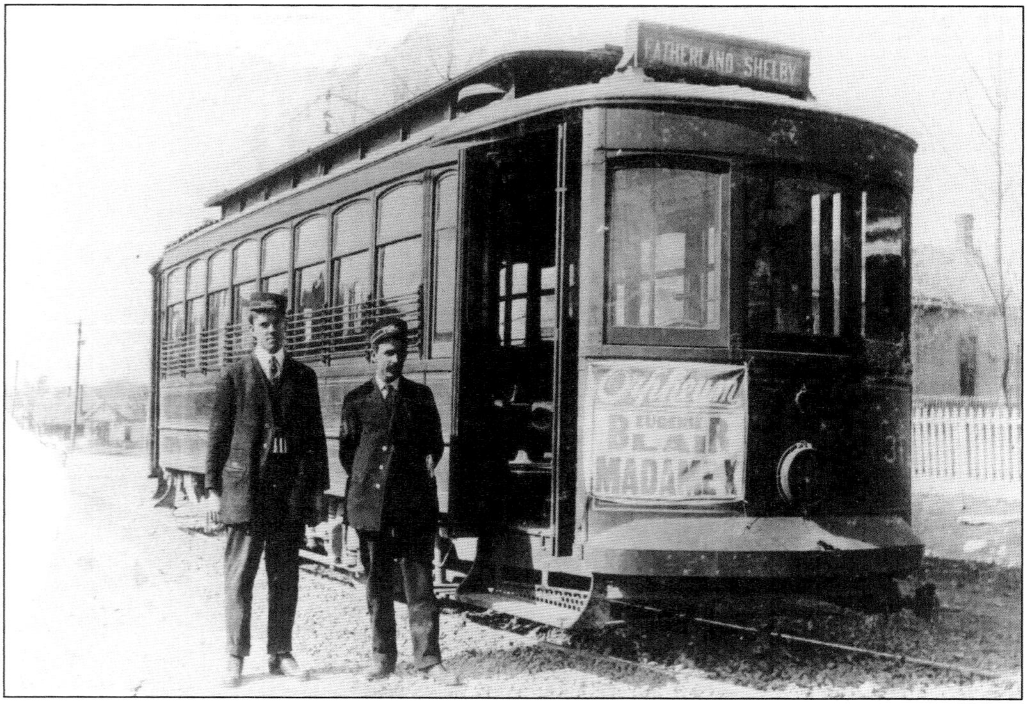

The Fatherland-Shelby line was one of five streetcar lines to radiate across the East Nashville community after crossing the Woodland Street Bridge over the Cumberland River from Public Square. Here, conductor W.W. Gunter (left) and motorman H. Price proudly pose next to their car at the end of their run near picturesque Shelby Park around 1929. (Mary G. Bray Collection)

Four years after the opening of Nashville's Transfer Station, the Nashville Railway & Light Company opened a sprawling carbarn a block north in 1906. The facility extended from College to Cherry Streets, later renamed Third and Fourth Avenues, respectively. While the brick structure was open at both ends, it provided shelter for much of the fleet with its 15 tracks and additional room on the second floor for offices. (Metro Nashville Archives, MTA Collection.)

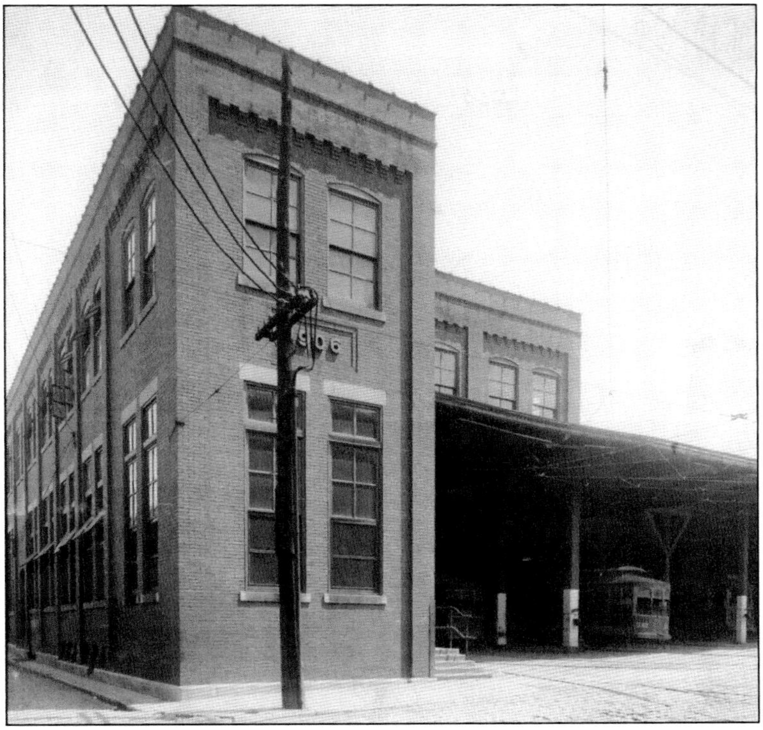

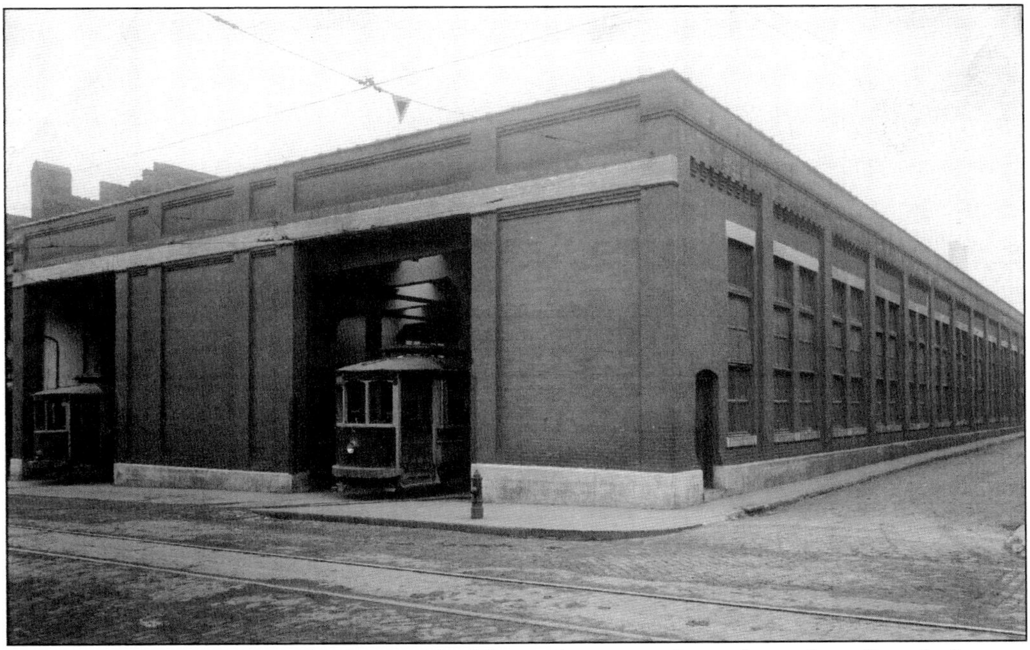

The street railway company had several buildings adjacent to the carbarn along Fourth Avenue where the vehicles were maintained and kept in tip-top order. The various structures included machine, electrical, and carpenter shops and a finishing building. The paint shop, shown here around 1920, was also important for keeping the fleet of aging cars looking new. Having the shop complex so close to the Transfer Station was a great advantage, allowing cars to be taken in and out of service quickly without affecting schedules. (Metro Nashville Archives, MTA Collection.)

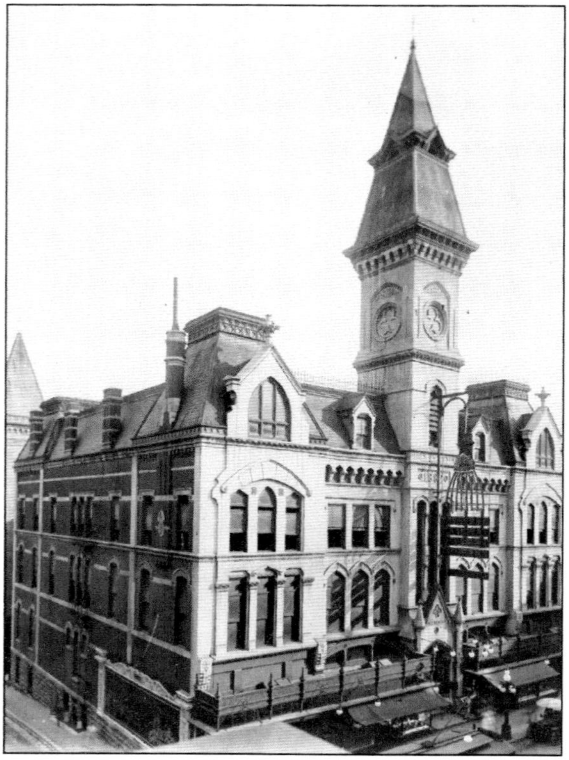

When the Watkins Institute Building opened in 1884, it was one of Nashville's most unique structures. For decades, its Gothic tower could be seen for miles. When the Nashville Railway & Light Company outgrew its offices in the Wilcox Building, it moved across the street to the stone structure at Church and High Streets in 1908. While the building was owned by the Watkins Institute, a respected education center, the streetcar company was its primary tenant, occupying the second floor for administrative offices. The street railway and utility company experienced rapid growth over the next several years and ultimately converted much of the main floor to a showroom for electric appliances. Customers could pay their electric bill, buy streetcar tokens, and purchase an electrical appliance without leaving the building. Sadly, this stately building was demolished in 1957. (Left, Tennessee State Library and Archives; below, Nashville Public Library, Special Collections.)

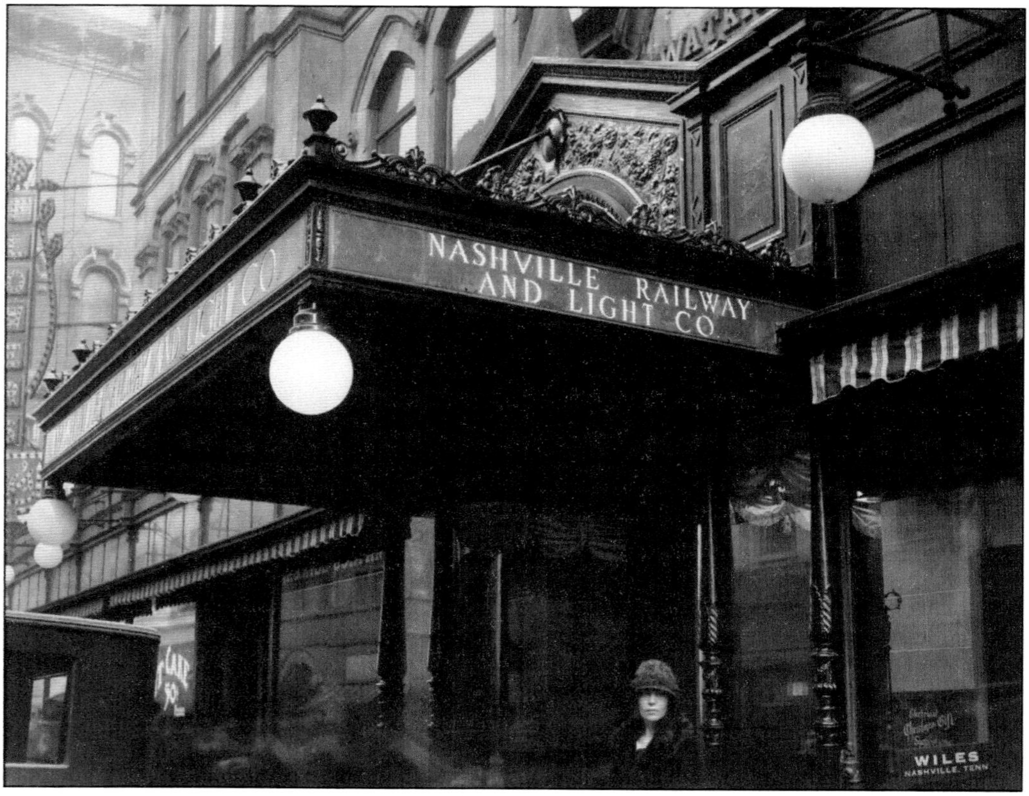

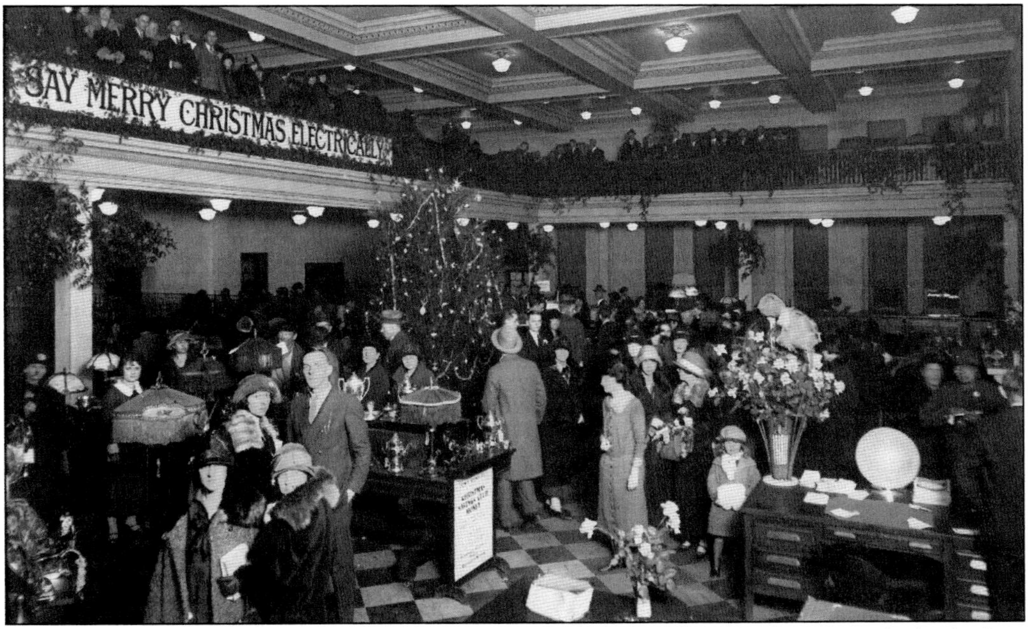

For decades, Nashvillians depended on the Nashville Railway & Light Company for both their transportation and electricity needs. In addition, the utility was a major retailer of lamps and every imaginable kitchen appliance, regularly running advertisements in the daily newspapers. In this view, its showroom, in the lobby of the Watkins Institute Building, is decorated for the holidays in the early 1920s as company officials look down from the mezzanine at the crowds. A prominent banner reads "Say Merry Christmas Electrically." (Nashville Public Library, Special Collections.)

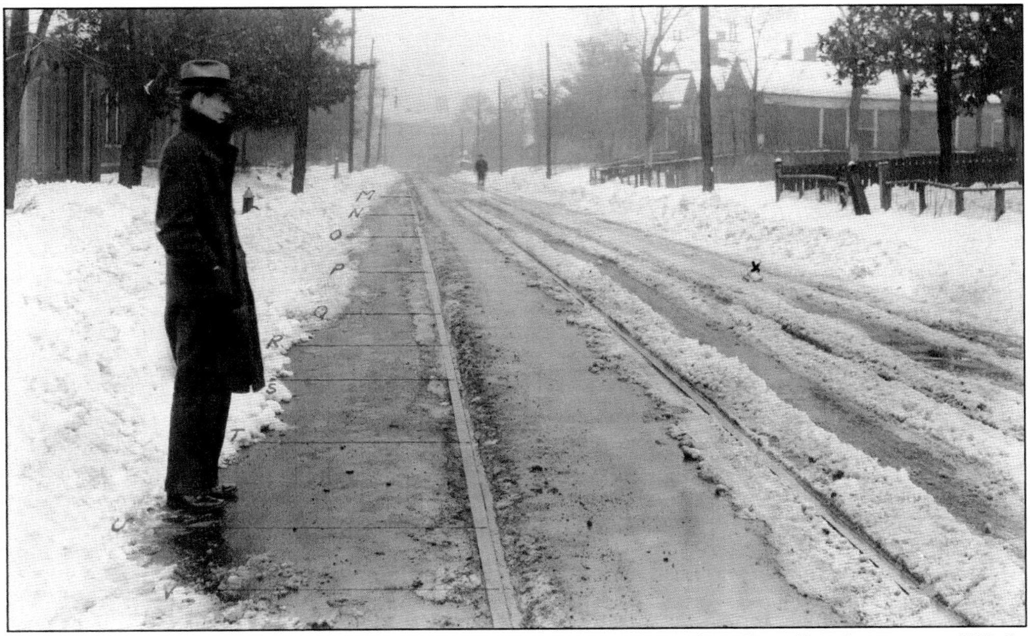

The lines and notations on this photograph indicate that it was taken for official purposes. While this Nashville location is unidentified, the unusual amount of snow in this 1929 scene serves as a reminder that over time, some things never change, such as waiting for a ride to work on a frigid day. (Tennessee State Library and Archives.)

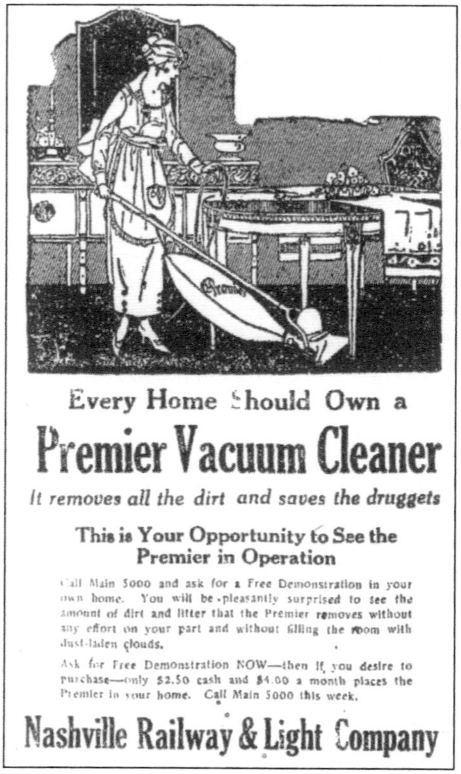

For many years, the Nashville Railway & Light Company ran advertisements in the larger Nashville newspapers promoting electric appliances sold at its showroom in the Watkins Institute Building. These also announced cooking demonstrations and promotions, often touting easy payment plans. The utility company seldom extended the same promotions to its street railway system; there was no need, since ridership remained high during those days. This advertisement from the early 1920s promotes Premier Vacuum Cleaners. (Author's collection.)

Electric household appliances were all the rage during the early 1920s; the Nashville Railway & Light Company wasted no time promoting and selling items from its downtown showroom. To draw attention to the new Universal Electric Washer, an attractive model demonstrates how easily the revolutionary machine could help wives free themselves from "washday drudgery." Music was provided by Tony Rose and several other musicians to liven things up. Rose's band performed regularly at the Glendale Park and Zoo and at company functions. (Nashville Public Library, Special Collections.)

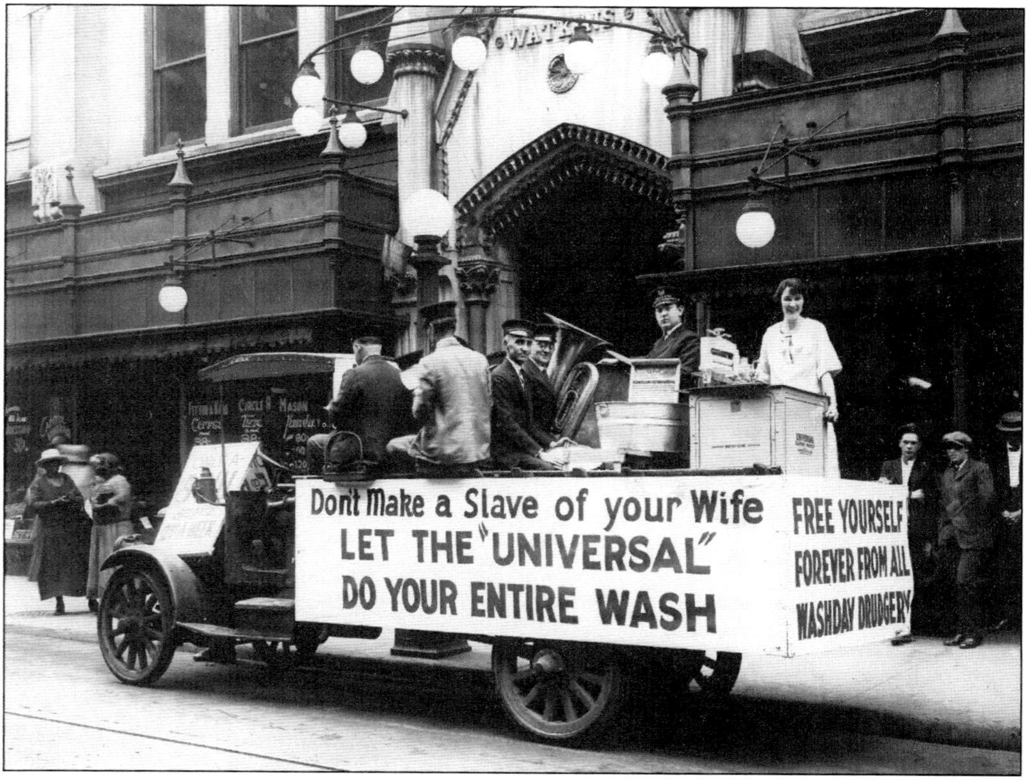

Three

Nashville's Golden Streetcar Era

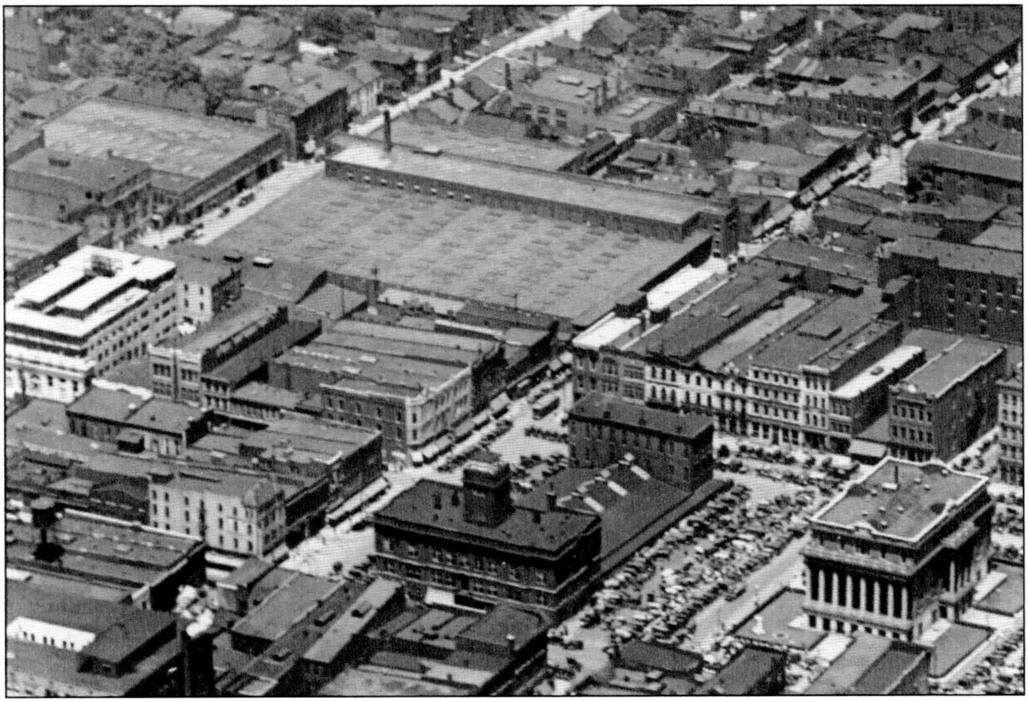

From Nashville's earliest days, its Public Square has been the center for commerce, shopping, and city and county government. The Transfer Station, where all of the city's streetcars lines converged, was conveniently across the street, facing the square's west side. In this early 1930s bird's-eye view of the Public Square, Nashville City Hall and the attached market house are at the bottom. The Davidson County Courthouse is at lower right. On market day, farmers from across the region brought their wagons to the square and lined up on both sides of the market house to sell their produce. This scene would change drastically a few years later, when a larger combination city hall and courthouse building consolidated the existing services and the market house moved to a more modern building on the opposite side of the square. Historically, Nashville's streetcar system always had a major presence at the square. In addition to the two-story Transfer Station between Third and Fourth Avenues near Deaderick Street, seen at lower left, the sprawling carbarn and maintenance shops were conveniently located a block north. This made it easy for employees to shuttle the streetcars between the three facilities as needed. All buildings seen here have since been demolished, with the exception of the Morris Memorial Building, constructed by the National Baptist Convention, at far left. (Metro Nashville Archives, MTA Collection.)

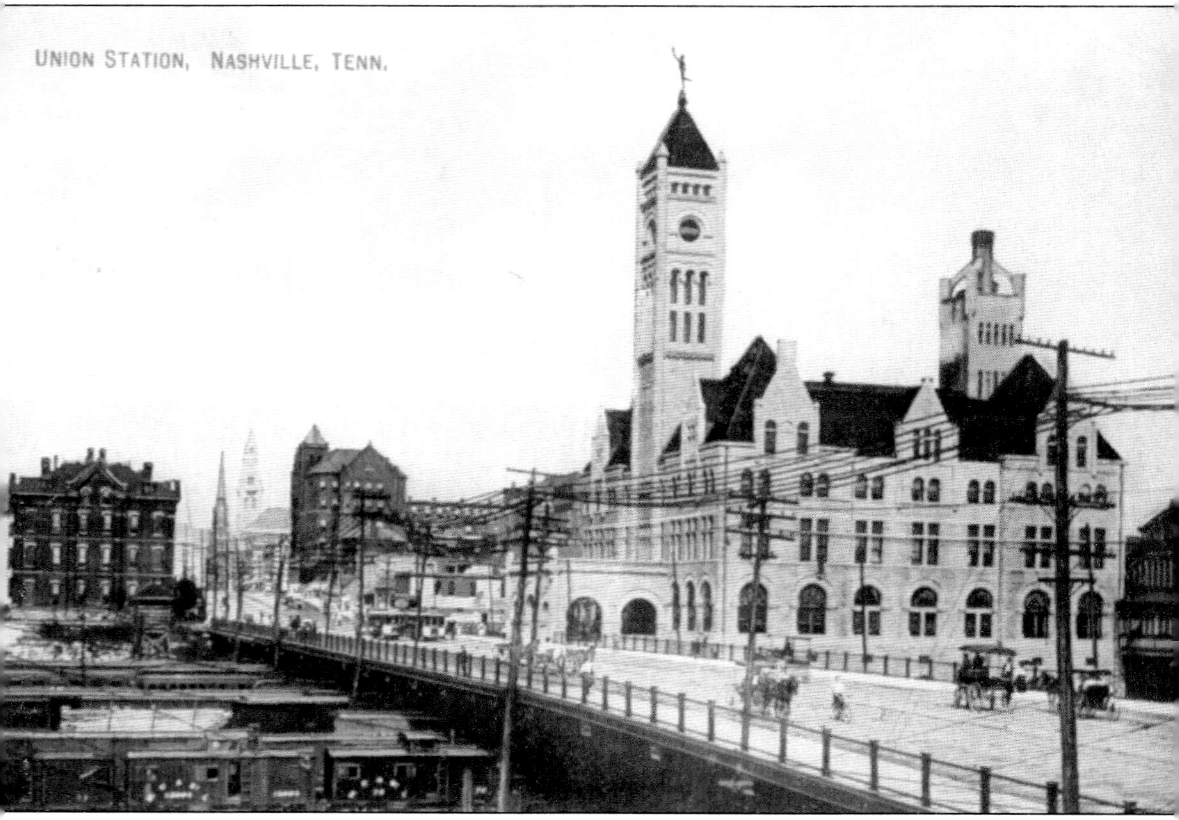

By 1910, the Nashville Railway & Light Company had a reputation as one of the safest and most efficient public transit systems in the nation. The various streetcar lines connected virtually all the city's attractions, colleges, parks, cemeteries, and even the company-owned Glendale Park and Zoo. One of the more important destinations for passengers, however, was Nashville's iconic Union Station. Served by both the Louisville & Nashville Railroad and the Nashville, Chattanooga & St. Louis Railway, this facility was the region's transportation center for decades. In this view looking east, two streetcars have stopped at the station to load and discharge passengers on Broadway at Tenth Avenue South. The building across the street is the general offices for the Nashville, Chattanooga & St. Louis Railway. In the background are the spires of the First Baptist Church, the federal courthouse–customs house, and the Vauxhall Apartments. (Metro Nashville Archives, Ridley Wills II Collection.)

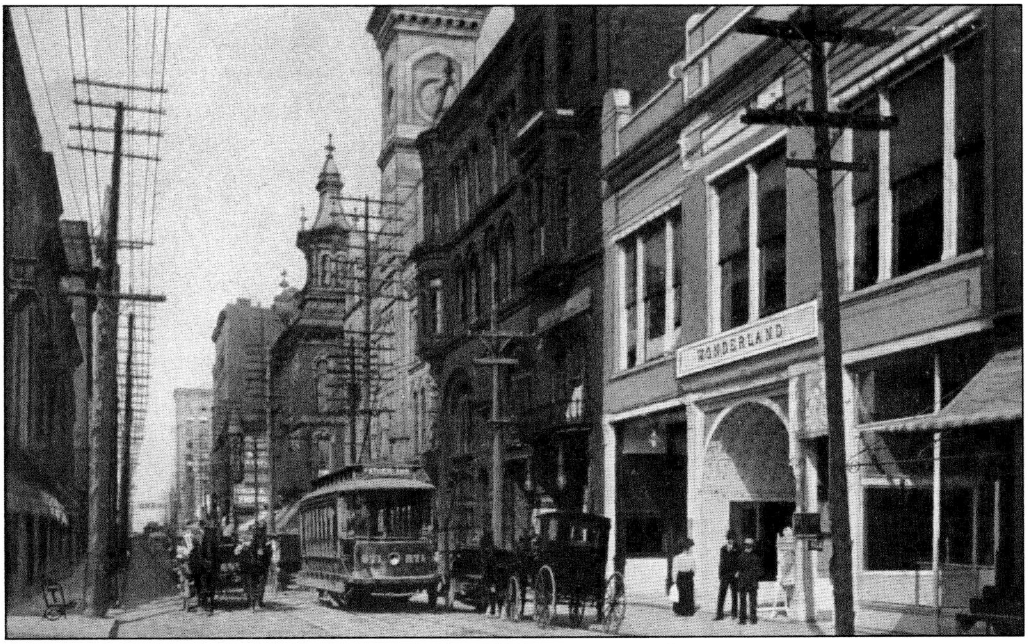

Car No. 271 is shown traveling east on Church Street approaching Sixth Avenue as it passes a horse-drawn wagon. Just to the right of the streetcar is the Watkins Institute Building with its majestic tower, where the offices of the Nashville Railway & Light Company are located. (Metro Nashville Archives, Ridley Wills II Collection.)

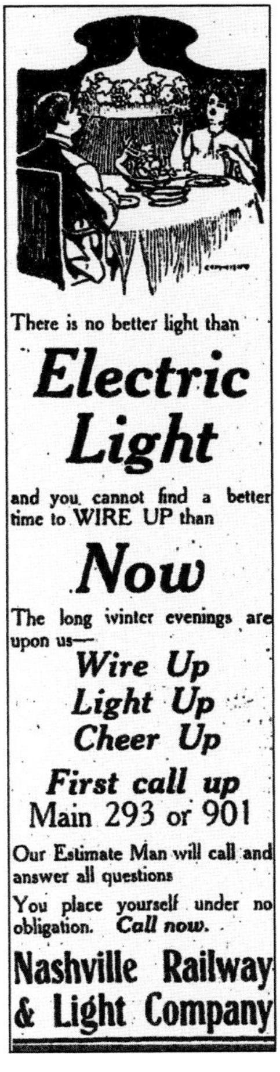

For decades, the Nashville Railway & Light Company was the city's only major utility company and generator of electricity. Not only did the firm own Nashville's street railway system, it also sold a variety of electric appliances and even wired houses for electric service. This advertisement from 1907 is an example of promotions regularly run in newspapers. This one encourages home owners to get their houses wired for electricity. (Author's collection.)

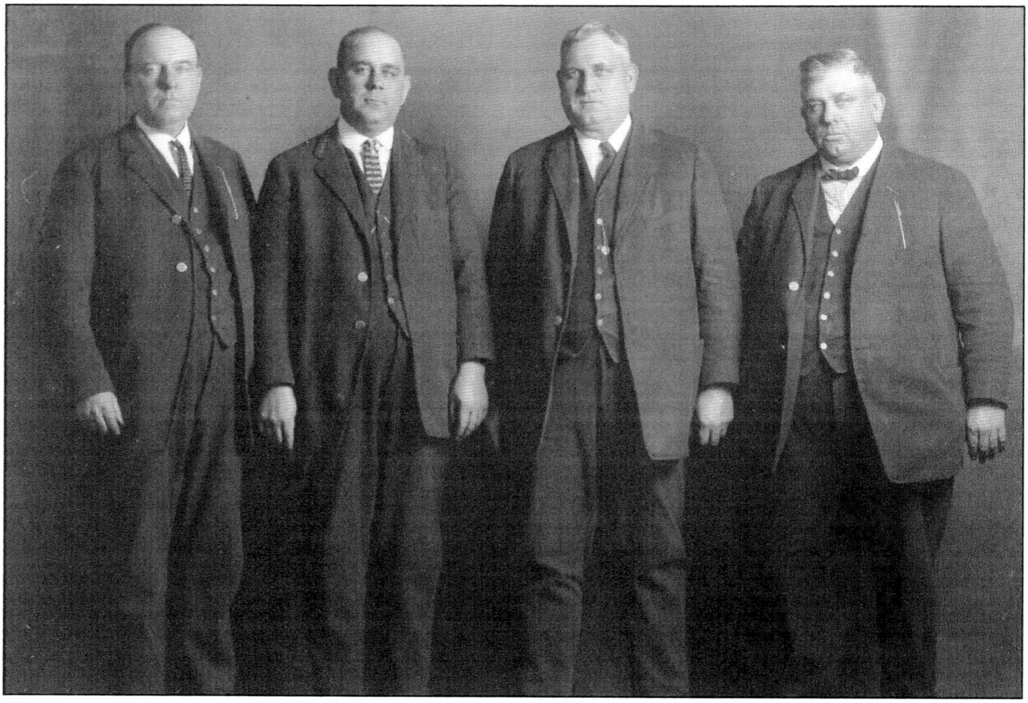

These NR&L company photographs were taken in the early 1920s. Above are four senior employees. While their titles are unknown, these men appear to be managers. Below, two motormen and two conductors strike a pose around the same time. Their employer ensured that the public knew who their crew worked for—the company's initials adorned their hat badges, embroidered lapels, and even the brass buttons on their uniforms. (Both, Metro Nashville Archives, MTA Collection.)

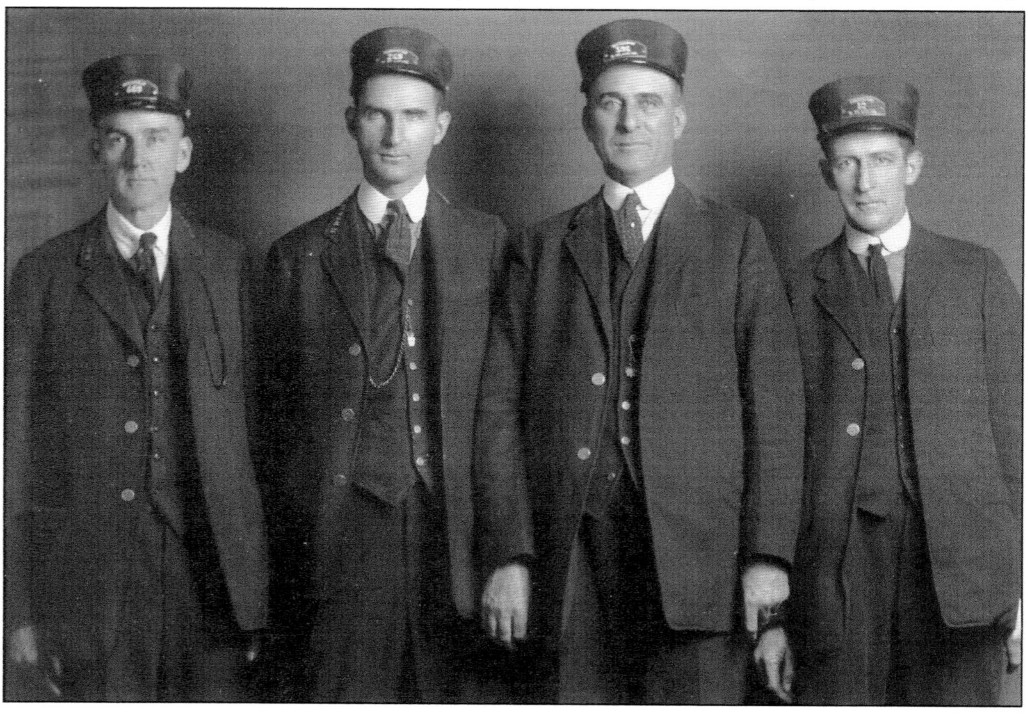

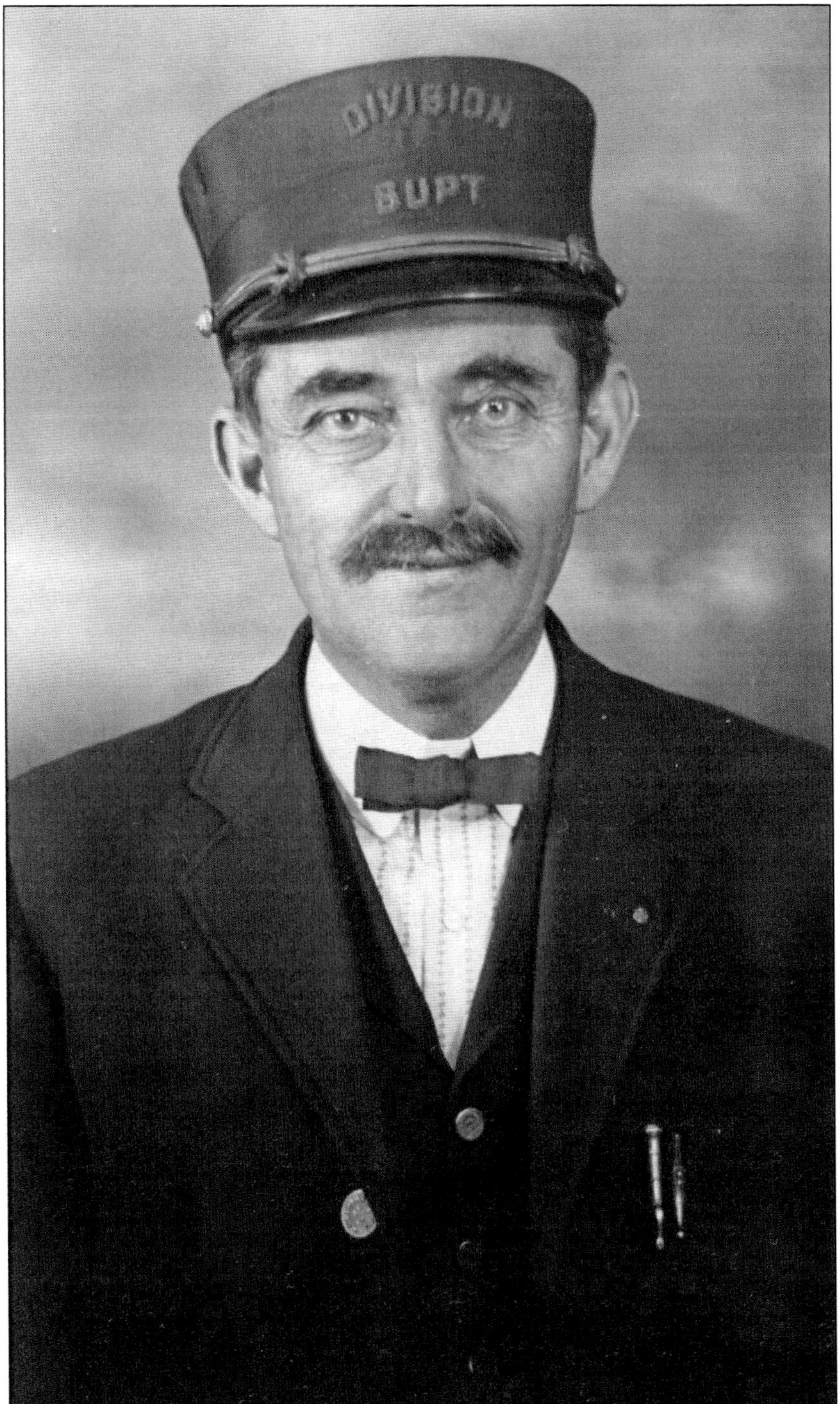

This portrait shows Leonard Jones, one of several division superintendents for the Nashville Railway & Light Company. It was his job to supervise the motormen and conductors of the streetcars in his sector, ensure that the cars ran on schedule, and solve any unexpected problems quickly. (Metro Nashville Archives, MTA Collection.)

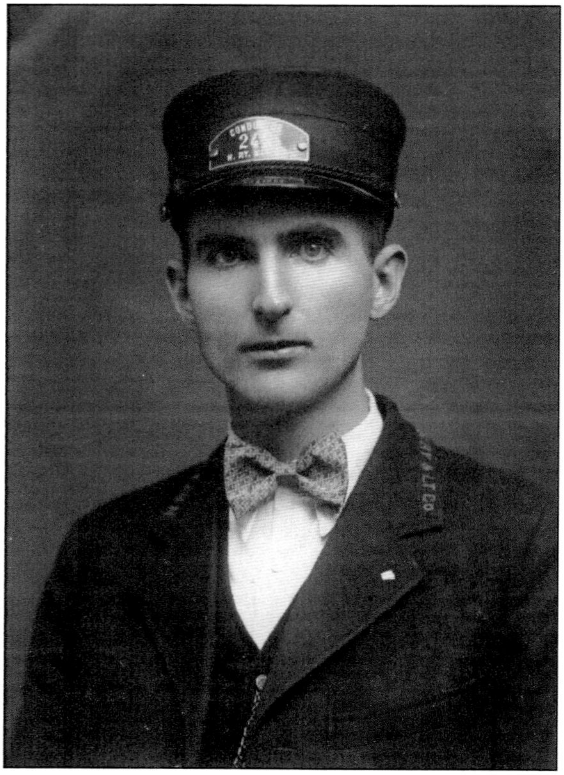

The streetcar conductor collected fares, assisted passengers during boarding and deboarding if necessary, and maintained order on his car. To the riding public, the conductor represented the Nashville Railway & Light Company. In this capacity, he was expected to look and act professionally at all times. The dress code was very strict: the standard NR&L uniform with a starched white shirt and gold chain. While most employees preferred bow ties, some favored neck ties instead. Wearing the traditional pillbox hat while on duty was mandatory. The attached badge gave the employee's title, employee number, and the company's initials, N.RY.&LT.CO. (Metro Nashville Archives, MTA Collection.)

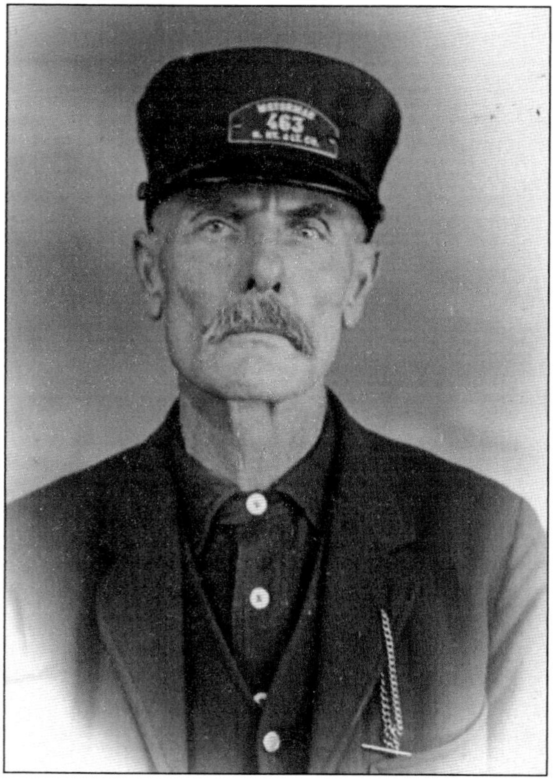

The motorman was responsible for operating the streetcar and for knowing all operational aspects of the cars and track he was operating over. Motormen normally began their careers as conductors. Garnering years of experience, conductors were later promoted to motormen when a position came open. In stark contrast to the previous photograph of the young conductor, this unidentified motorman, a seasoned veteran of the Nashville Railway & Light Company, has probably worked the streetcars most of his life. While transit workers never made good wages, they were very dedicated to the company. It shows in this motorman's face. (Metro Nashville Archives, MTA Collection.)

In this staged image, two employees of the Nashville Railway & Light Company pose with a Simplex Electric Iron. It is unknown if this image was intended for publicity purposes or to promote sales of electric irons, which were one of many types of appliances sold by the company in its showroom in the Watkins Institute Building downtown. (Metro Nashville Archives, MTA Collection.)

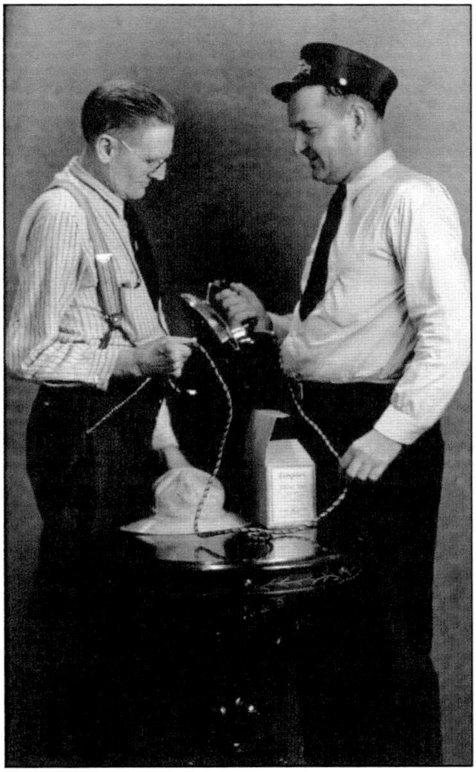

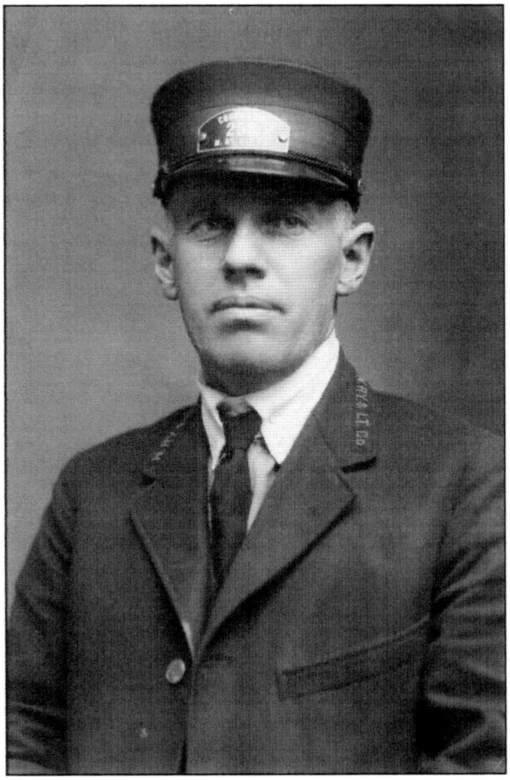

This company portrait of NR&L conductor C.C. Pitt was taken in the early 1920s. (Metro Nashville Archives, MTA Collection.)

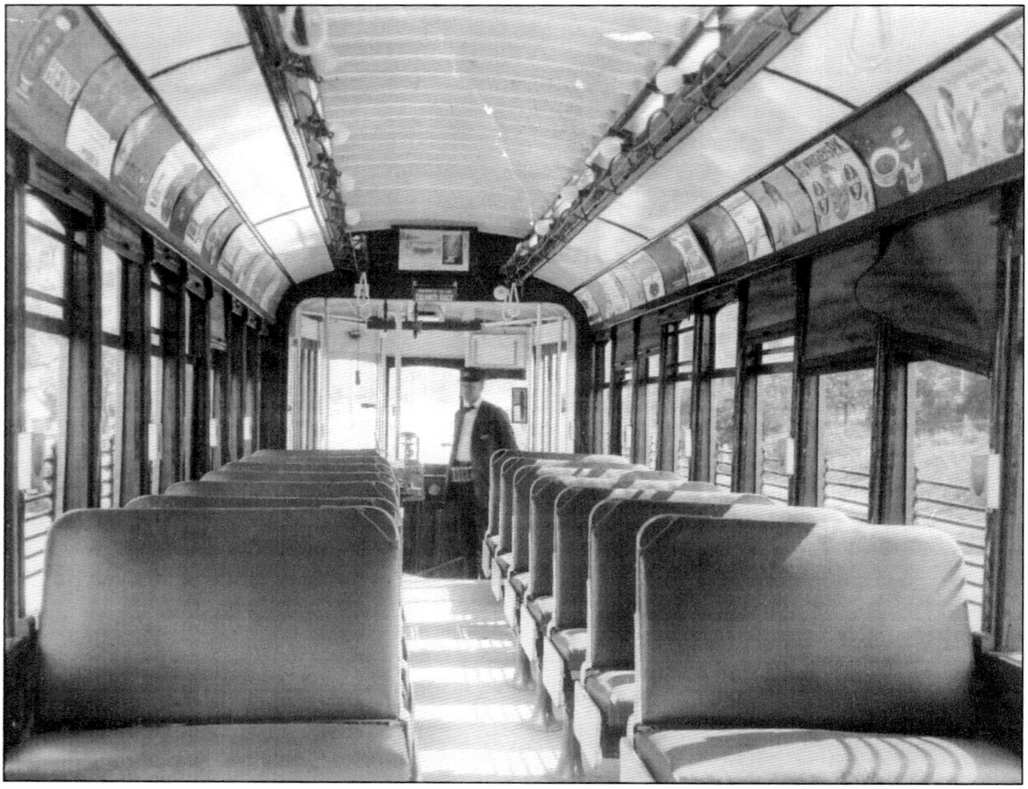

A Nashville Railway & Light conductor poses with a newly remodeled streetcar in 1926. New appointments included leather seats, linoleum flooring, improved lighting, and new paint for the walls and ceiling. (Metro Nashville Archives, MTA Collection.)

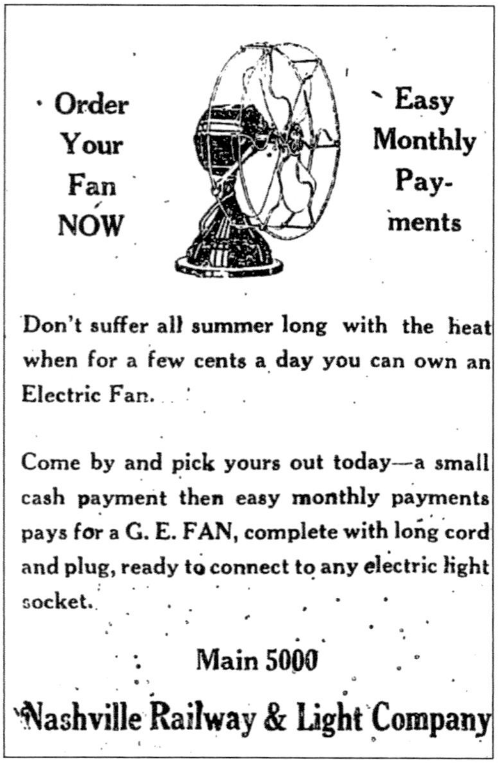

Here is another example of an advertisement run by the Nashville Railway & Light Company, this time for electric fans in 1922. (Author's collection.)

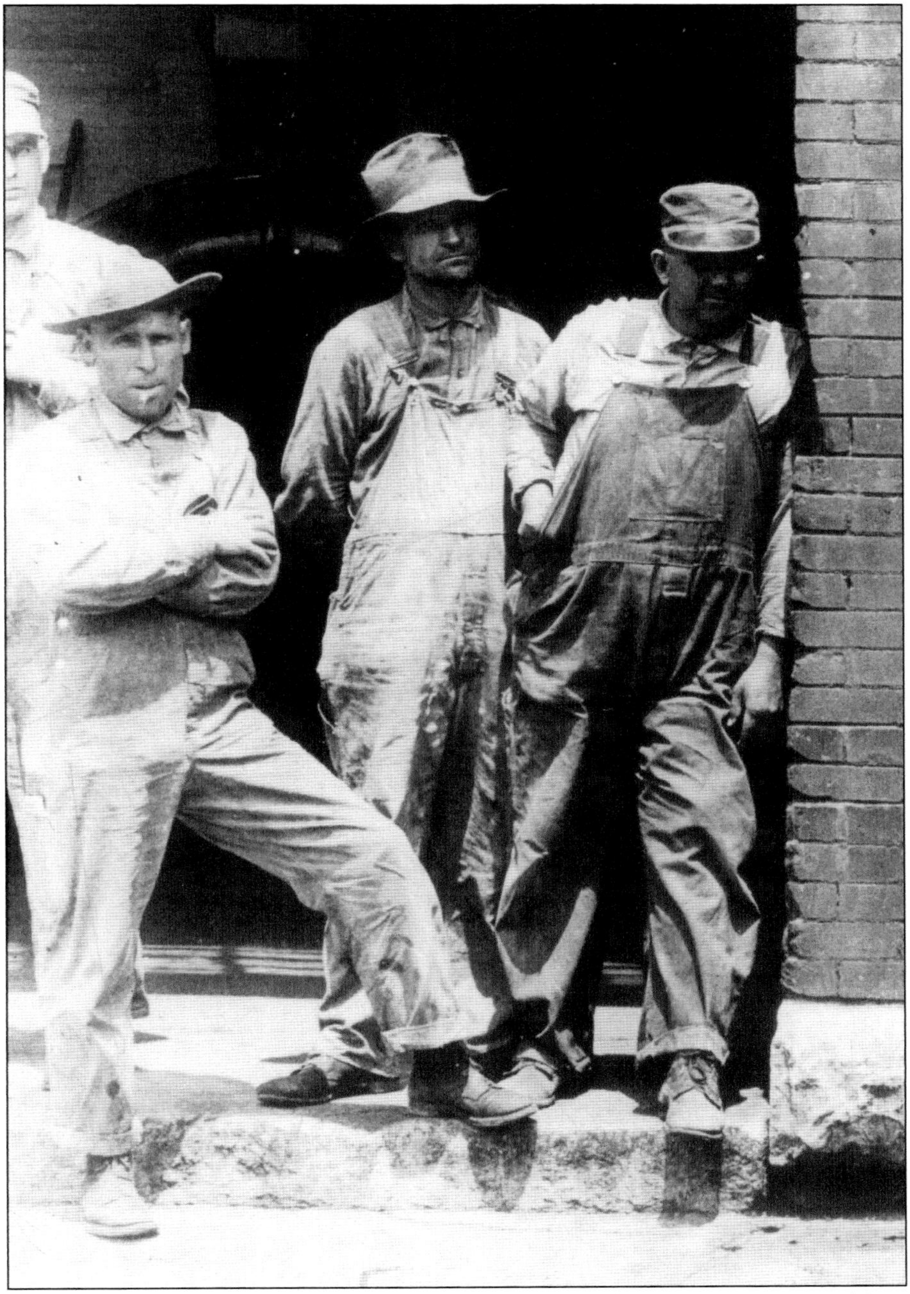

While much of the public spent a considerable part of their adult lives commuting to and from work on streetcars, they seldom came in close contact with any transit employees other than the conductor while he collected their fare or perhaps the car's motorman as they disembarked at the end of their journey. Passengers rarely considered that it took hundreds of other employees to keep the cars and tracks maintained in good working order. This included an army of mechanics, electricians, machinists, carpenters, painters, maintenance-of-way workers, and laborers to maintain and repair the rolling stock and tracks. It was rare that the often-forgotten shop employees had their photographs taken, but the company photographer recorded these men casually standing in front of the car shop on Fourth Avenue North in the early 1920s. (Metro Nashville Archives, MTA Collection.)

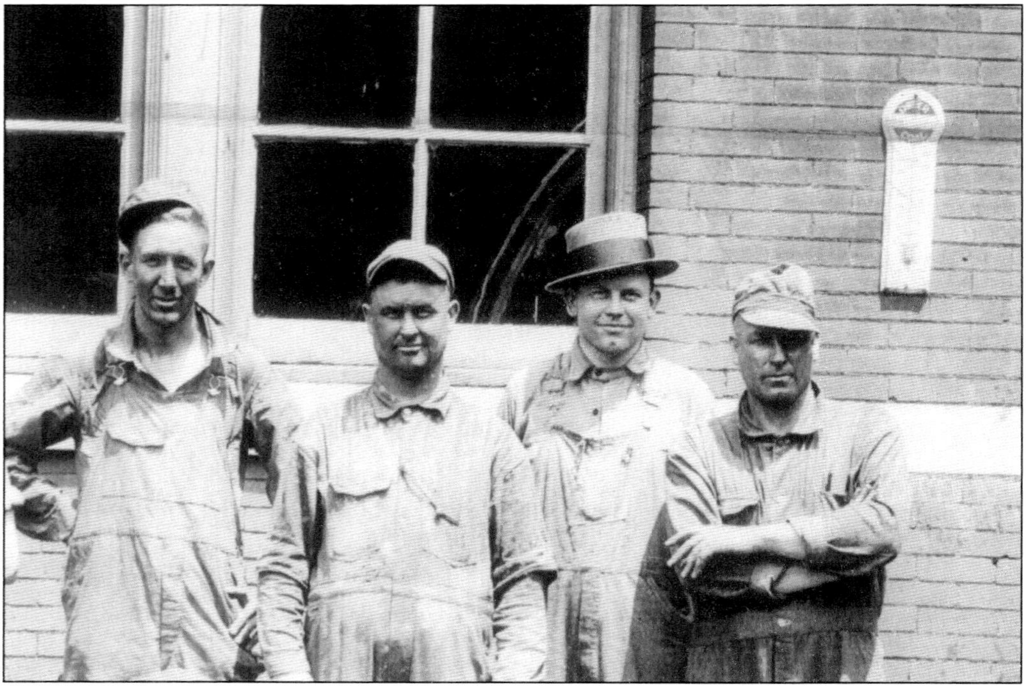

These two photographs were also taken in front of the NR&L shops, most likely at the same time as the image on the previous page but depicting additional shop employees. (Both, Metro Nashville Archives, MTA Collection.)

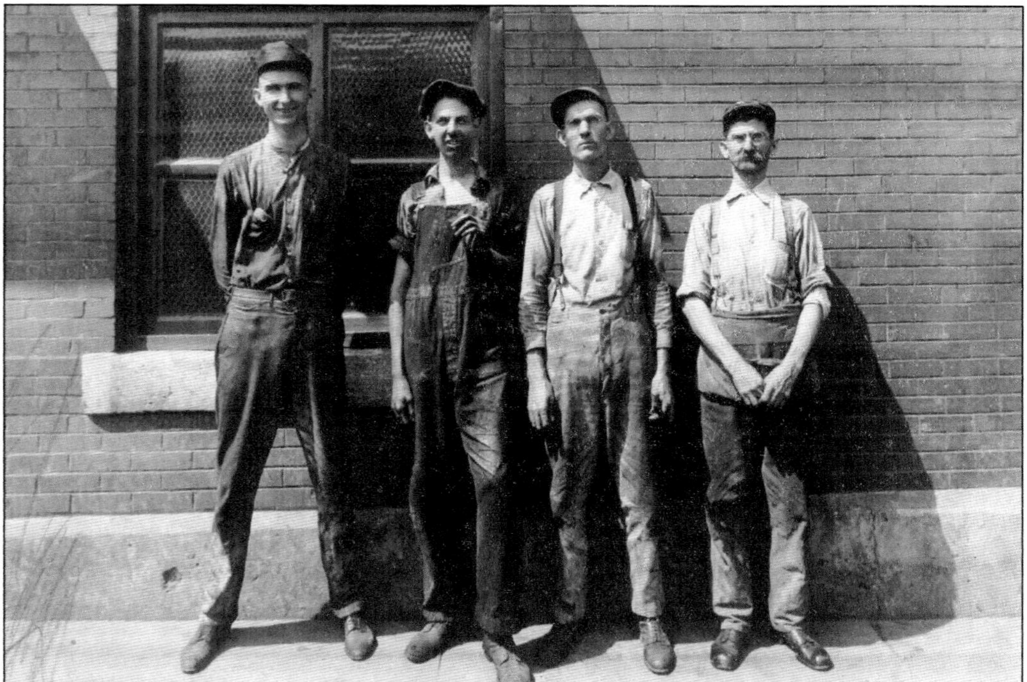

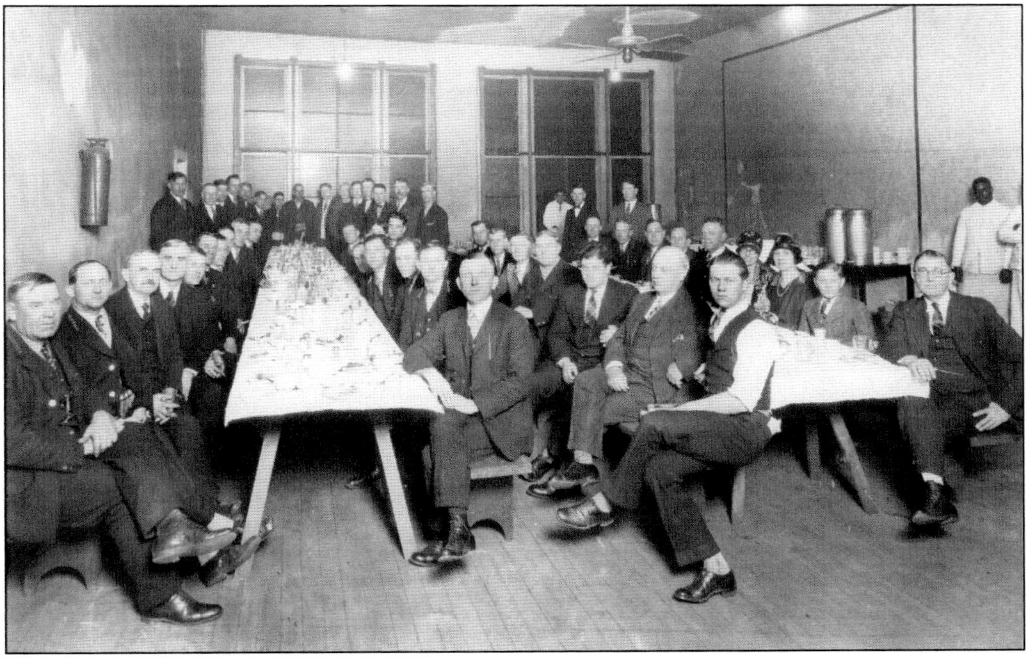

In the undated photograph above, several employees of the Nashville Railway & Light Company have assembled for a meeting that included a meal. Nearly all the men are motormen and conductors, along with perhaps the superintendent and other NR&L brass. Although the event appears to be an official gathering to discuss company business, one can't help but notice the drab condition of the room, with its unpainted plaster, simple light fixtures, and wooden benches. Below, the employees pose for another portrait while some finish their meals. The three men at far left in the back row appear to be musicians who provided entertainment for the event. (Both, Metro Nashville Archives, MTA Collection.)

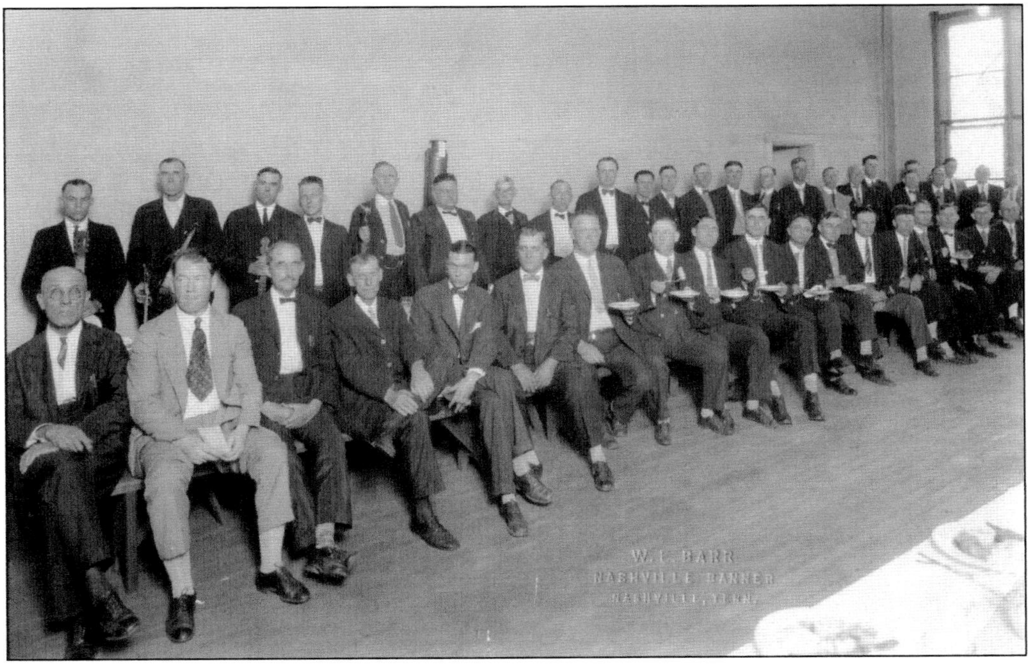

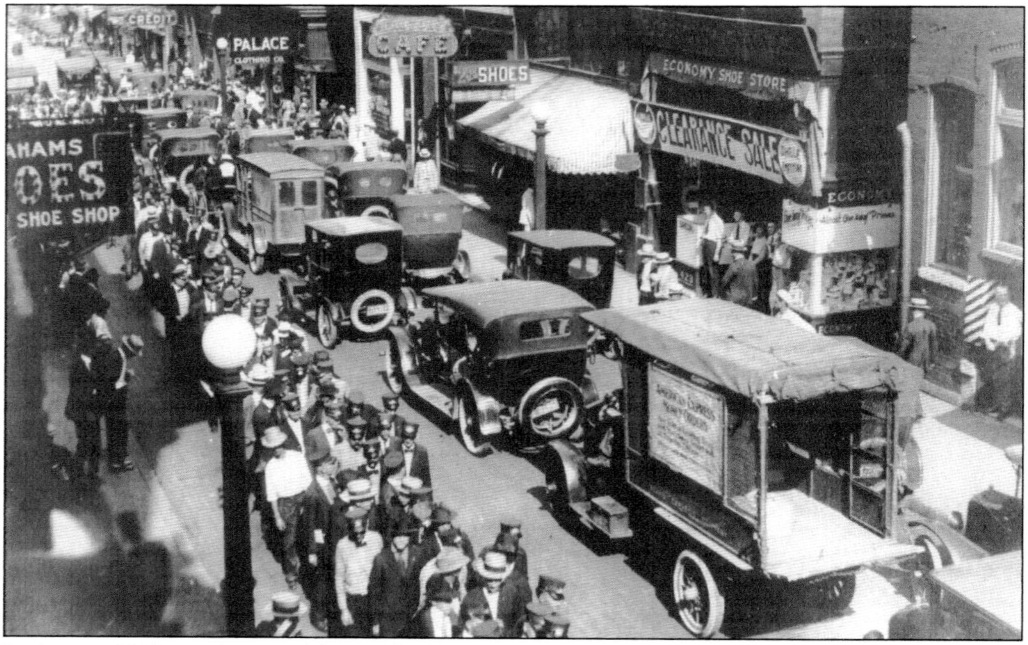

In August 1919, employees of the Nashville Railway & Light Company went on strike demanding better pay and working conditions. Motormen, conductors, and other employees march down Union Street near their union headquarters in a show of solidarity. (David H. Steinberg collection.)

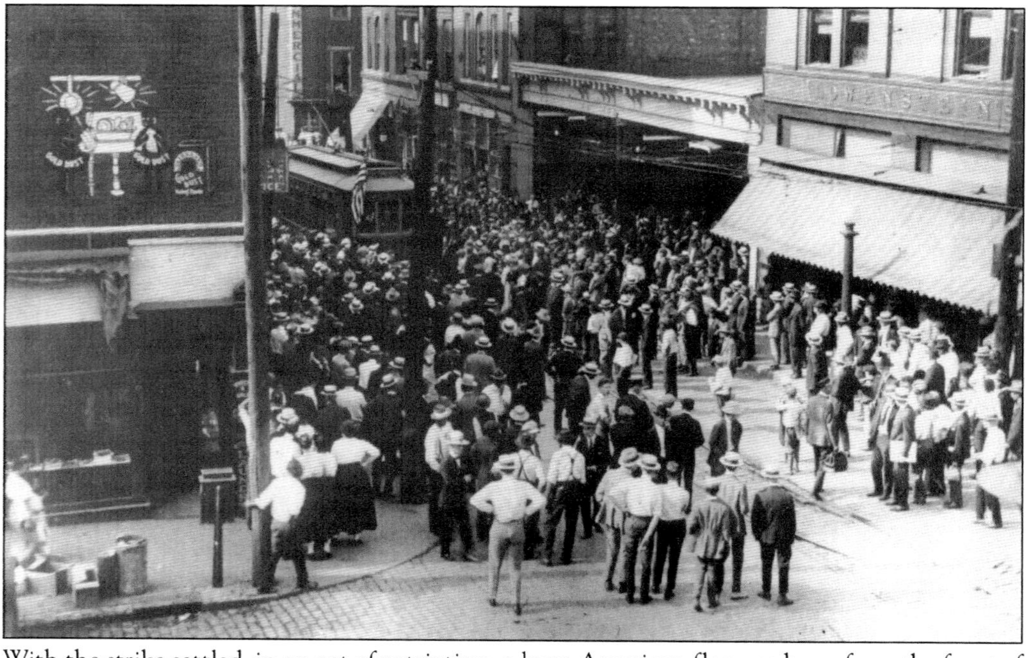

With the strike settled, in an act of patriotism, a large American flag was hung from the front of a West Nashville streetcar by motorman J.H. Gardner, the first man discharged for joining the union. A throng of cheerful employees of the Nashville Railway & Light Company crowd Fourth Avenue to watch the first streetcar arrive at the Transfer Station from the carbarn on the hot afternoon of August 21, 1919. Moments later, passengers boarded the first revenue run since the shutdown, and business resumed. (Tennessee State Library and Archives.)

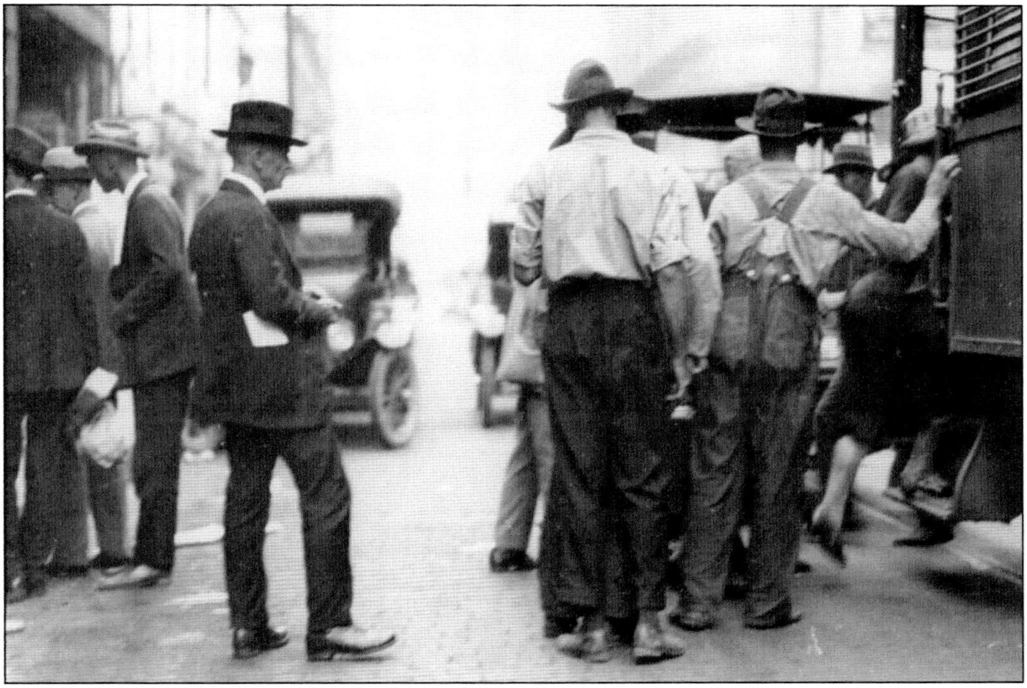

Passengers dodge downtown vehicles while boarding a streetcar on Fourth Avenue one late afternoon in 1925. One safety risk posed by streetcars was having to load and disembark in the center of congested streets. (Metro Nashville Archives, MTA Collection.)

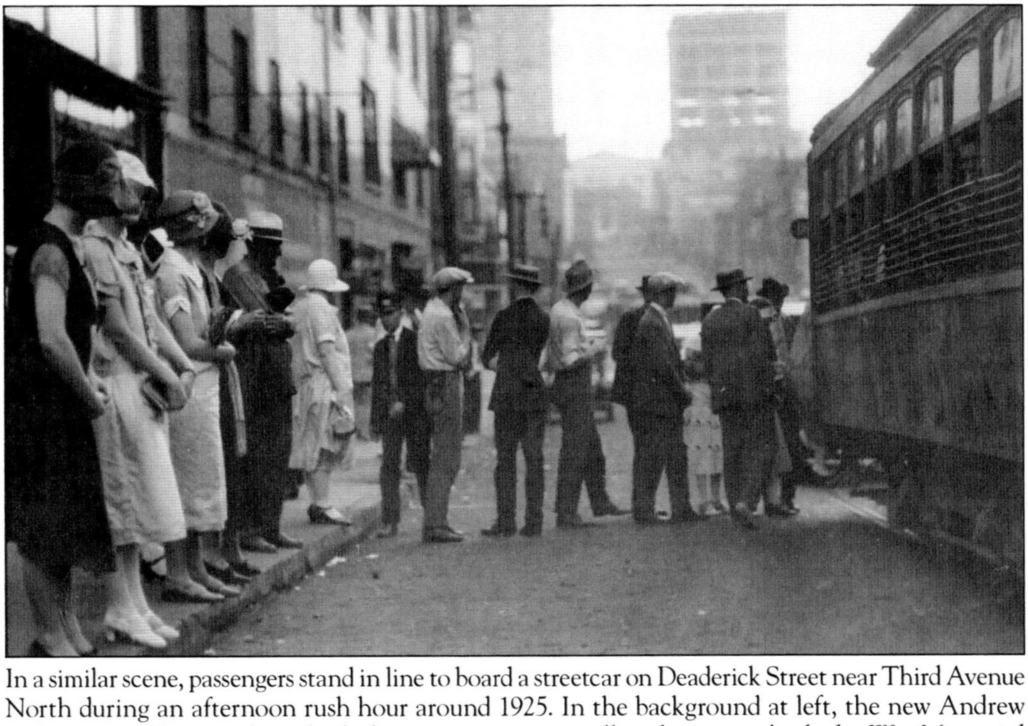

In a similar scene, passengers stand in line to board a streetcar on Deaderick Street near Third Avenue North during an afternoon rush hour around 1925. In the background at left, the new Andrew Jackson Hotel has just been built, but construction is still underway on both the War Memorial Auditorium and the Cotton States Building. (Metro Nashville Archives, MTA Collection.)

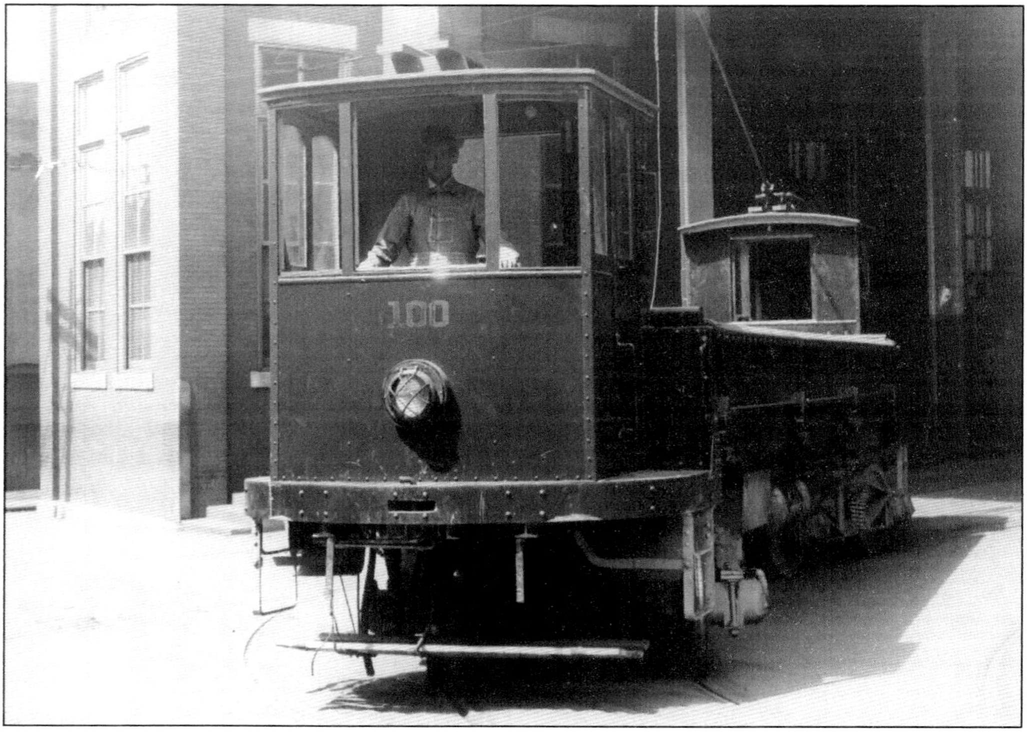

To keep a street railway in good running order, maintenance on both the tracks and right-of-way is an ongoing chore requiring special equipment. Part of this equipment was car No. 100, an air-operated side-dump car built by the Differential Steel Car Company of Findley, Ohio. These 1920s photographs were taken at the Nashville carbarn on Third Avenue North by the Nashville Railway & Light Company photographer to possibly publicize the newly acquired piece of equipment. They show the car from different angles: from the front showing the motorman at the controls, and from the side to better illustrate its unloading feature. (Both, Metro Nashville Archives, MTA Collection.)

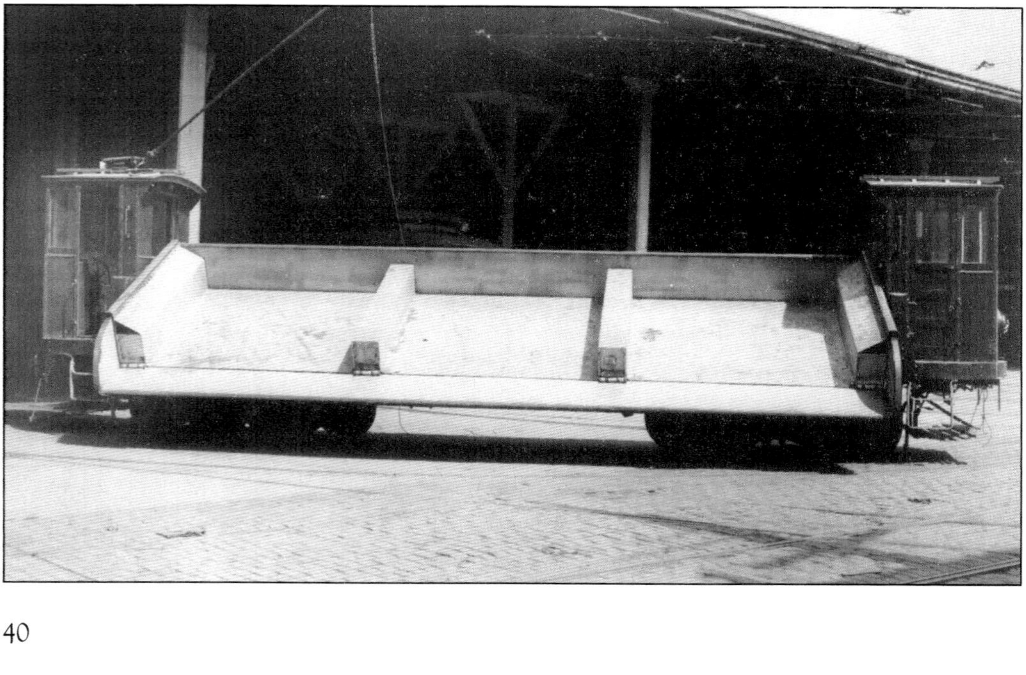

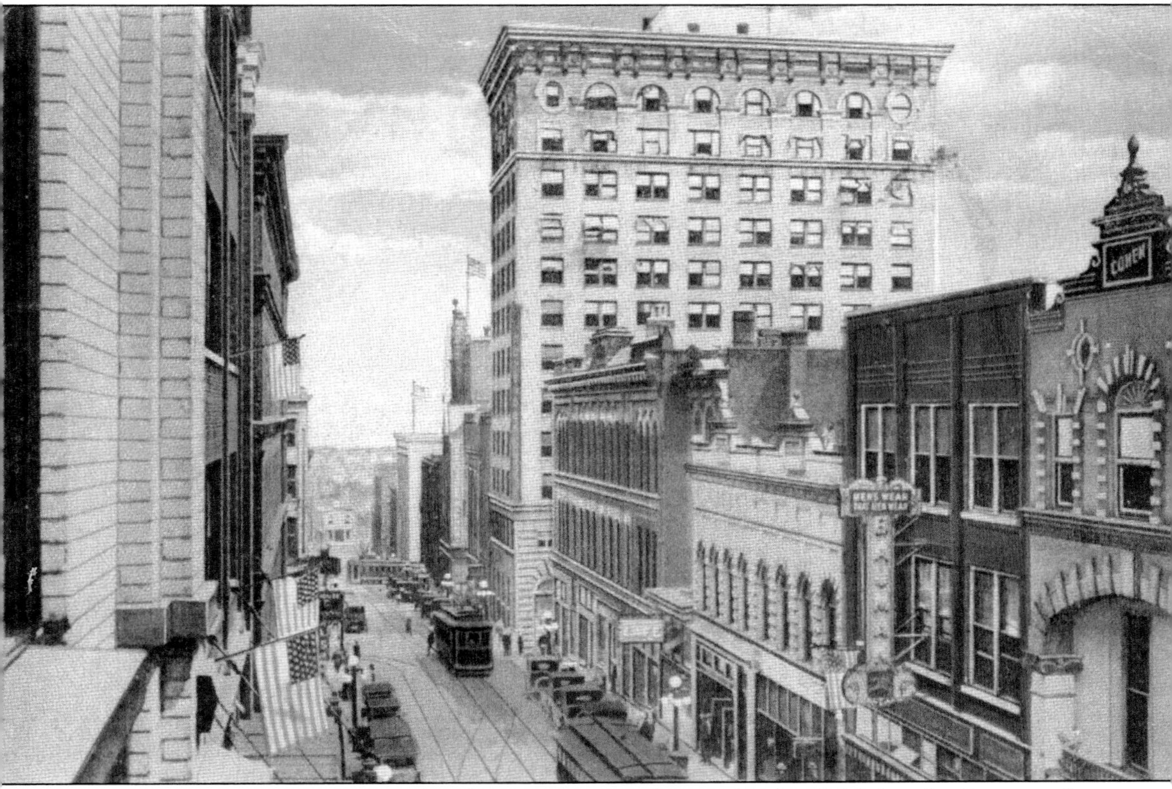

For many of the streetcar lines heading west or south from Nashville's Transfer Station, the tracks proceeded north on Fourth Avenue before turning west on Church Street, where many of the city's prominent businesses were located. The four blocks between Fourth and Eighth Avenues included department stores, hotels, theaters, restaurants, doctors' offices, and a variety of other merchants. Once the streetcars reached Eighth Avenue, the tracks diverged. One set continued west on Church Street, while the other set turned south toward Broadway. Looking east on Church Street toward Fourth Avenue, two streetcars travel away from the photographer going toward the Transfer Station, while another car crosses in the distance. Landmarks in this photograph include the 12-story Independent Life Building, once Nashville's tallest structure, and the Cohen Building. Both notable buildings still survive. (Metro Nashville Archives, Ridley Wills II Collection.)

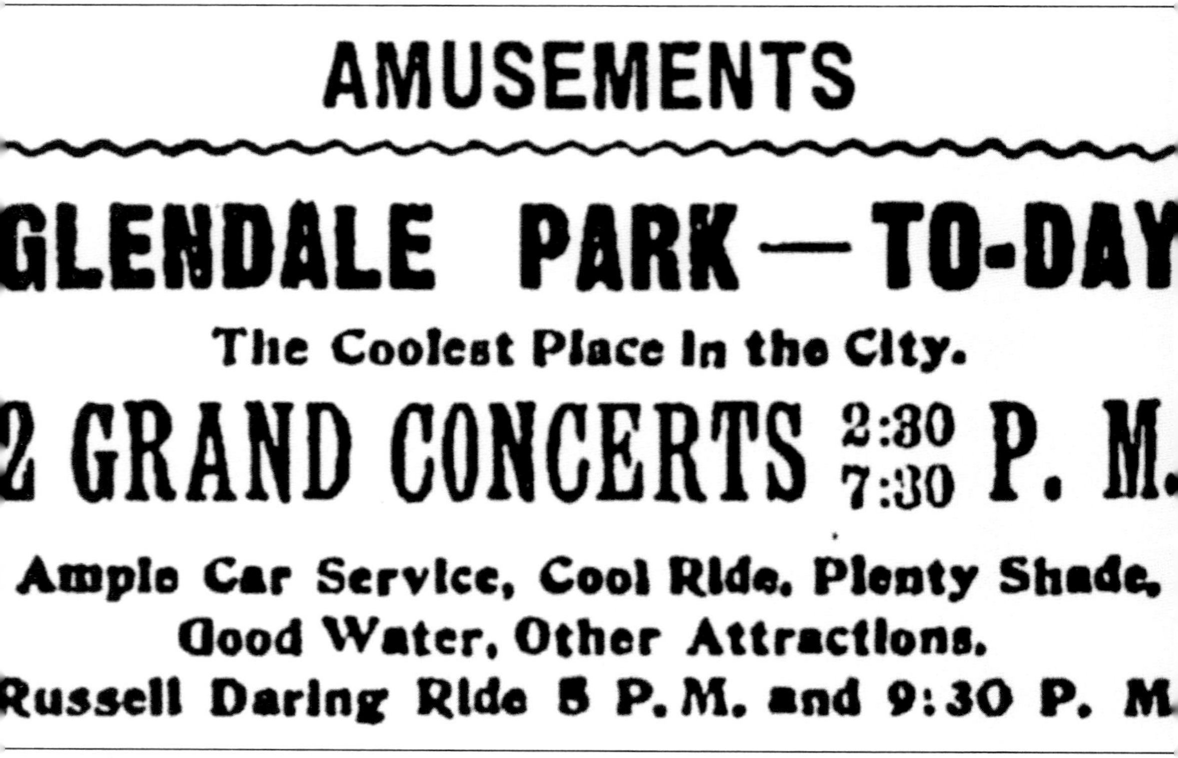

The Nashville Railway & Light Company routinely advertised in the Nashville newspapers, primarily promoting electric appliances, but it also regularly touted its company-owned Glendale Park. During the early 20th century, the popular Nashville attraction featured a zoo, carnival rides, roller rink, tennis court, croquet ground, bandstand, and casino. In an era before automobiles were affordable, the only way to travel to the park was by streetcar. For those living in the city, Glendale Park was a welcome respite where visitors could leave their worries behind. The venue was billed by its owners as the "coolest place in the city," an important selling point before air-conditioning. (Author's collection.)

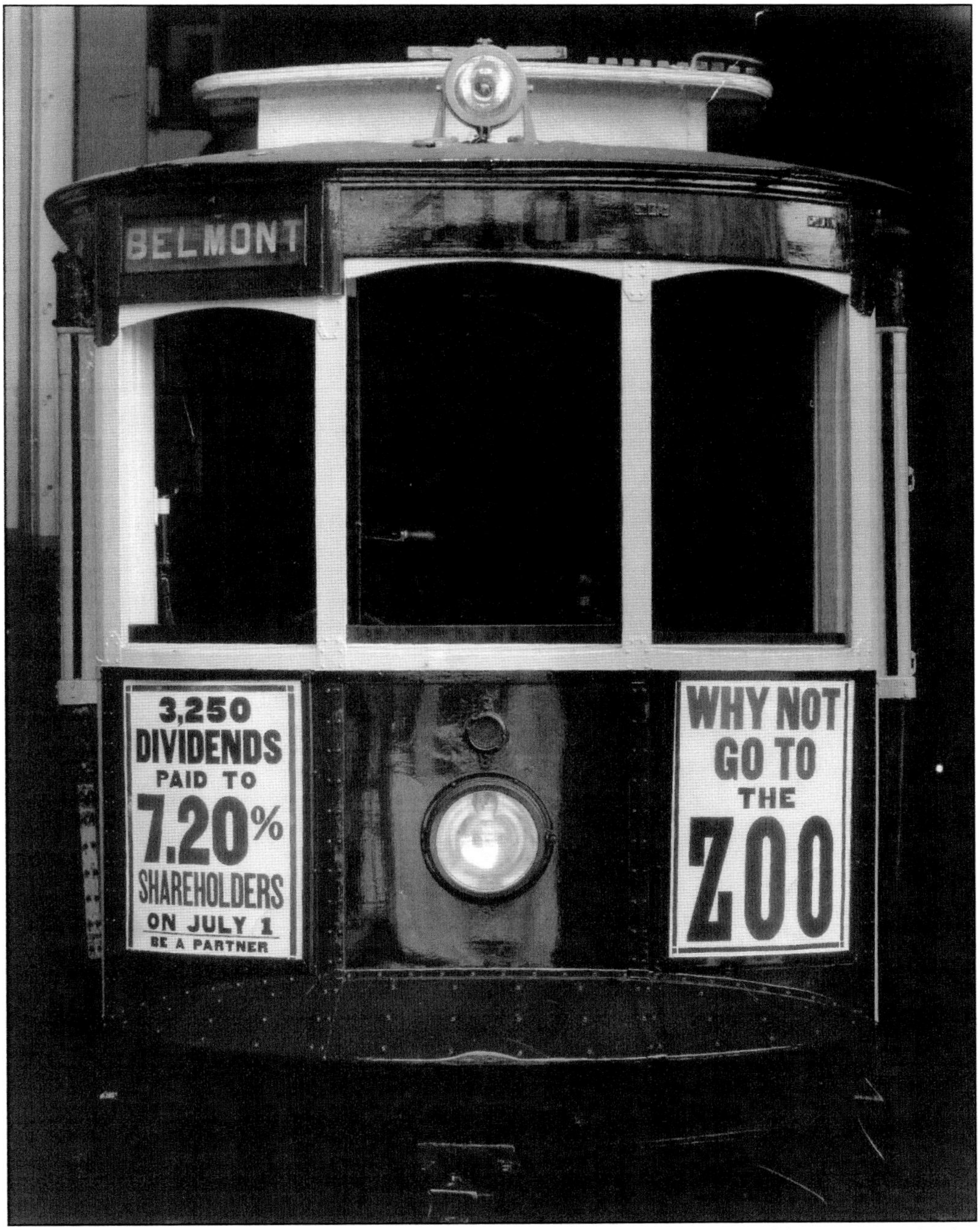

The placement of advertisements on both the interior and exterior of public transit vehicles began during the late 1800s with horse-drawn trolleys. The practice continues to this day on transit vehicles. Advertising on the exterior of Nashville's streetcars was limited to only the front and rear of the vehicles, unlike modern buses, where ads are plastered on all sides. It was not uncommon for the Nashville Railway & Light Company to promote itself or its interests. In this view, No. 410 is shown at the company's paint shop on Fourth Avenue after being freshly shopped and sporting two new ads. The sign on the left refers to a shareholder program being endorsed by the company. The other publicizes the NR&L-owned zoo at Glendale Park. (Metro Nashville Archives, MTA Collection.)

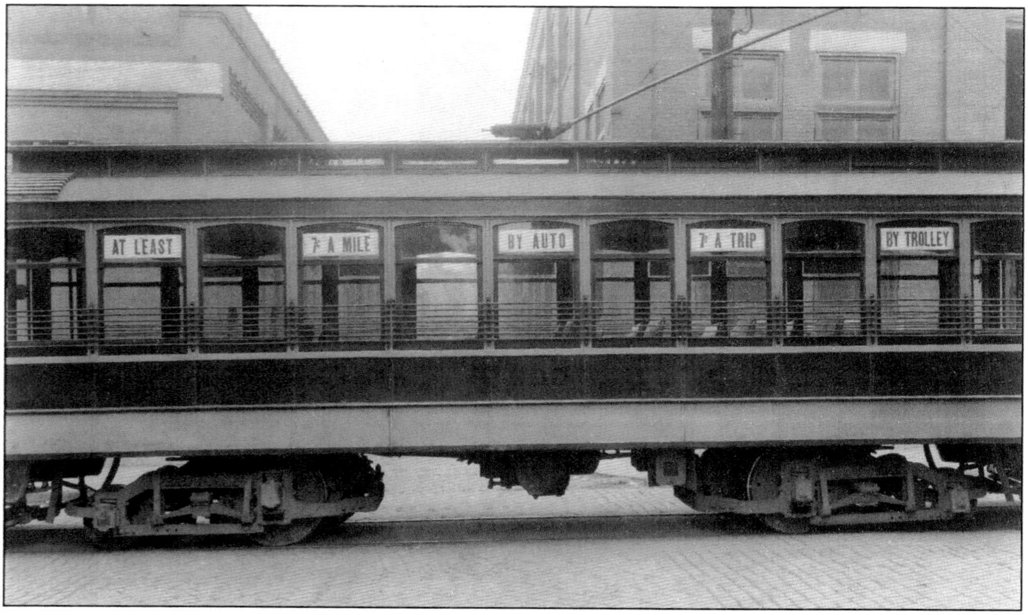

Car No. 500 is seen in front of the Fourth Avenue car shops with signage that reads "At least 7¢ a mile by auto 7¢ a trip by trolley" in an effort to lure motorists out of their cars. During the 1920s, streetcars and other forms of public transit were beginning to experience a drop in ridership as automobiles became affordable for the middle class. (Metro Nashville Archives, MTA Collection.)

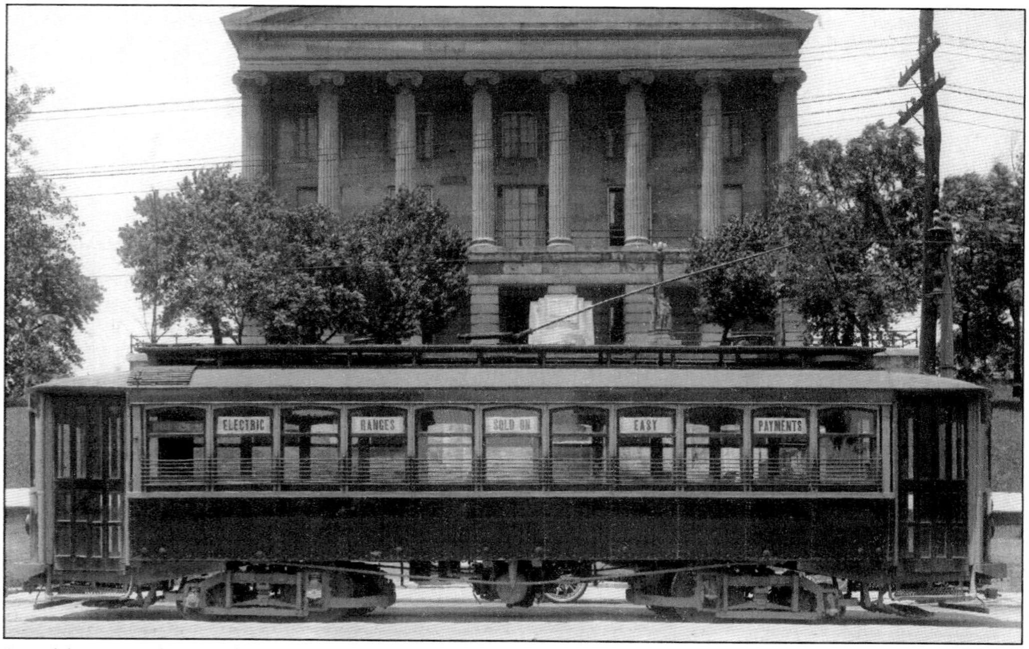

In addition to being the owner of the city's street railway system, the city's power company, and Glendale Park, the Nashville Railway & Light Company also sold a wide variety of electric appliances in its downtown showroom inside the Watkins Building on Church Street. In another example of self-promotion, car No. 418 is adorned with window signs that read "Electric ranges sold on easy payments." This scene was staged on Cedar Street using the Tennessee State Capitol as a backdrop. (Metro Nashville Archives, MTA Collection.)

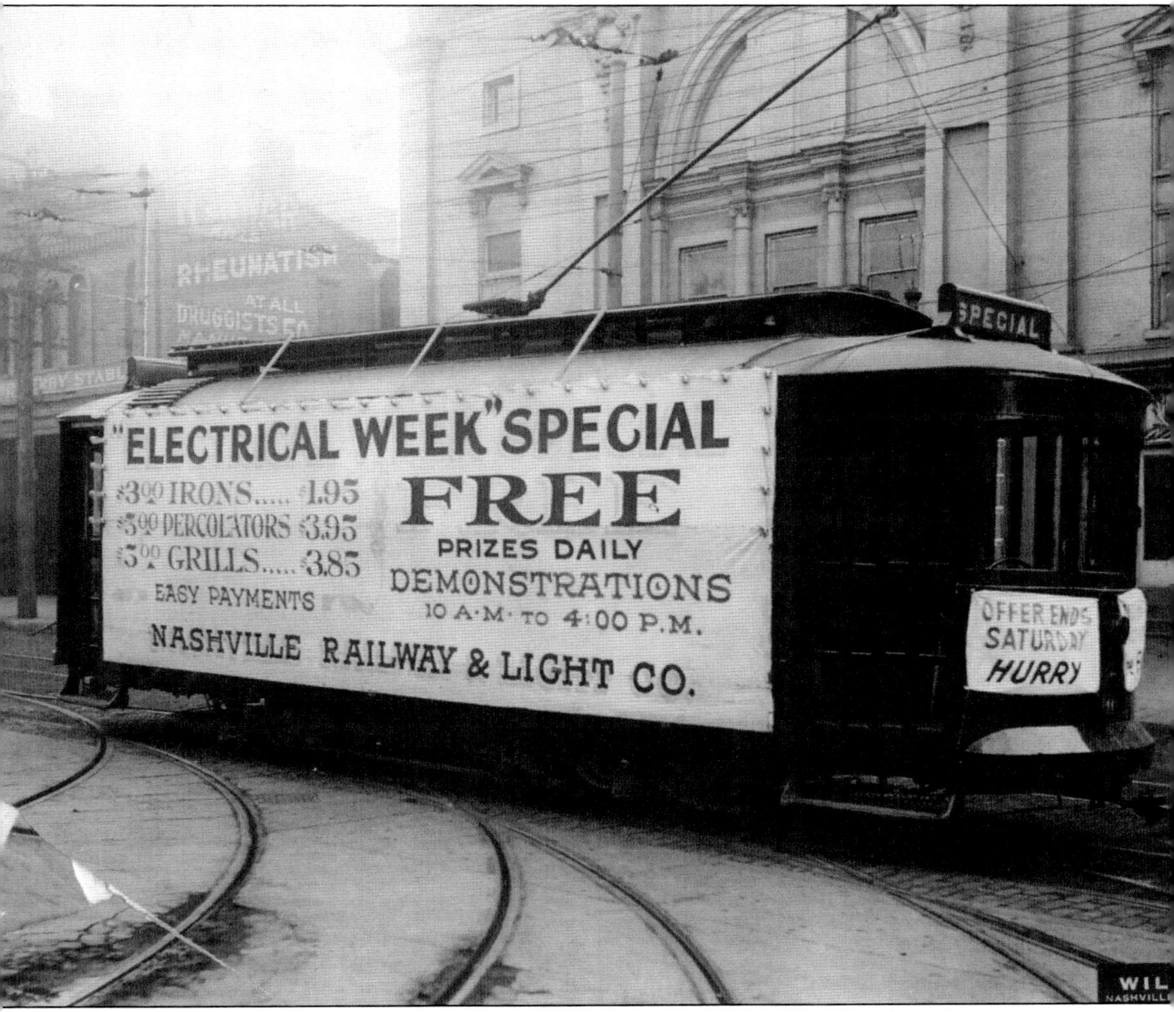

For more than 25 years, the Nashville Railway & Light Company was a very lucrative enterprise branching out into various related endeavors. The company regularly ran advertisements in most of Nashville's newspapers promoting the latest in chore-saving gadgets, including washing machines, ranges, and percolators. Not wanting to waste resources, the NR&L also regularly utilized streetcars to double as mobile billboards, getting its message across efficiently. In what may be one of the earliest examples of "wrap advertising," such a car is spotted in front of the Bijou Theater on Fourth Avenue in the 1920s. (Nashville Public Library, Special Collections.)

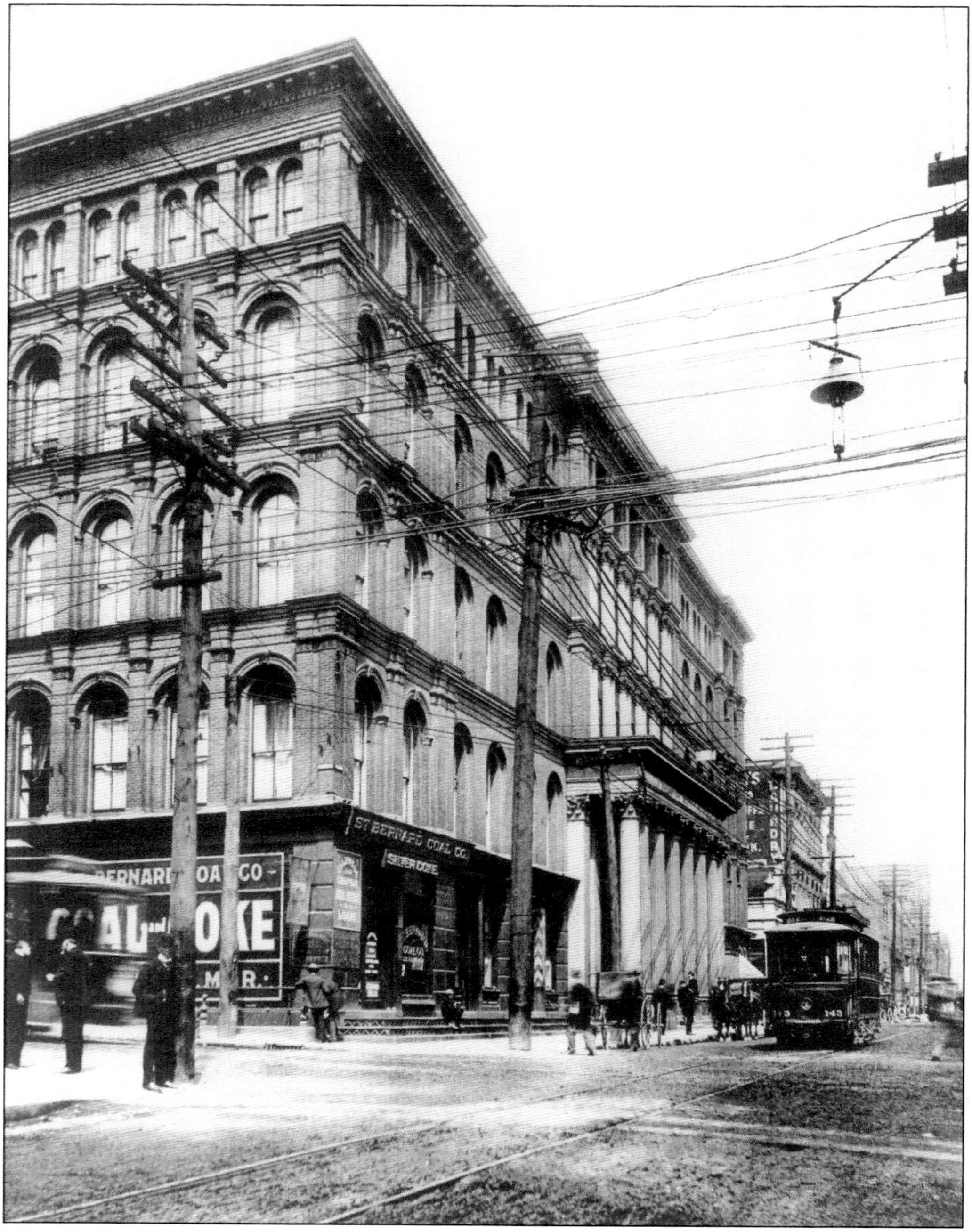

With Nashville's Historic Maxwell House Hotel as a backdrop, car No. 143 makes a brief stop while heading south on Fourth Avenue as another streetcar, at left, heads west on Church Street and out of the camera's view. In 1910, around the time this photograph was taken, film speeds were so slow that virtually all motion was blurred. (David H. Steinberg collection.)

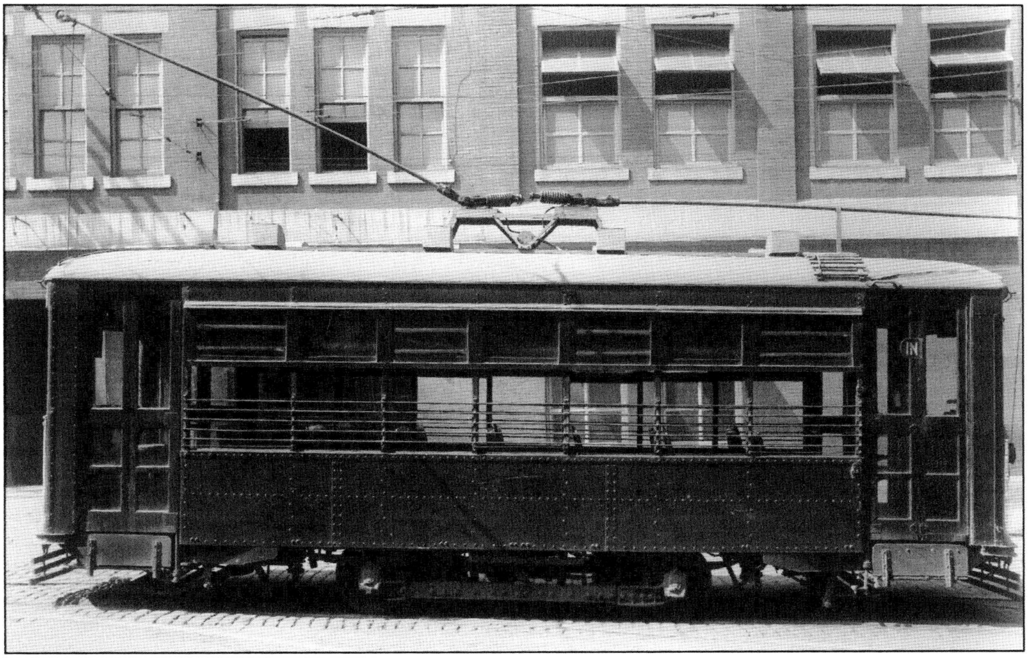

Nashville Railway & Light Company No. 52 was built by the American Car Company in 1919. The car has been staged in front of the shops on Fourth Avenue for the company photographer, most likely soon after it arrived on the property. (Metro Nashville Archives, MTA Collection.)

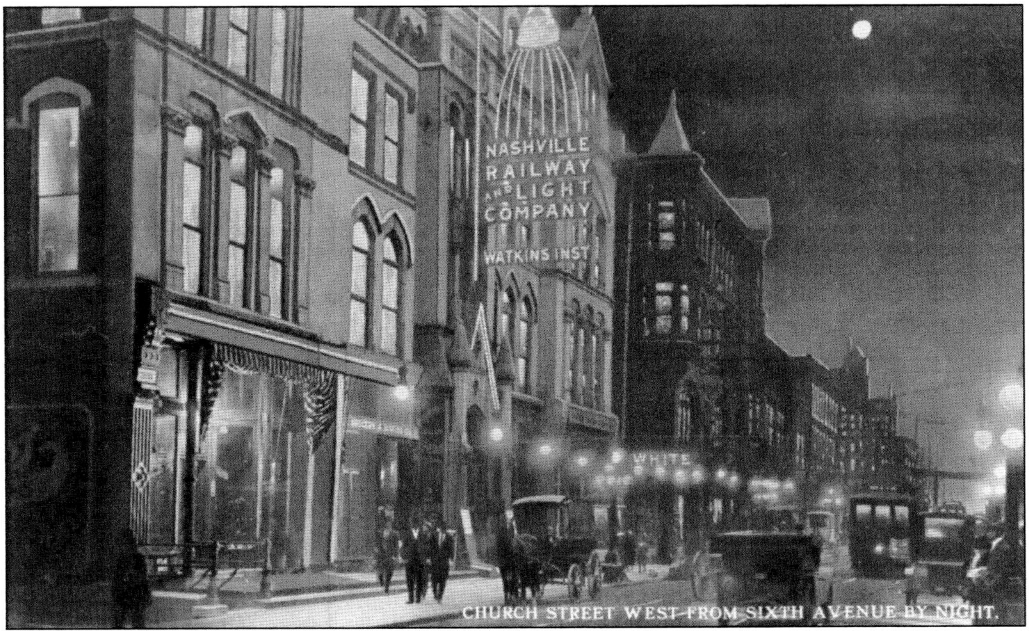

For decades, the stately Watkins Institute Building on Church Street was where the administrative offices were based for the Nashville Railway & Light Company and successor Tennessee Electric Power Company. During this time, the utility company could boast of having the largest electric sign in Nashville. The sign shown in this simulated night view from around 1915 was replaced by a larger and more impressive one 10 years later (see page 63). (Metro Nashville Archives, Ridley Wills II Collection.)

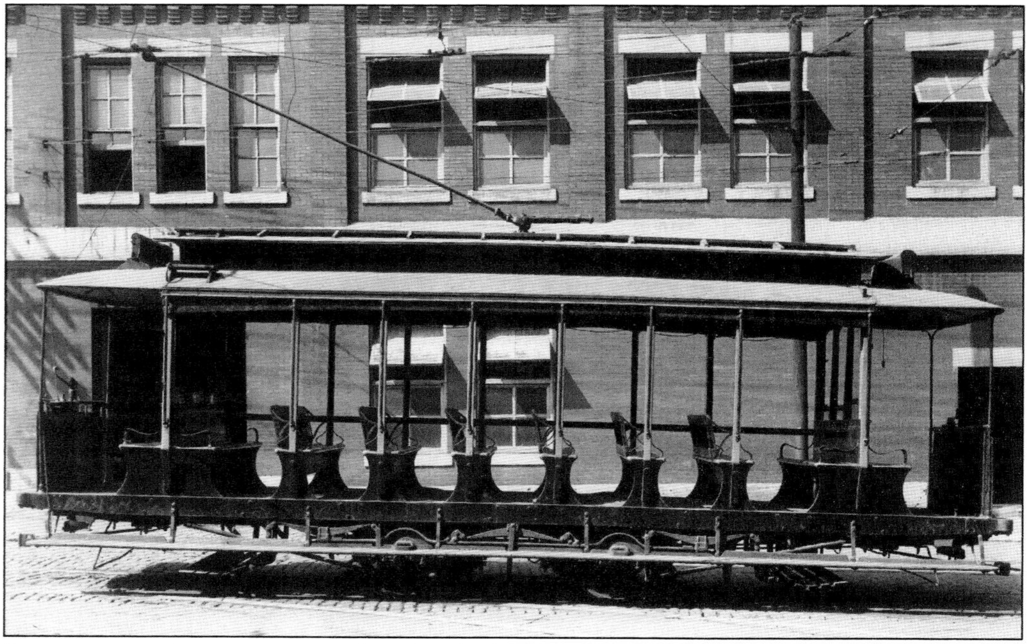

For operations during warm weather, the Nashville Railway and Light Company owned several open cars. The motorman's controls are at both ends of the vehicle, and seat backs are reversible for operation in either direction. This company photograph of an unidentified car was taken in front of the car shops on Fourth Avenue. (Nashville Public Library, Special Collections.)

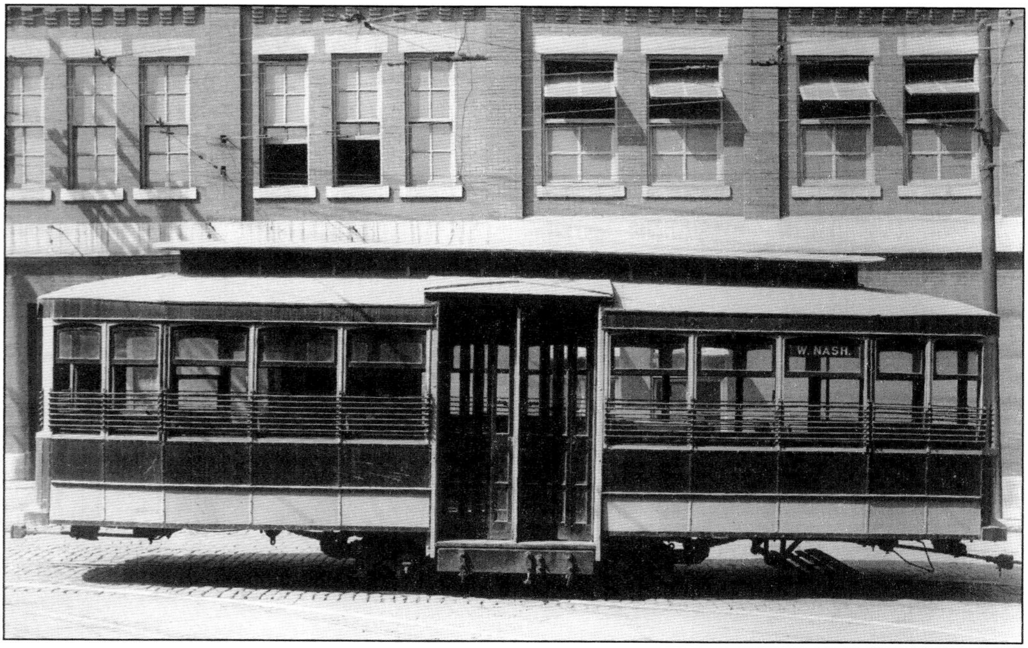

Over the years, Nashville's street railway companies owned a wide variety of equipment built by various manufacturers, including the Birney, American, and St. Paul Noiseless car companies. One of the more unique cars on the roster was No. 326, a center-door non-powered trailing car shown in front of the shops on Fourth Avenue. During special events or when hauling heavier crowds, this car could be coupled to powered cars, increasing capacity. (Metro Nashville Archives, MTA Collection.)

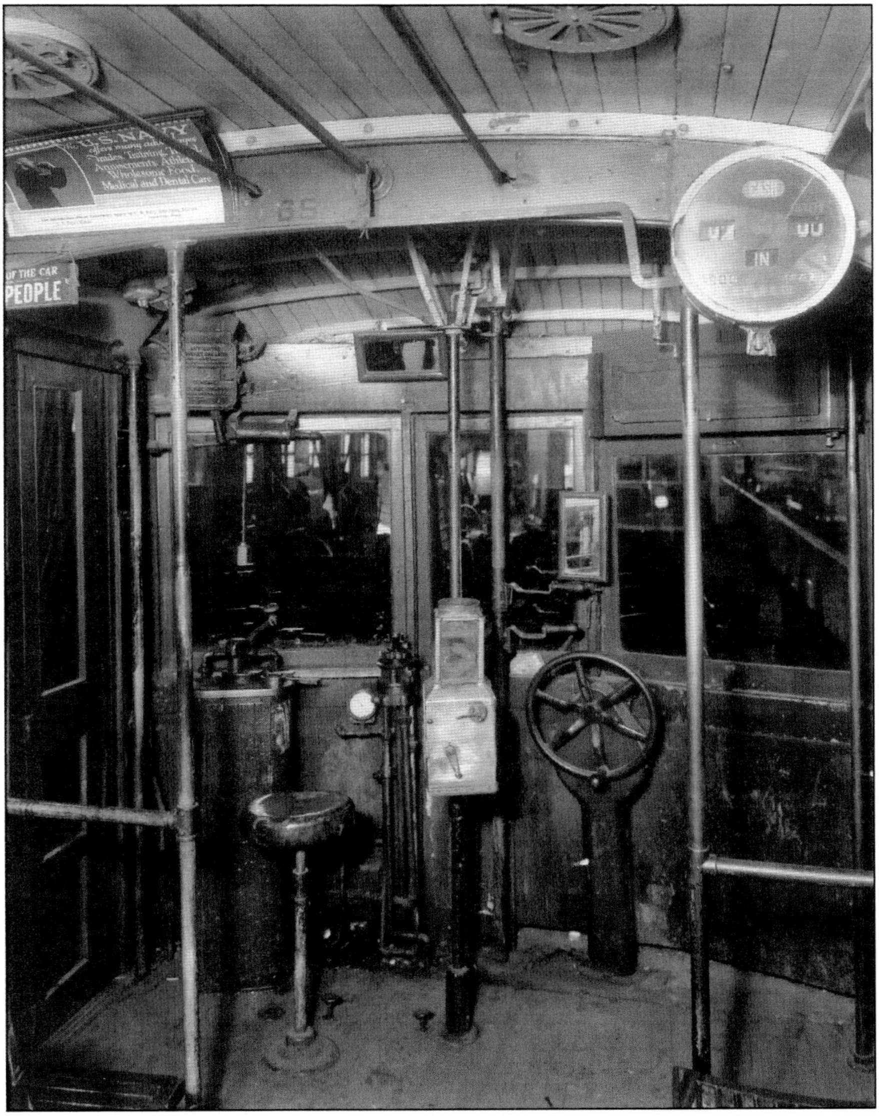

This is a typical motorman's control stand in an early electric streetcar. The job of a motorman was an important one; he had to be familiar with all the controls and how the car reacted with each application of acceleration or brakes. Over the years, the arrangement of the controls was relatively standard, with some variations depending on the car builder. The motorman's stool was on the left, facing the direction of travel. To the left of the stool was the handle for the controller. As the name implies, this device controls the speed of the streetcar in the same manner as the accelerator of an automobile. To the immediate right of the control handle is the directional key, allowing the vehicle to go forward or reverse. In the upper left is the handle for the automatic circuit breaker box, permitting the motorman to quickly cut power in the event of an emergency. Located on the floor beneath the stool were two pedals. One of these controlled the gong, which served to warn nearby autos or pedestrians. The other was known as the dead man's control. If the motorman were to release this pedal when the car was in motion, the brakes would automatically be applied. Between the stool and the brake wheel is the fare box, which had to be manually cranked by the motorman each time coins or tokens were inserted. The round device at upper right is a fare register/counter, which registered the number of fares boarding. (Metro Nashville Archives, MTA Collection.)

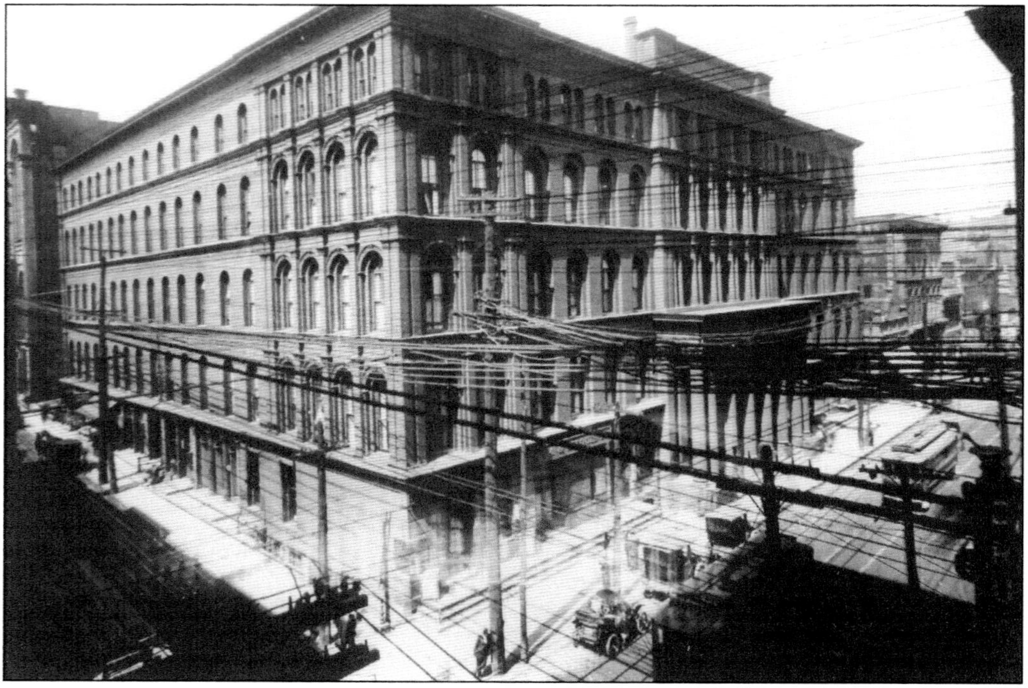

Nashville's historic Maxwell House was the city's largest and most impressive hotel when it formally opened in 1869 (previously, the unfinished structure had served as a barracks, prison, and hospital during the Civil War). Two cars are southbound on Fourth Avenue near Church Street, partially obscured by a web of electric lines. This eyesore was eliminated when the poles were removed and the lines moved underground. (Tennessee State Library and Archives.)

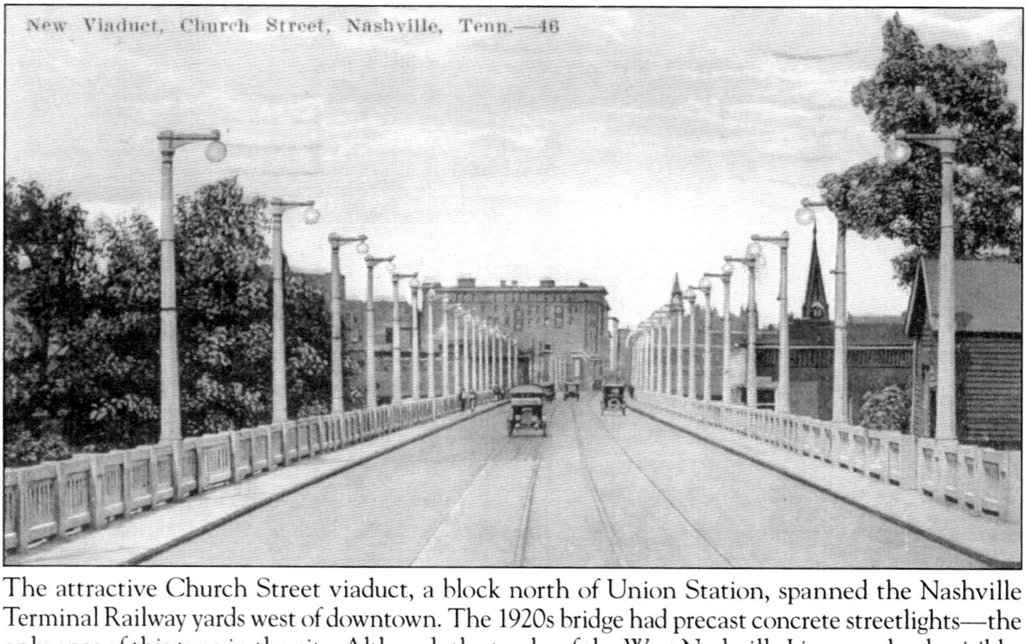

The attractive Church Street viaduct, a block north of Union Station, spanned the Nashville Terminal Railway yards west of downtown. The 1920s bridge had precast concrete streetlights—the only ones of this type in the city. Although the tracks of the West Nashville Line are clearly visible, the trolley and support wires were retouched out of the scene for aesthetic reasons on this postcard. The Hotel Tulane is in the background. (Metro Nashville Archives, Ridley Wills II Collection.)

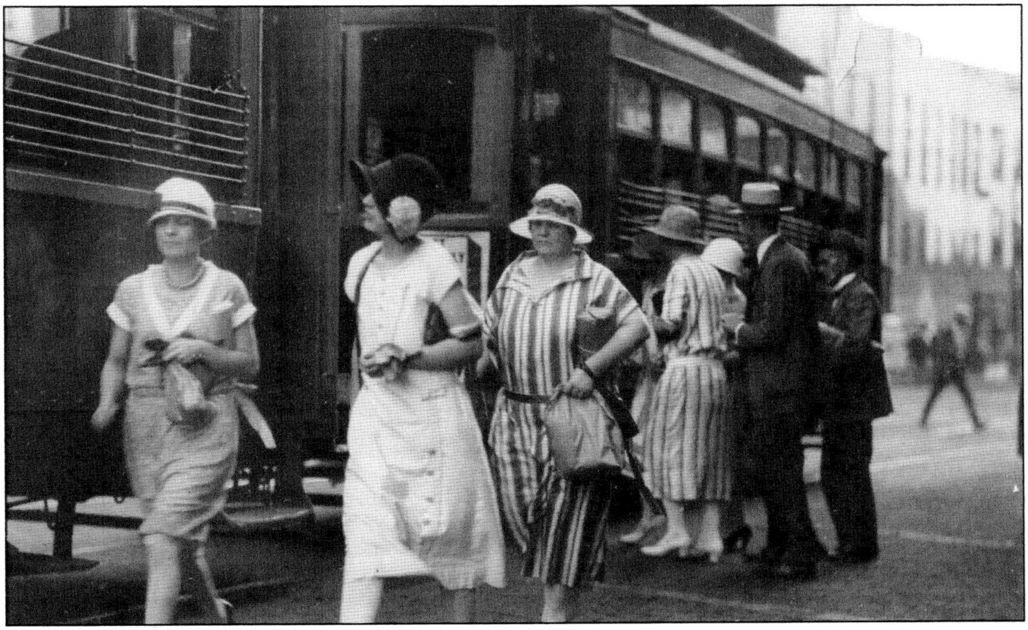

Over the past century, the time-honored ritual of commuting to work has changed little except for the style of clothing worn and the type of conveyance taken. In this scene from the 1920s, three women have just disembarked from a Nashville Railway & Light car on an unidentified downtown Nashville street. In the background, people line up to board at the rear of the car. (Metro Nashville Archives, MTA Collection.)

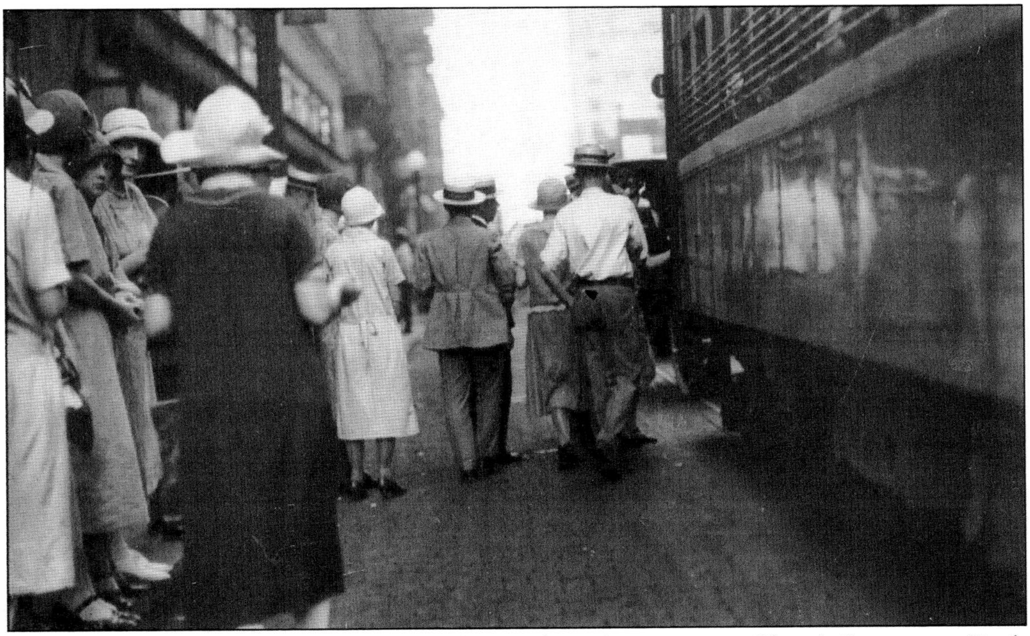

A line forms as people board at the rear of an outbound streetcar on Church Street near Sixth Avenue in downtown Nashville after a hard day's work. The Independent Life Building, once Nashville's tallest structure, can be seen in the distance. During the early 20th century, everyone wore a hat while outdoors; no self-respecting person would leave home without one. (Metro Nashville Archives, MTA Collection.)

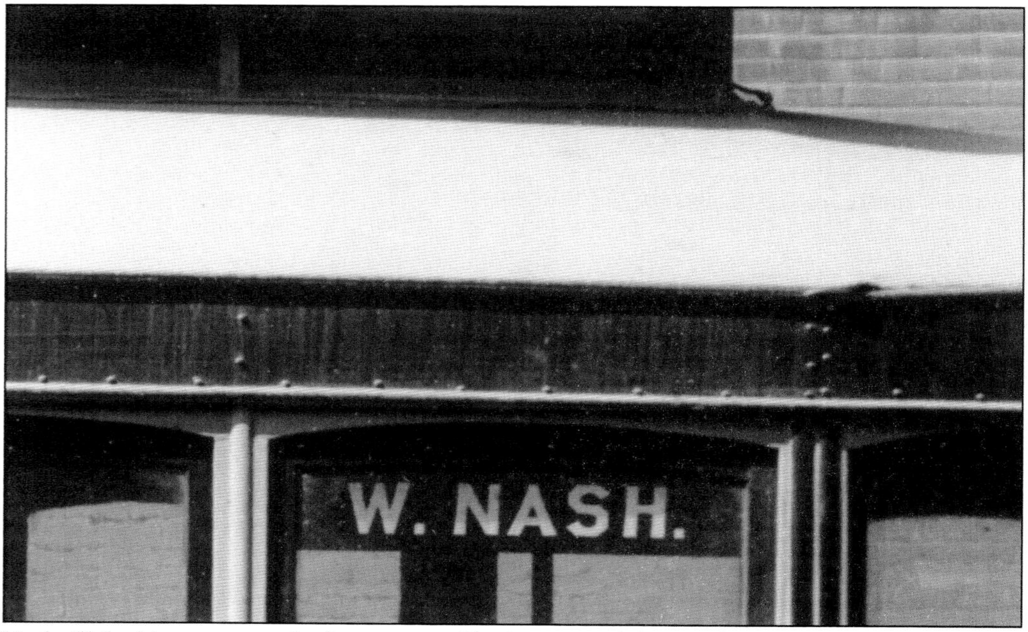

Nashville's older streetcars had unique profiles because of their 19th-century-style overhanging clerestory roofs. Newer-style cars built after 1920 sported simplified curved roofs that eliminated this characteristic, giving the vehicle a more modern look, affectionately nicknamed "baldies" by street railway employees. (Author's collection.)

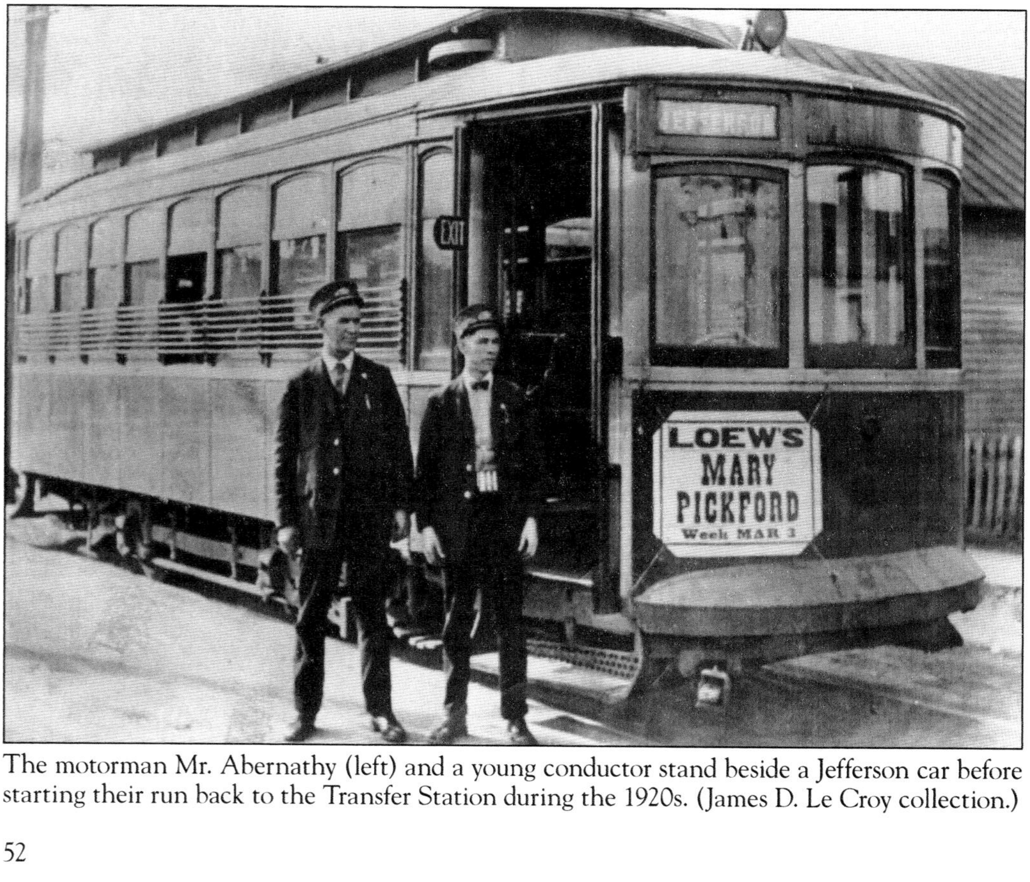

The motorman Mr. Abernathy (left) and a young conductor stand beside a Jefferson car before starting their run back to the Transfer Station during the 1920s. (James D. Le Croy collection.)

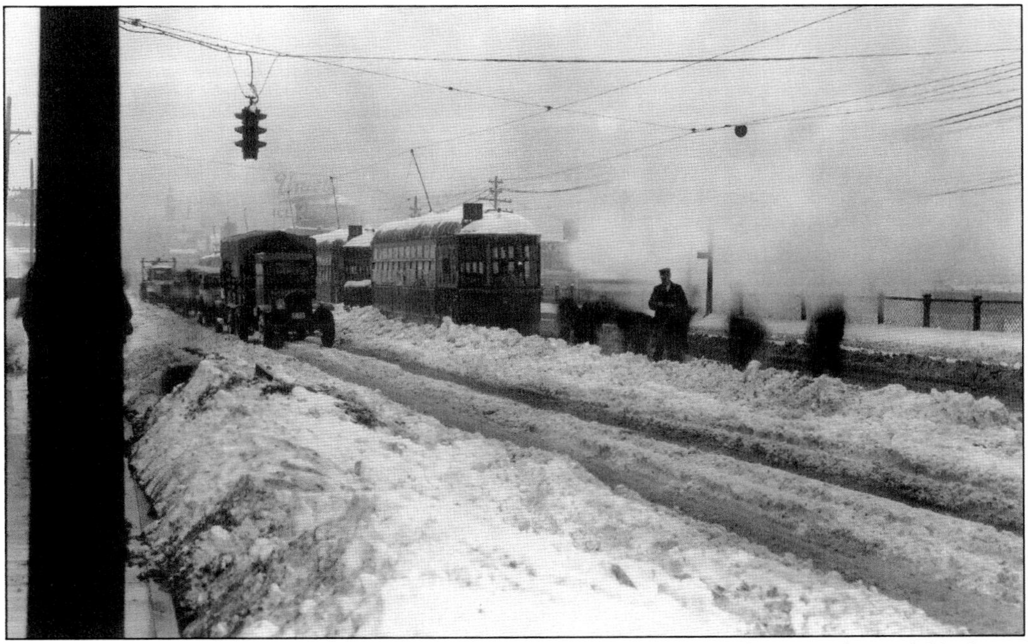

Over the years, inclement weather has occasionally hampered even the most dependable forms of public transportation. On February 20, 1929, Nashville was hit with an ice storm followed by 15 inches of snow. Automobiles packed the white stuff on the streetcar tracks, completely incapacitating the system. Borrowed city, county, and state road scrapers proved insufficient, and the trolley operators themselves warily wielded pick and shovel to loosen the frozen mass. These two photographs were taken looking in opposite directions at a line of six streetcars stranded on the Broadway viaduct between Tenth and Twelfth Avenues. The overcast sky and coal smoke made for a very bleak day, requiring the photographer to make a long exposure. (Both, Metro Nashville Archives, MTA Collection.)

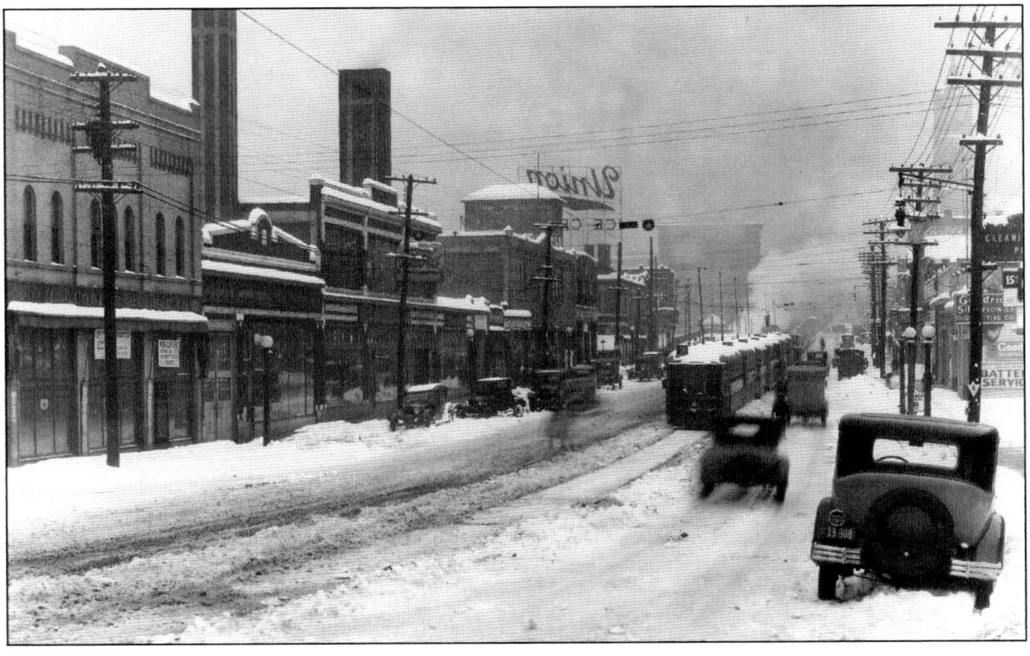

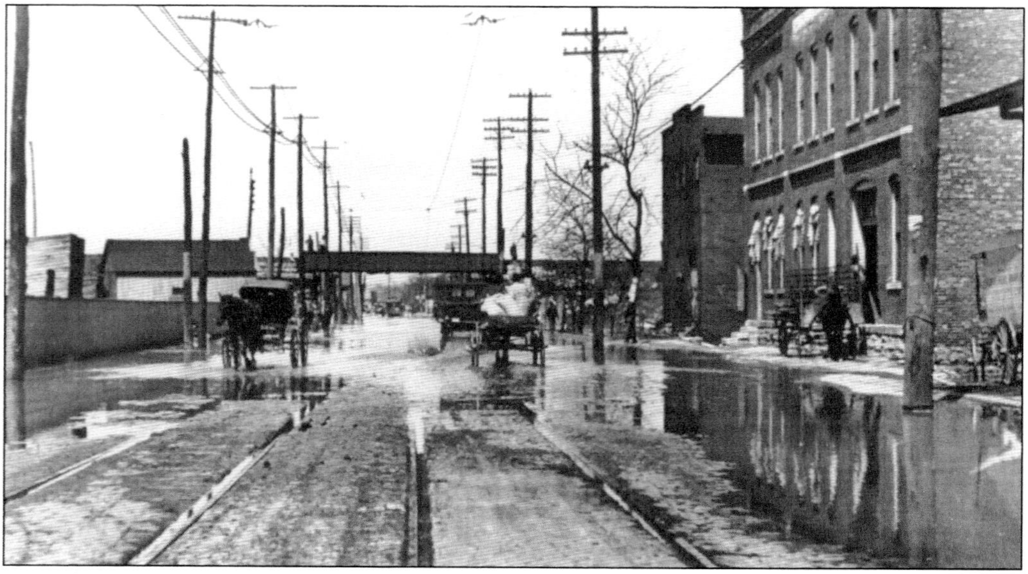

Over the years, the Nashville Railway & Light Company has experienced its share of weather-related hardships. Before the winter storms in 1929, several devastating floods in 1926 and 1927 caused property damage across the city. As a result, the street railway company sustained serious property losses and service interruptions on numerous lines. This scene illustrates the extent of damage as horse-drawn wagons plod slowly down First Street near the Louisville & Nashville Railroad overpass, immediately east of the Cumberland River. A stranded streetcar can be seen in the distance. (Tennessee State Library and Archives.)

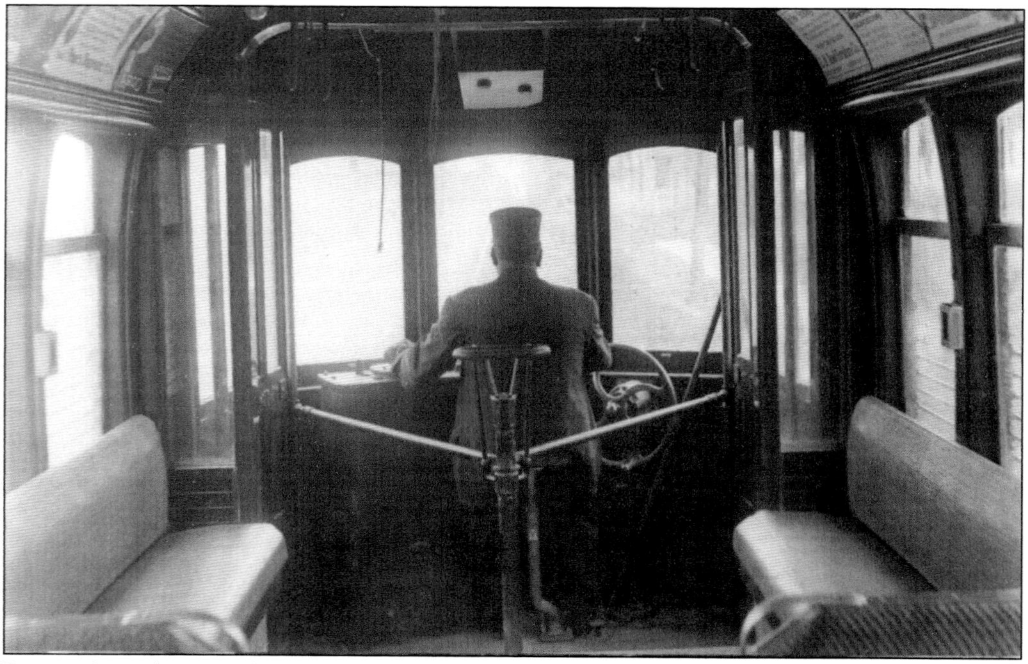

During the early years of street railway operation, cars were normally staffed by two men. Passengers boarded from the rear door, where the conductor collected the fare. Upon leaving, they would pass the motorman to exit through the front of the car. The absence of a fare box in this photograph illustrates such an operation. (Metro Nashville Archives, MTA Collection.)

Four

Tennessee Transportation Company

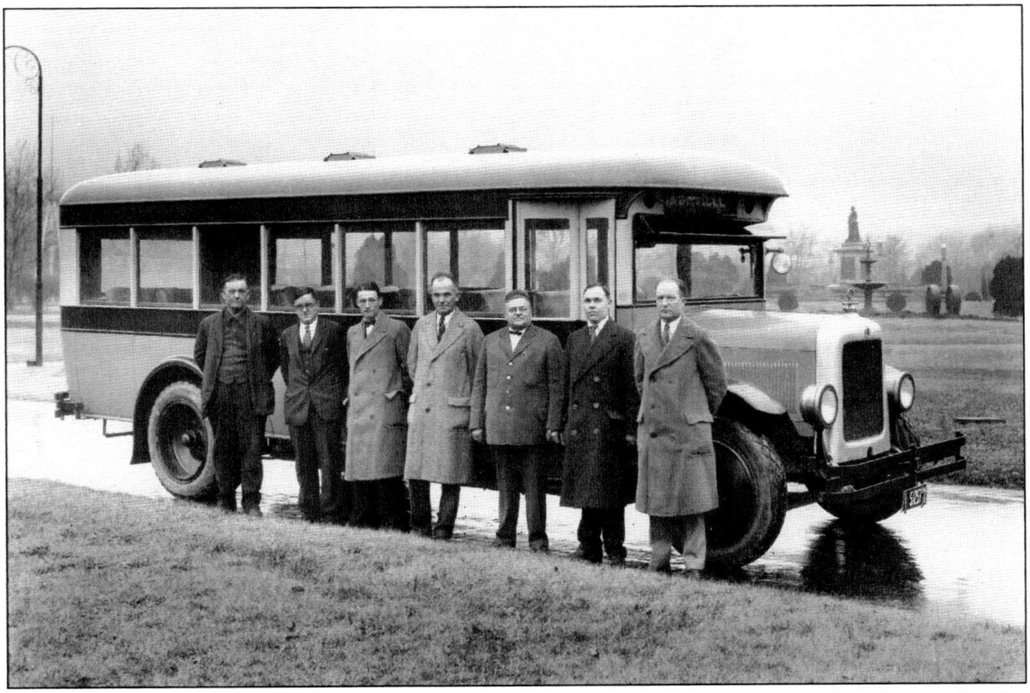

In 1926, the Nashville Railway & Light Company requested and was granted a charter for the incorporation of the Tennessee Transportation Company (TTC). The purpose for the new subsidiary was to expand rather than replace the existing street railway system using motorized buses. The mayor and city council of Nashville issued the fledgling company a license under an ordinance in October of that year. Two months later, TTC purchased 13 new Model Z-29 buses from the Yellow Coach Manufacturing Company. Soon, service was initiated on five new bus routes: Bordeaux, Dickerson Road, Granny White Pike, Inglewood, and Sunset Park. Nashville's Centennial Park was used as a location for this company photograph, taken on a cold and rainy day in 1927. Officials of TTC proudly pose in front of one of their new buses shortly after its delivery. (Metro Nashville Archives, MTA Collection.)

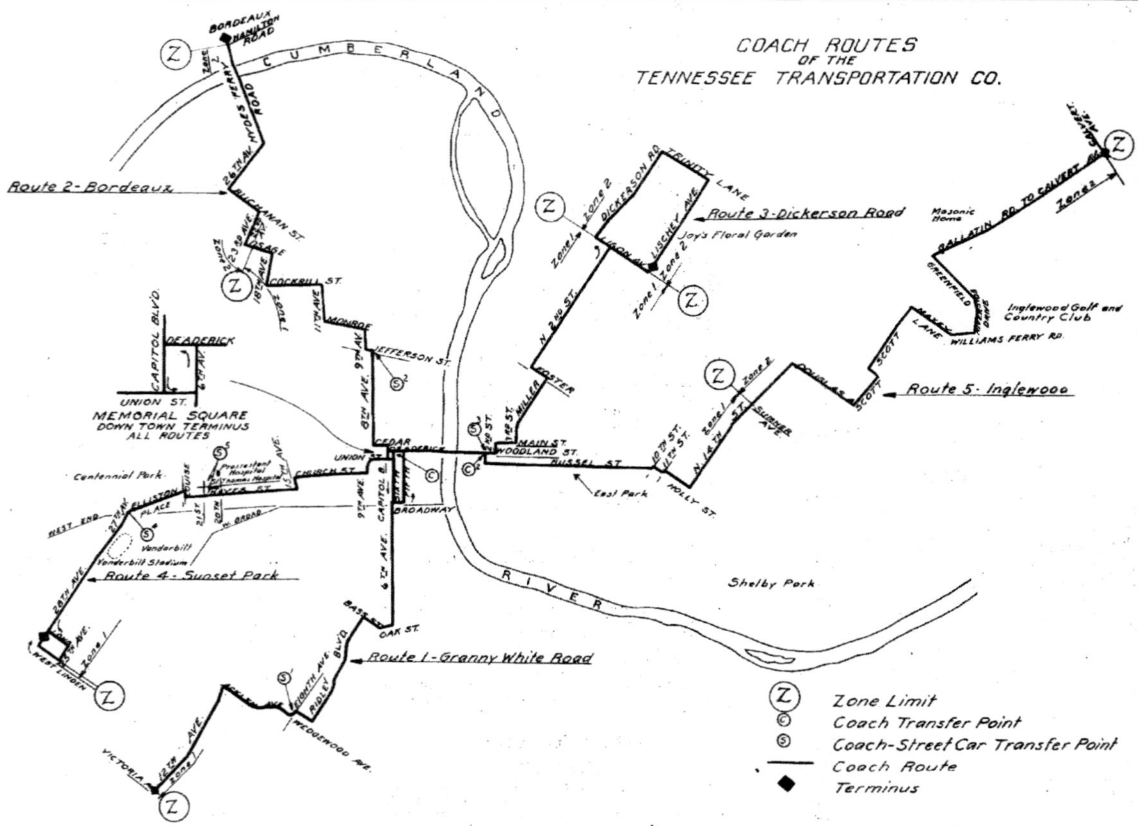

After the Tennessee Transportation Company launched its new motor coach service in early 1927, it wasted little time promoting its five new routes. The schedules were protected by 13 new buses that served new suburban markets not covered by the city's street railways. All of TTC's buses terminated at Nashville's Memorial Square as opposed to the Transfer Station, which had always been the central hub for the city's streetcars. Unlike the flat 7¢ fare charged by streetcars, TTC introduced fare zones, a practice that continues on many modern bus systems to this day. (David H. Steinberg collection.)

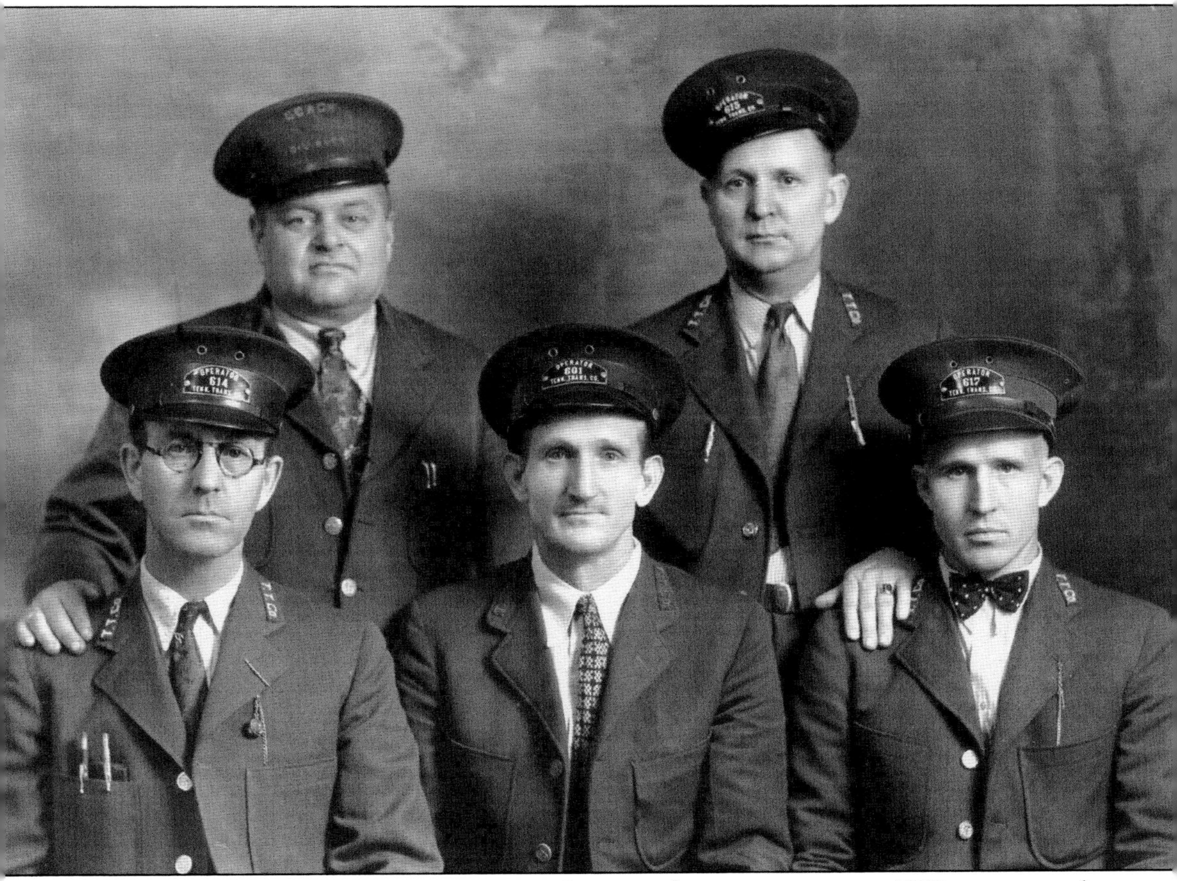

At the time the Tennessee Transportation Company began operation in 1927, motor coach transit was still in its infancy. Electric streetcars were still the primary means of transit for cities. To project a more up-to-date image for employees, TTC management provided uniforms with a sharper and more modern look. The dark uniforms traditionally worn by streetcar motormen and conductors were replaced by a medium gray material and the traditional pillbox hat with a service cap. In addition, since motor coaches were staffed by one man instead of two, the driver's title was now operator rather than motorman. This official employee portrait from the late 1920s illustrates the new appearance. (Metro Nashville Archives, MTA Collection.)

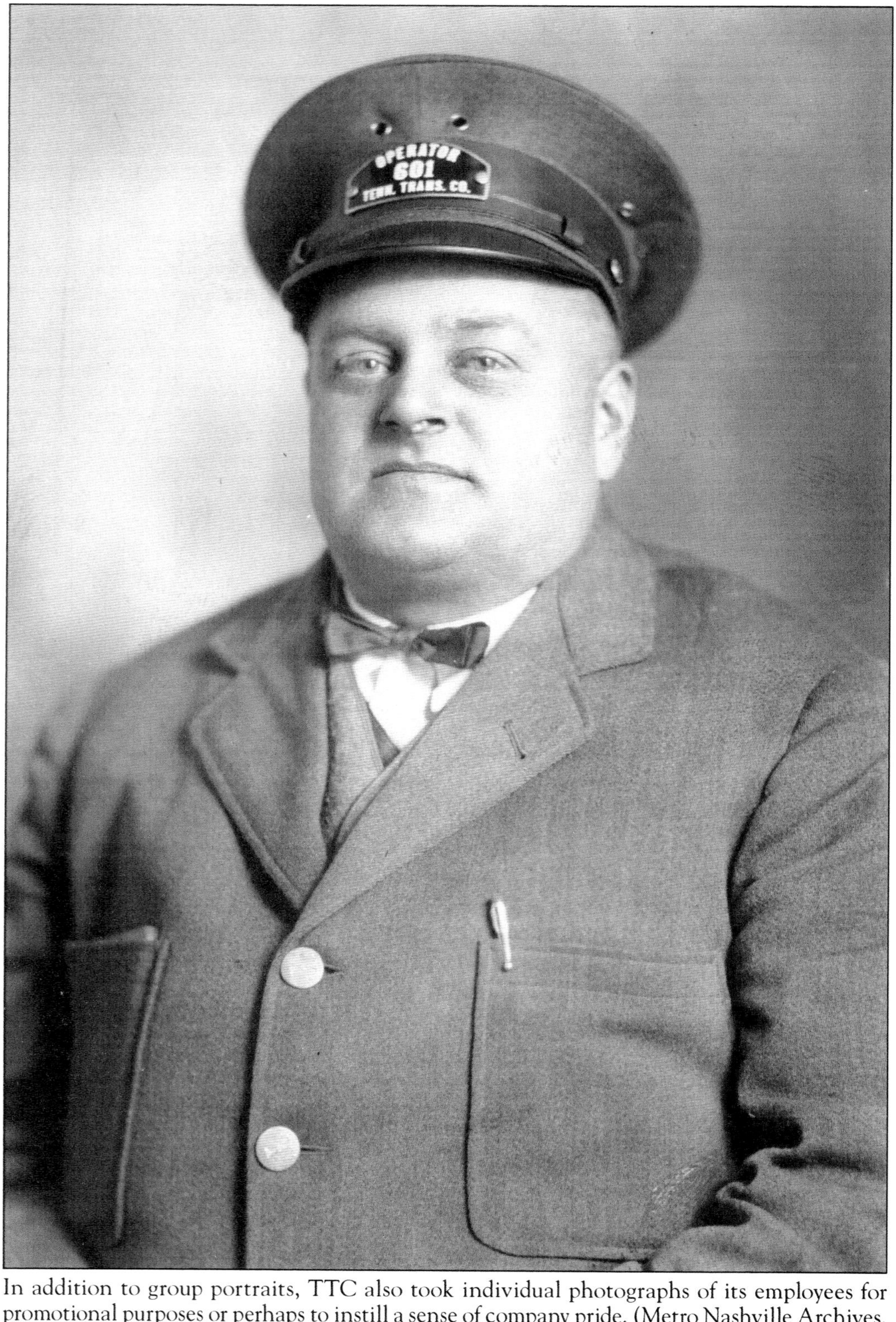

In addition to group portraits, TTC also took individual photographs of its employees for promotional purposes or perhaps to instill a sense of company pride. (Metro Nashville Archives, MTA Collection.)

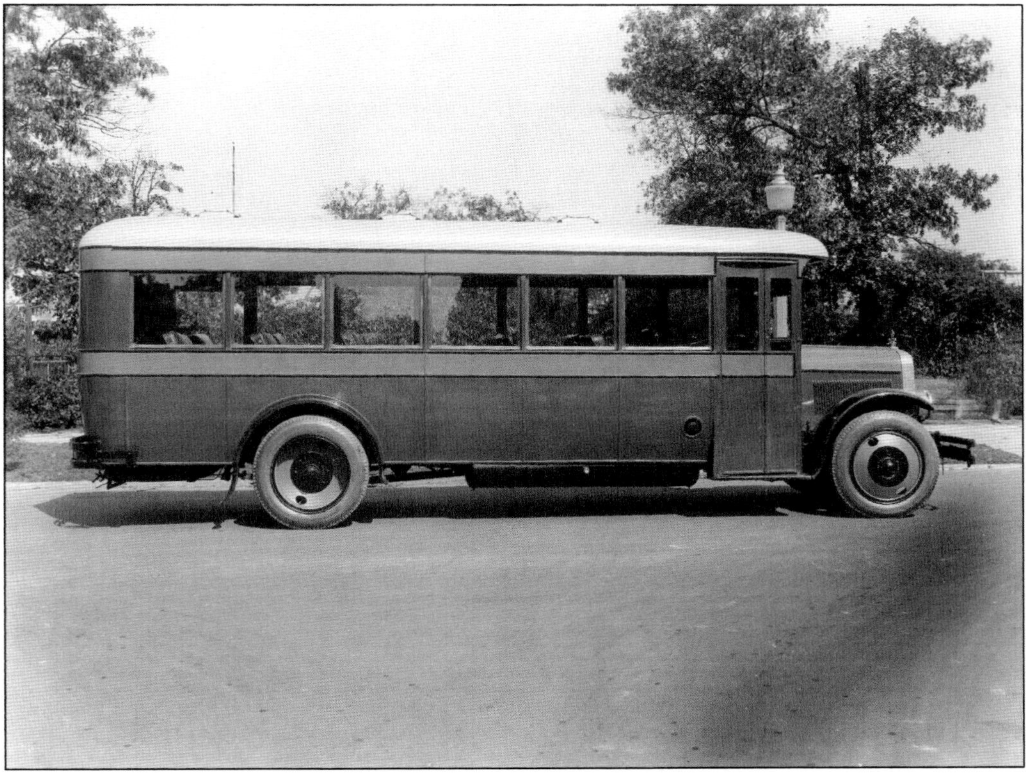

In some views of the new motor coaches acquired by Tennessee Transportation Company in 1927, it appears that some of the models sported different color schemes. (Both, Metro Nashville Archives, MTA Collection.)

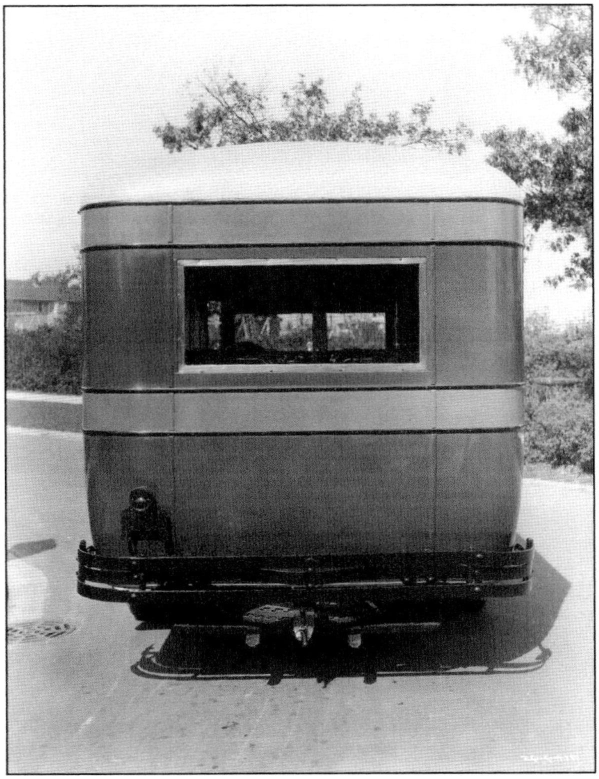

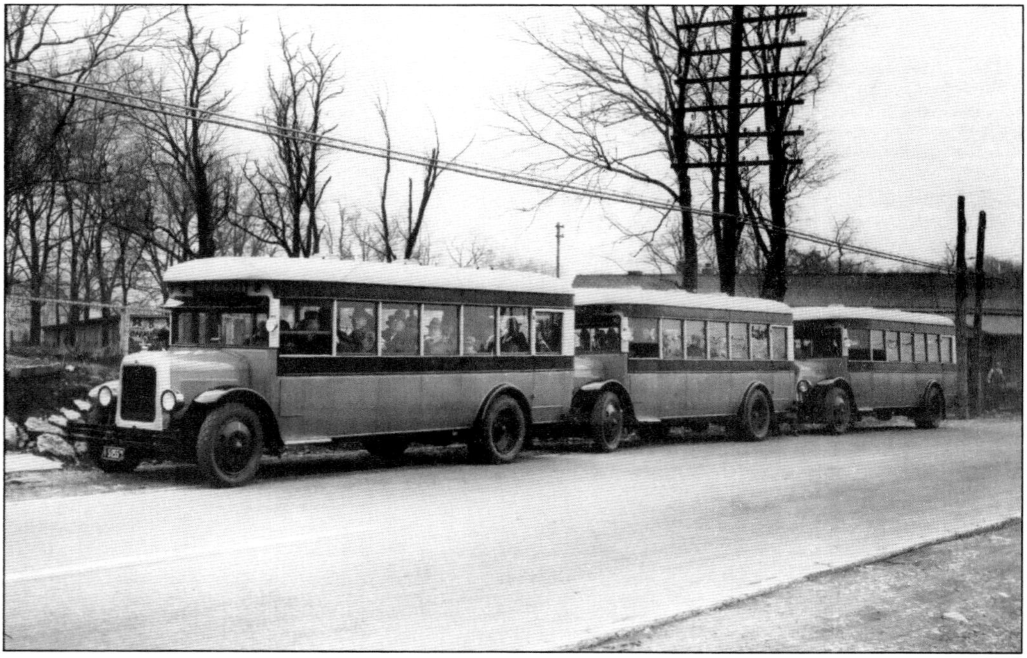

In this scene, TTC motor coaches Nos. 112, 113, and 114 are staged for a company photograph near the Bordeaux community in early 1927 during a charter trip for dignitaries and company officials. These vehicles represented the first city buses for Nashville. (Metro Nashville Archives, MTA Collection.)

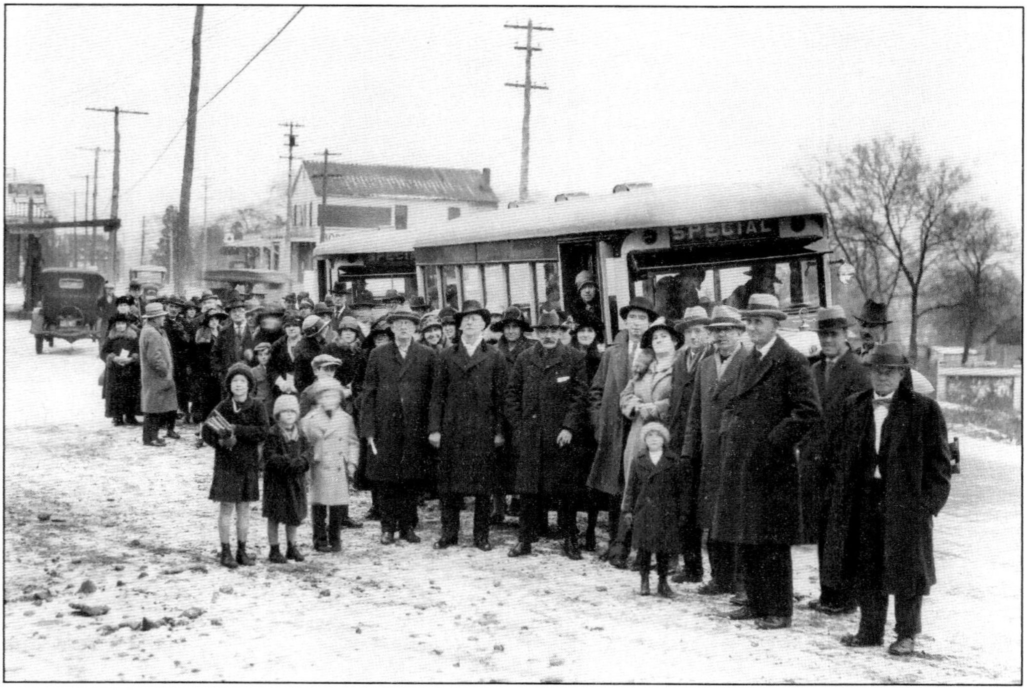

A group of dignitaries, invited guests, and their families pose for a photograph in front of two new Yellow Coach buses on the same wintry day as the previous scene. (Metro Nashville Archives, MTA Collection.)

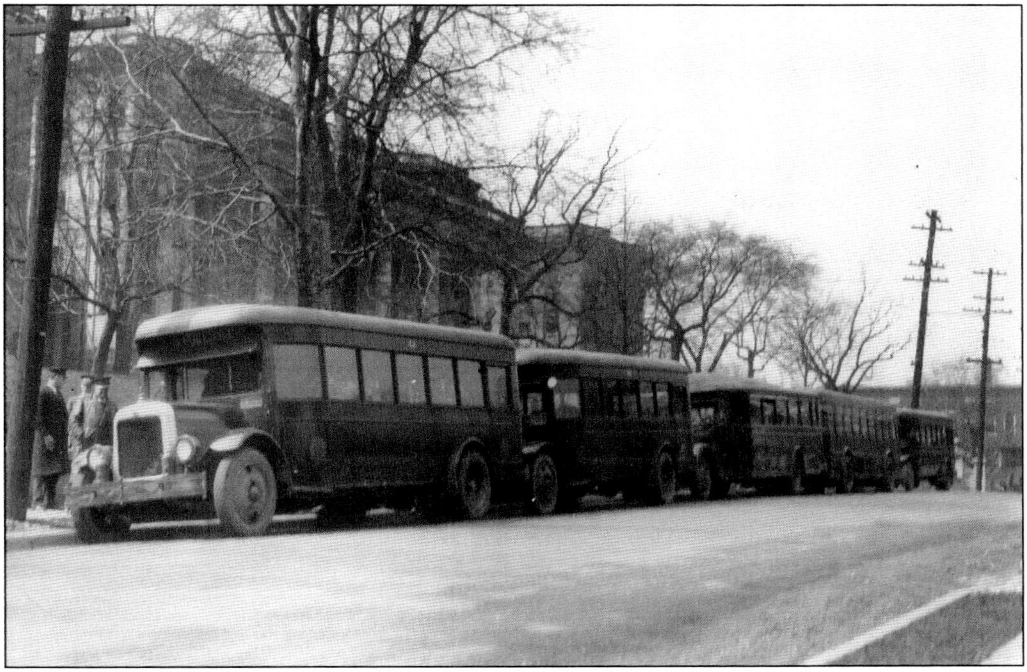

These photographs were taken nearly five years after the images on the previous pages. In 1930, the Tennessee Transportation Company was absorbed by the Tennessee Electric Power Company. During this time, the Nashville Railway & Light Company was also part of the consolidation with TEPCO, which was now operating Nashville's streetcars and buses. During a charter trip, several TEPCO buses are parked in front of Nashville's Ward-Belmont College to pick up students for an outing in the early 1930s. Charter trips such as this have always been a good revenue producer for transit companies. (Both, Metro Nashville Archives, MTA Collection.)

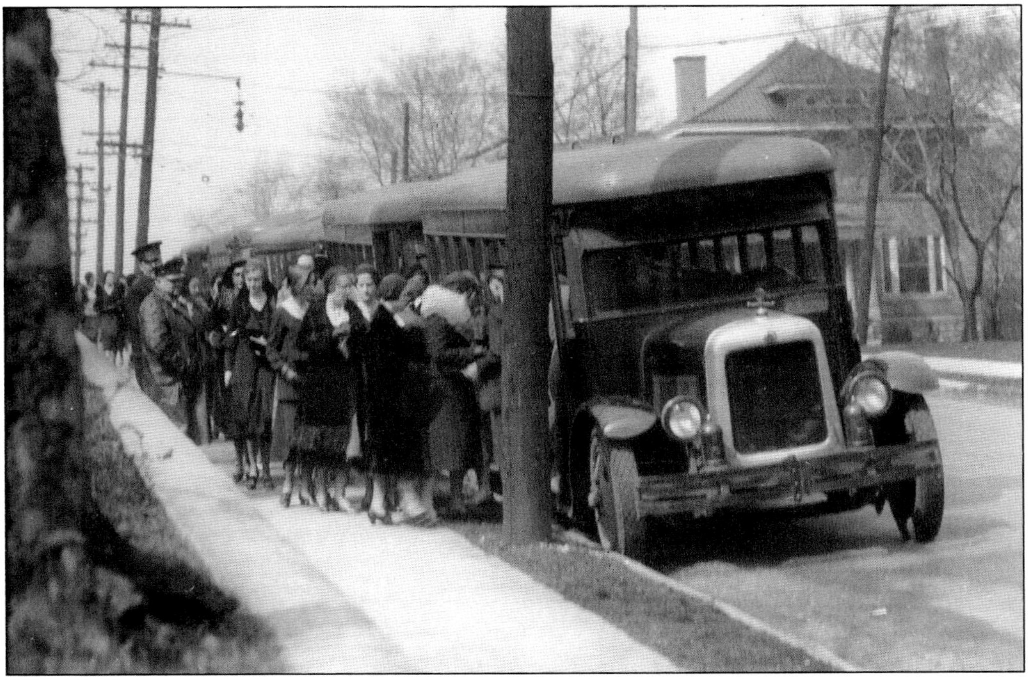

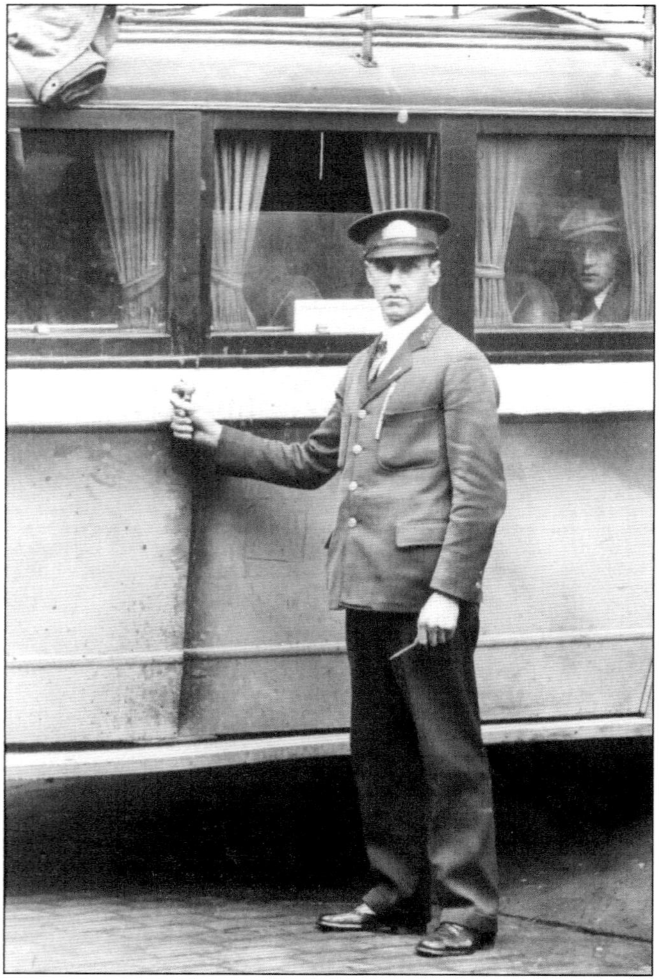

An unidentified driver for the Tennessee Transportation Company poses for a picture as he prepares to board his bus and begin his run to Old Hickory on an overcast day in the early 1930s. (Metro Nashville Archives, MTA Collection.)

In an earlier view from 1927, Tennessee Transportation Company No. 108, a product of the Yellow Coach Manufacturing Company, is seen during a tour. The operator and passengers are clearly becoming impatient with the photographer and are ready to resume their trip. (Metro Nashville Archives, MTA Collection.)

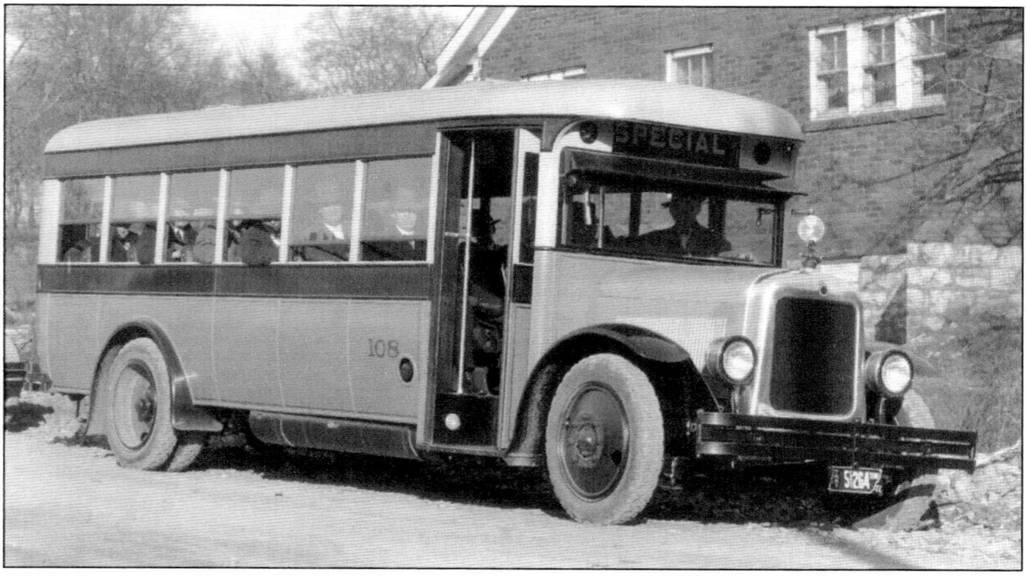

Five

TEPCO TAKES OVER

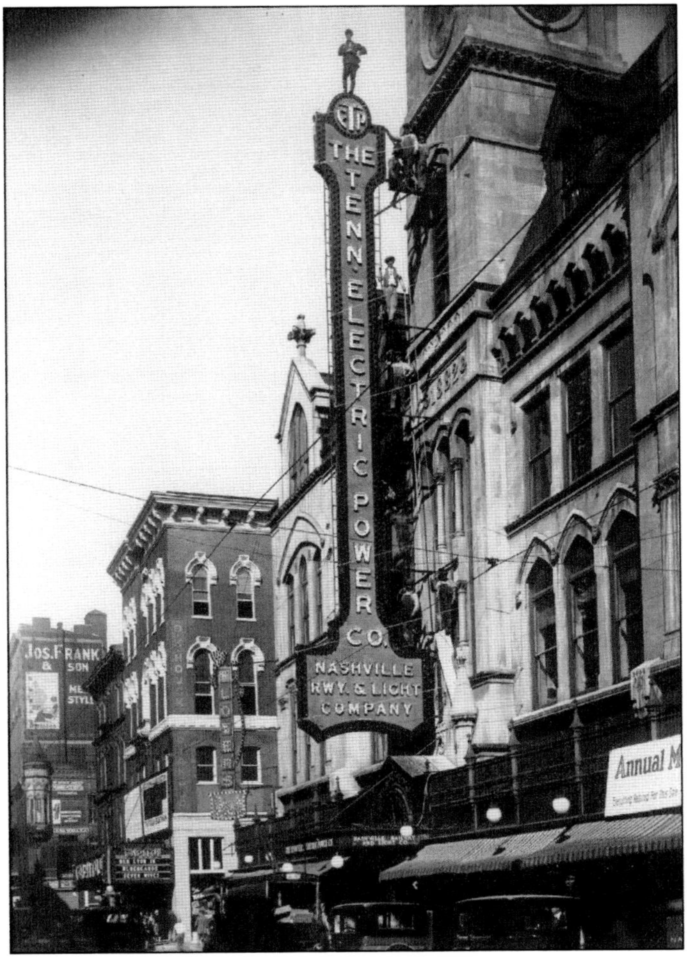

By 1912, the Philadelphia-based E.W. Clark and Company had absorbed several Tennessee utility companies, including the locally owned NR&L. In 1922, the Tennessee Electric Power Company was incorporated, consuming the assets of 45 Tennessee companies, including the Chattanooga Railway & Light Company and the Nashville Railway & Light Company. The latter company retained its identity for several more years before being merged into TEPCO in 1930. From the beginning, the offices of the NR&L, and later TEPCO, occupied the first floor of the distinctive Watkins Building. TEPCO wasted no time erecting what is arguably the largest electric sign in Nashville. In this publicity photograph, 10 TEPCO employees pose precariously on the impressive new display. (David H. Steinberg collection.)

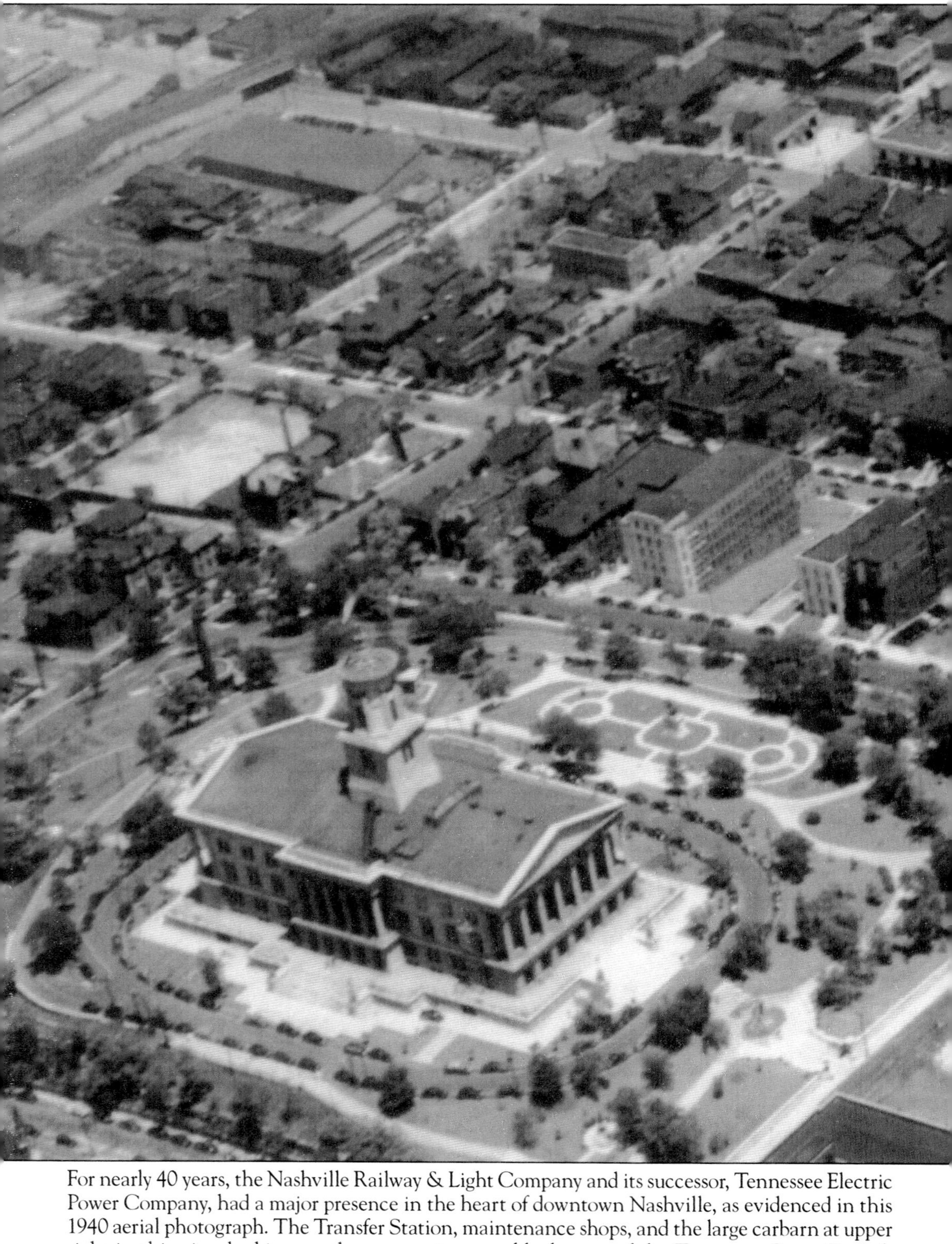

For nearly 40 years, the Nashville Railway & Light Company and its successor, Tennessee Electric Power Company, had a major presence in the heart of downtown Nashville, as evidenced in this 1940 aerial photograph. The Transfer Station, maintenance shops, and the large carbarn at upper right in this view looking northeast were just two blocks east of the Tennessee State Capitol.

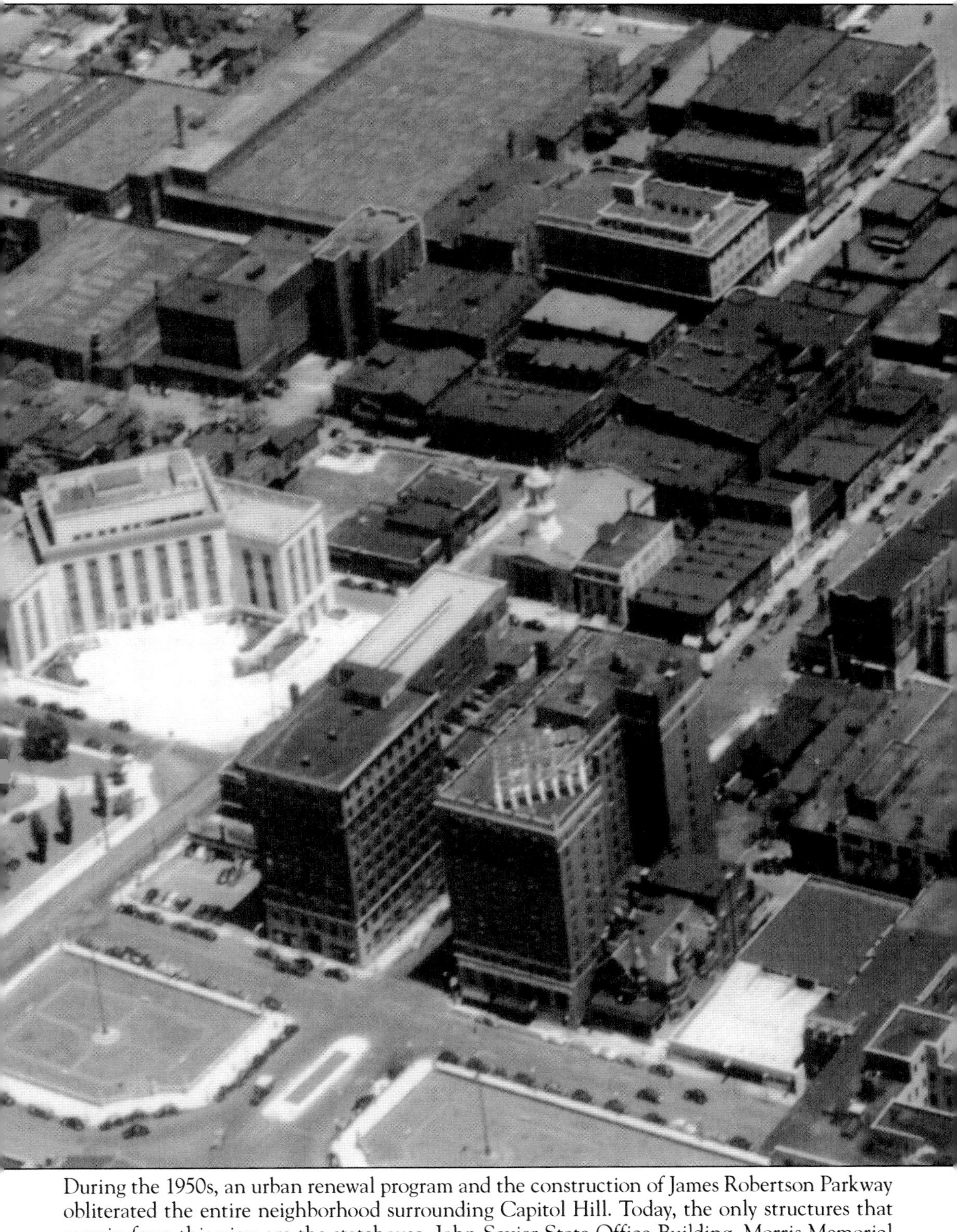

During the 1950s, an urban renewal program and the construction of James Robertson Parkway obliterated the entire neighborhood surrounding Capitol Hill. Today, the only structures that remain from this view are the statehouse, John Sevier State Office Building, Morris Memorial Building, and St. Mary's Catholic Church. (Metro Nashville Archives, MTA Collection.)

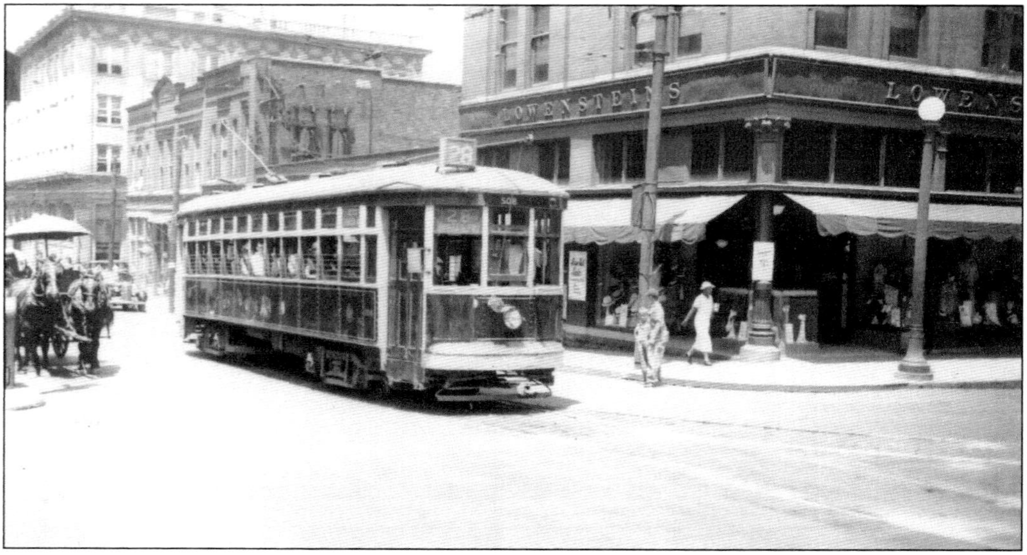

On a warm day in the late 1930s, a TEPCO streetcar has just turned south out of the Transfer Station and begins its turn east onto Deaderick Street. From there it will pass through Public Square, cross the Cumberland River via the Woodland Street Bridge, and enter East Nashville over the Porter Road line. (James D. Le Croy collection.)

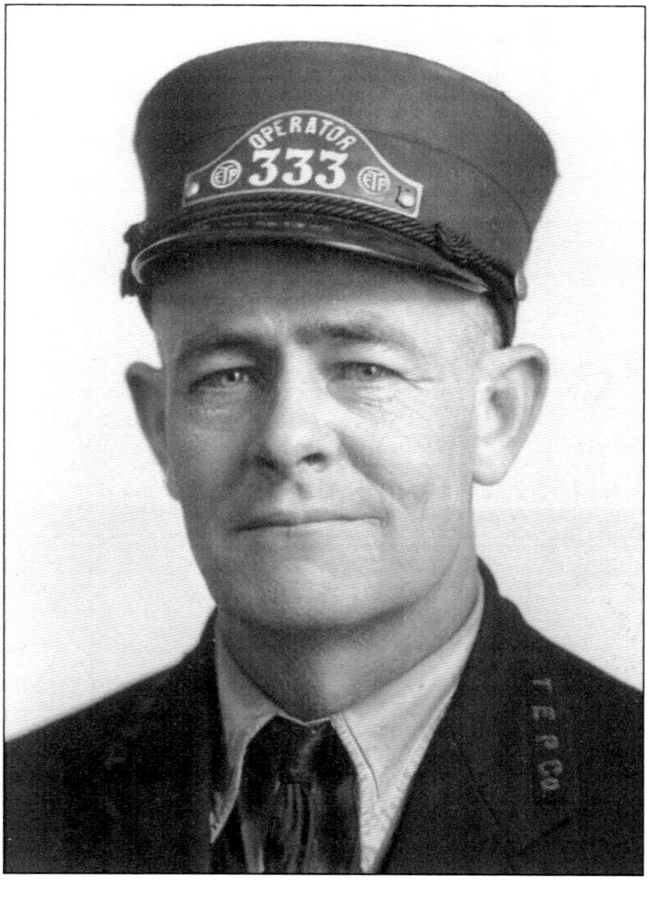

Changes to the appearance of streetcar personnel uniforms came quickly after the Tennessee Electric Power Company acquired the Nashville Railway & Light Company in the 1920s. The new company applied its initials and logo in every conspicuous place. The jacket now sported an embroidered "TEPCO" on both collars. The hat badge was now larger, with TEPCO logos adorning each side of the more prominent badge number. The title "motorman" was also changed to "operator" by the new regime. The employee shown is D. Reeves. (Metro Nashville Archives, MTA Collection.)

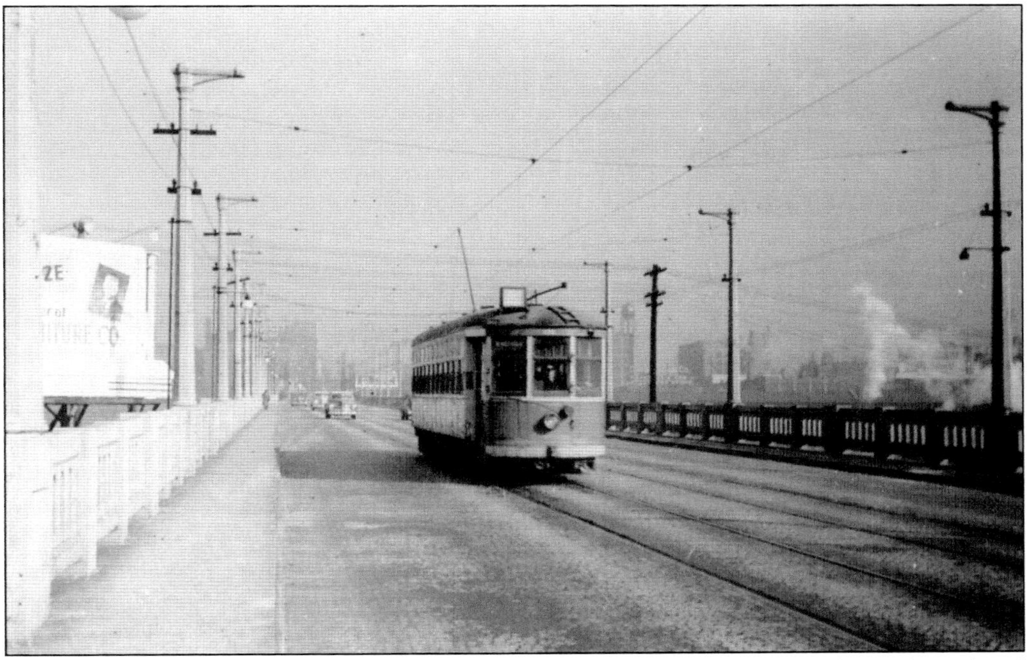

An outbound West Nashville car rambles across the Church Street viaduct and over the railroad gulch on a cold winter day around 1940. Nashville's smoky skyline can be seen in the distance. (Nashville Public Library, Special Collections.)

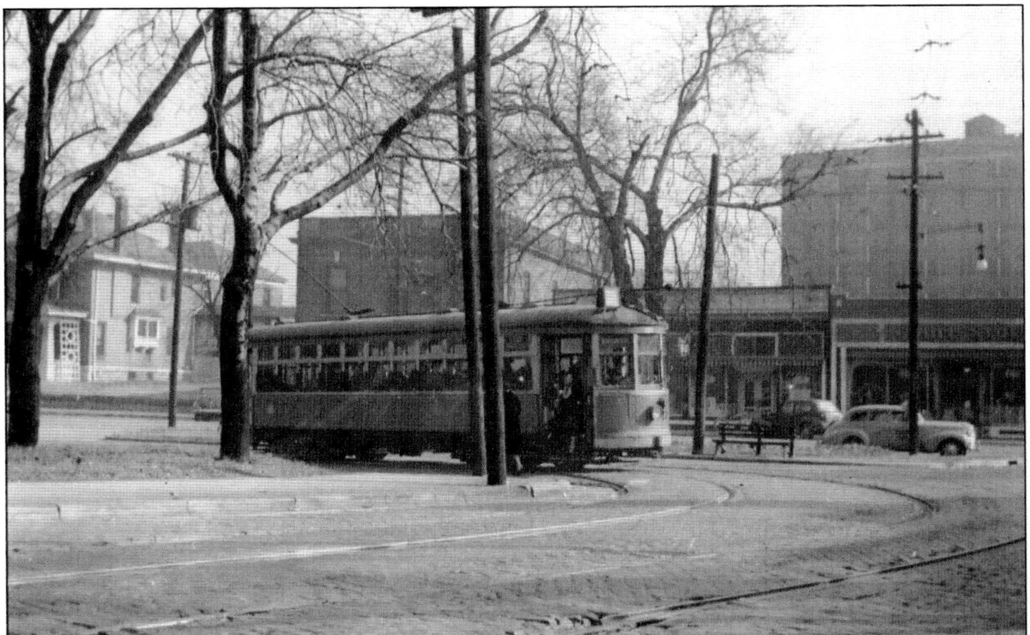

A westbound TEPCO streetcar discharges passengers on Church Street at Twenty-Second Avenue in the late 1930s. In moments, the car operating over the West Nashville line will turn north onto Twenty-Second Avenue toward Charlotte Avenue, then continue west before terminating its run at the Tennessee State Penitentiary. Many of the buildings in the background survive today. (Nashville Public Library, Special Collections.)

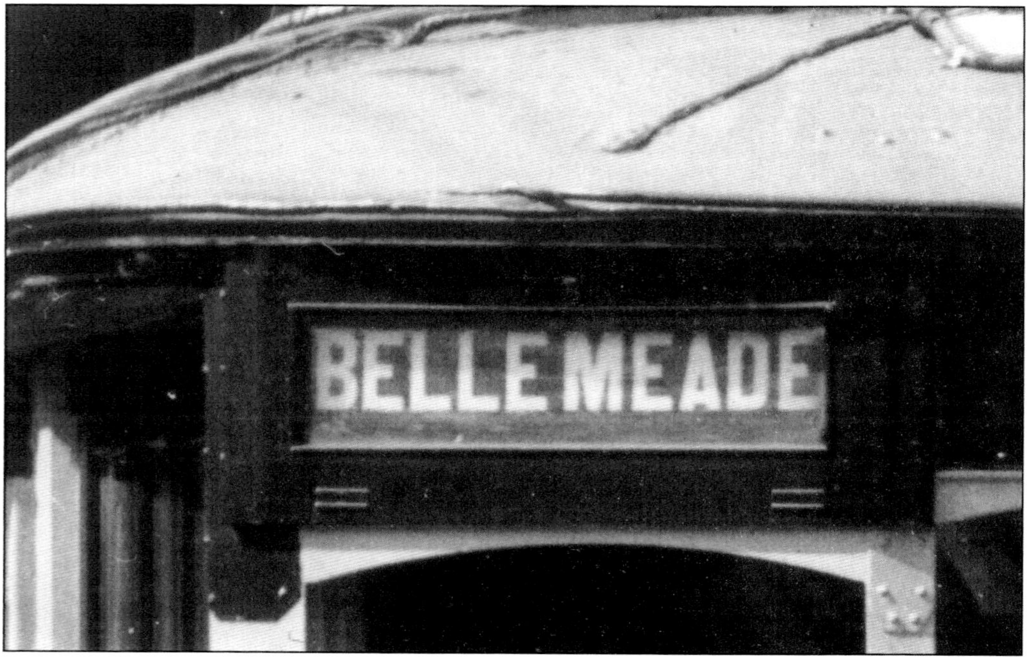

In terms of mileage, the Belle Meade line was the longest of any of Nashville's street railway routes, operating via Broadway, West End Avenue, and Belle Meade Boulevard. On an early winter morning in 1940, TEPCO No. 400 is seen at the end of the line on Belle Meade Boulevard near Percy Warner Park. With several passengers already on the car, the operator stands by, waiting for last-minute stragglers moments before leaving for downtown. (Both, Metro Nashville Archives, MTA Collection.)

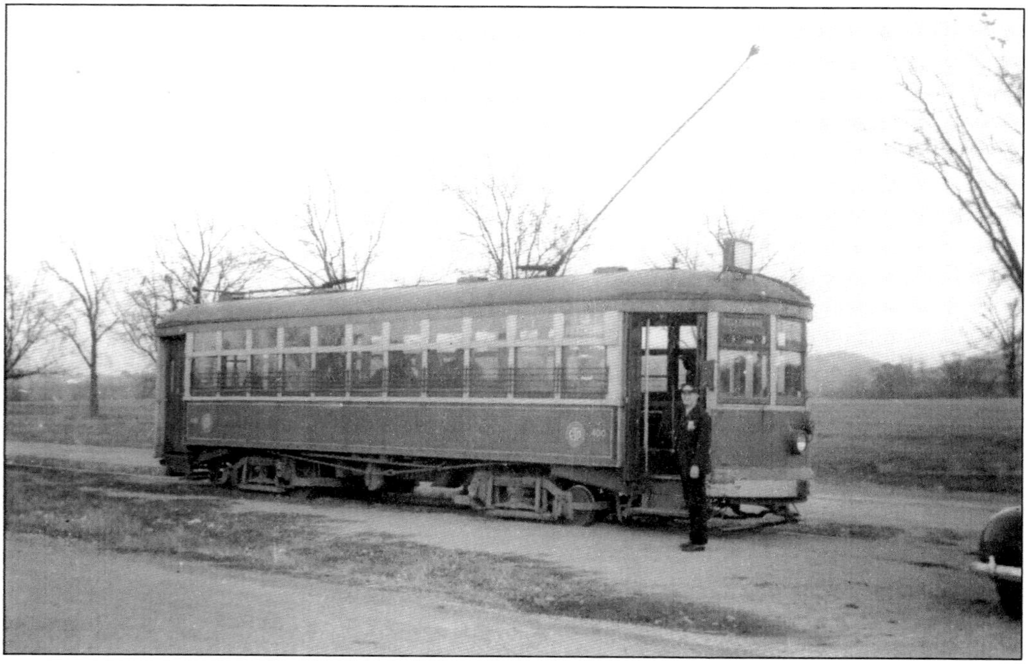

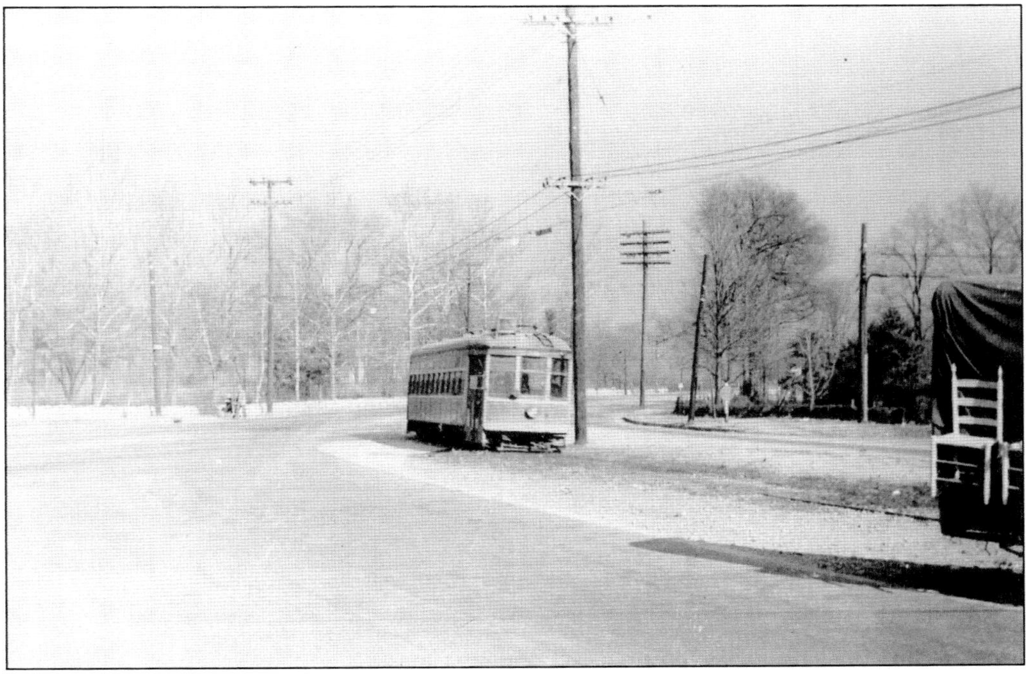

A TEPCO car on the Belle Meade line is shown turning south down Belle Meade Boulevard. From this point to the end of the line, the track will travel on a grassy median to the line's terminus near Percy Warner Park. (Nashville Public Library, Special Collections.)

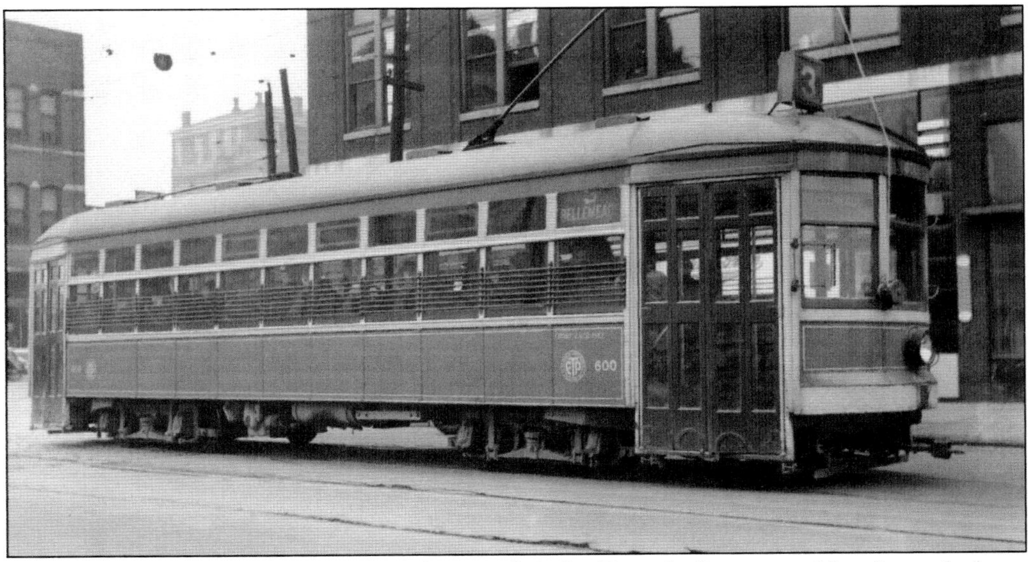

On an overcast day, TEPCO No. 600 has just left the Transfer Station and heads south down Fourth Avenue toward Broadway, where it will turn west for the trip to Belle Meade Boulevard. Along the journey, the route will pass Union Station, Vanderbilt University, and Centennial Park. (David H. Steinberg collection.)

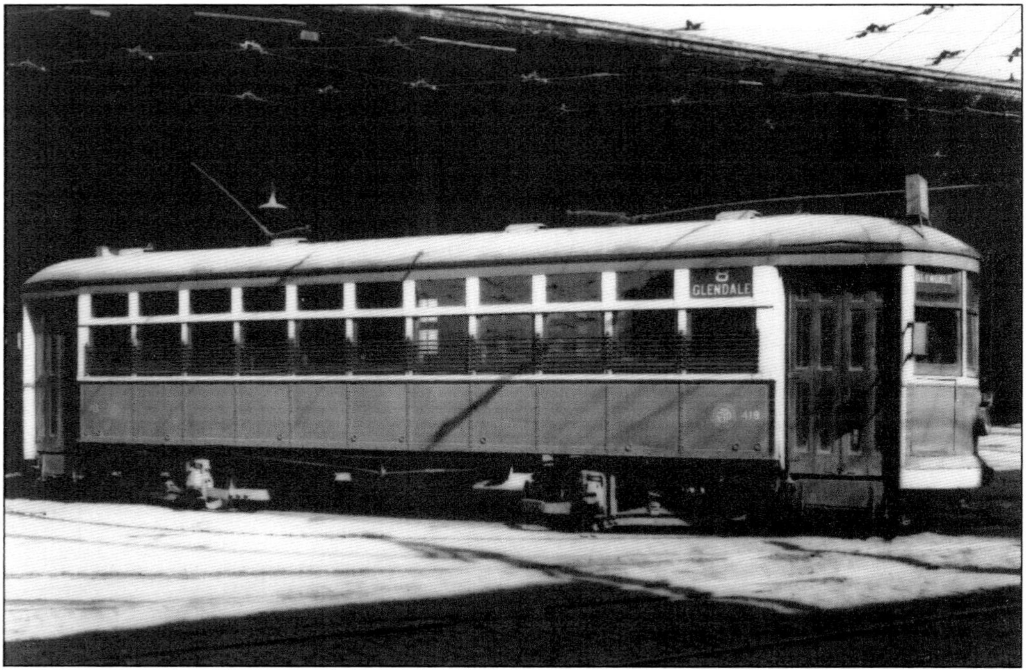

During an afternoon in the late 1930s, TEPCO No. 419 has been moved out of the carbarn and into the sun prior to starting its run on the Glendale line. (David H. Steinberg collection.)

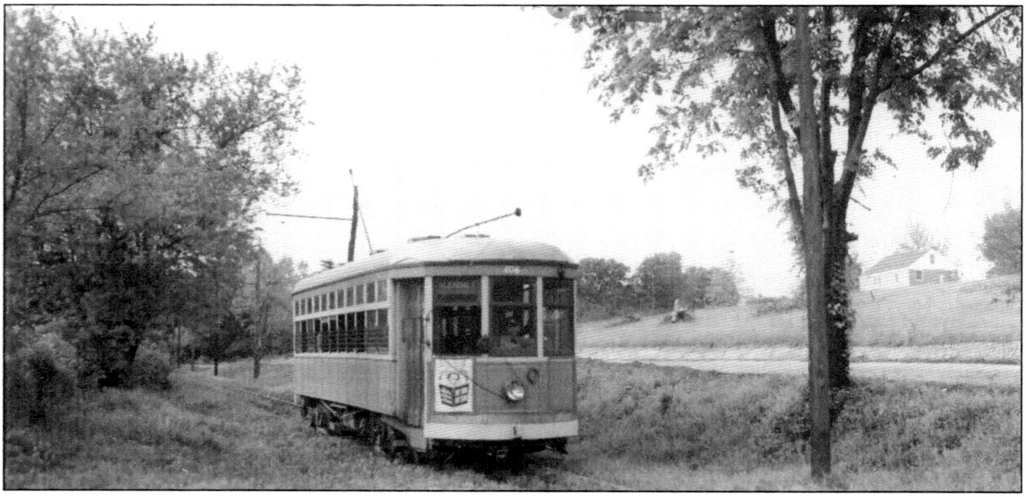

One of the more unique and picturesque streetcar lines operating in Nashville was the line to Glendale Park. Originally built as the Overland Dummy Railway Company in 1887, this was the city's first steam dummy railroad. During the era of horse-drawn streetcars, before electrification, a few street railways were powered by dummy steam locomotives. Over the years and several mergers later, the Overland was folded into the operations of the Nashville Railway & Light Company, and years later, the Tennessee Electric Power Company (TEPCO). It was initially built to connect Nashville with Glendale Park and Zoo, which also happened to be owned by the same businessmen who owned Nashville's streetcar system. Within the city, the route ran down Eighth Avenue South to Douglas, then west to Tenth Avenue. For the remainder of the journey, the track operated over private right-of-way. This scene shows a Glendale car in a rural area believed to be near Lealand Lane as it approaches the end of its run in the late 1930s. (David H. Steinberg collection.)

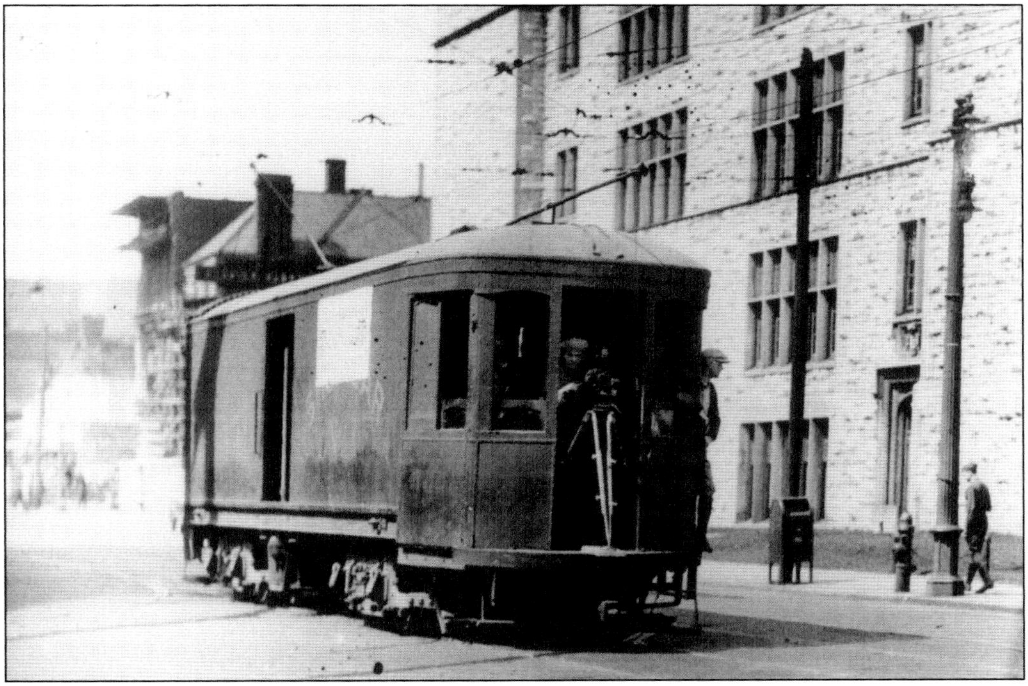

A unique non-revenue streetcar that would occasionally make an appearance was TEPCO's shop car. This vehicle was used for various functions including transporting tools and supplies to various sites where track maintenance was required. On this occasion in 1926, the car is being used to transport a movie crew and its camera to film the tracks and right-of-way. In this scene, the car is traveling south on Eighth Avenue near Broadway. The building to the immediate right is Hume-Fogg High School, which is still in use as the city's oldest high school. (David H. Steinberg collection.)

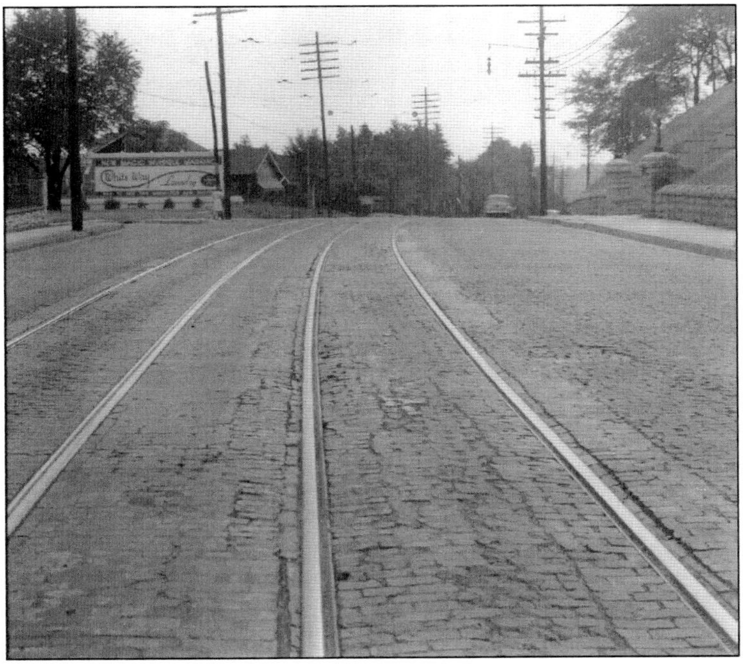

Just months before the Glendale streetcar line was converted to bus operation in 1940, this photograph was taken from the motorman's point of view looking south on Eighth Avenue near Hamilton Avenue. The entrance to the Nashville City Reservoir can be seen at right. (Metro Nashville Archives, MTA Collection.)

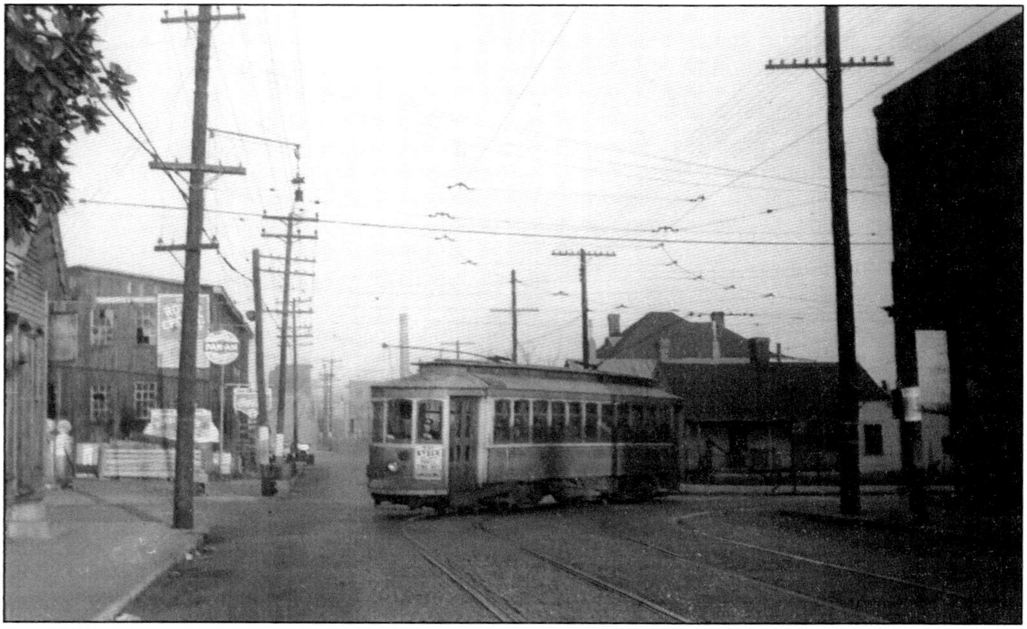

A TEPCO car negotiates a curve in an unidentified Nashville neighborhood as the evening sun begins to set. Due to the numerous turns on some lines, streetcars did not travel very fast. (Nashville Public Library, Special Collections.)

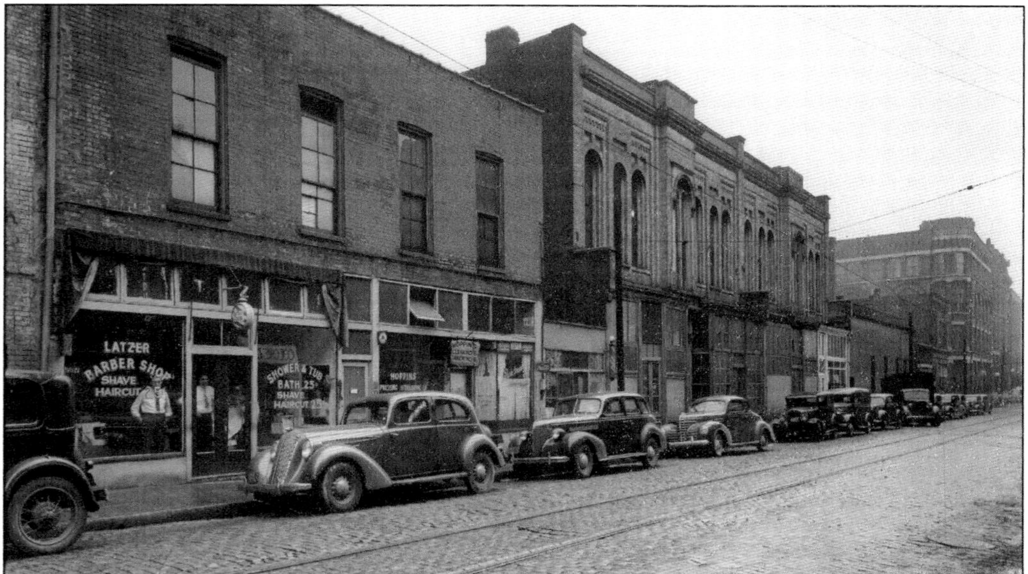

With the proliferation of automobiles after the 1920s, streetcar operation began to fall out of favor with city leaders, as the fixed-route vehicles often created bottlenecks for drivers, especially in urban areas. Diesel-powered buses were soon considered the transit choice of the future. The rubber-tired vehicles offered a smoother ride for patrons, and unlike street railways, could operate on any route or drive around congestion. This photograph looking west on Cedar Street towards Fourth Avenue illustrates how a line of parked cars and a streetcar track could quickly create congestion and potential safety problems. The four-story building on the corner is the Duncan Hotel. (Metro Nashville Archives, MTA Collection.)

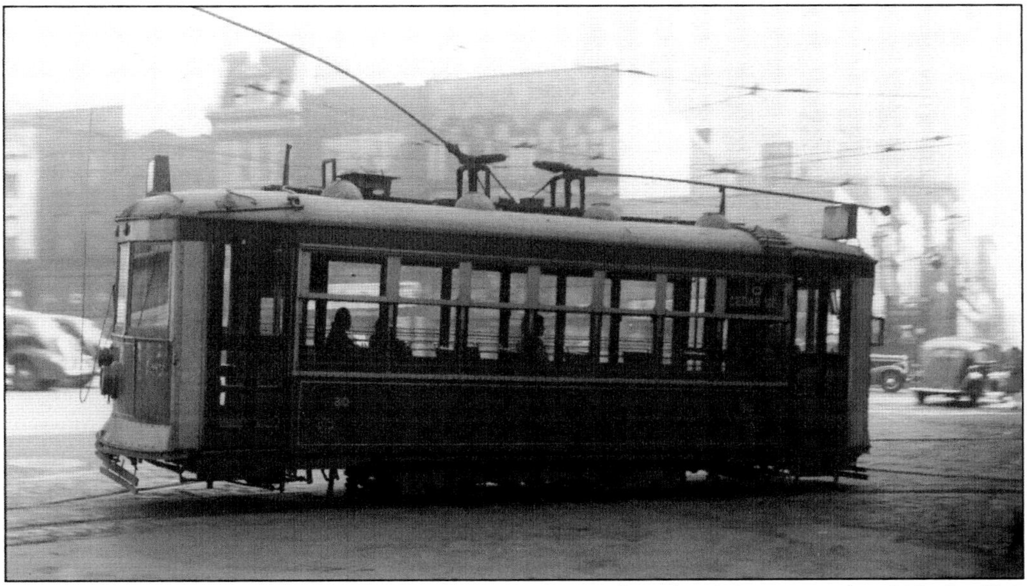

TEPCO No. 80, a single-truck Birney car, turns into the Third Avenue side of Nashville's Transfer Station after completing its run on the Cedar Street line. A few years later, Cedar Street would be renamed Charlotte Avenue. The Public Square is visible in the background. (David H. Steinberg collection.)

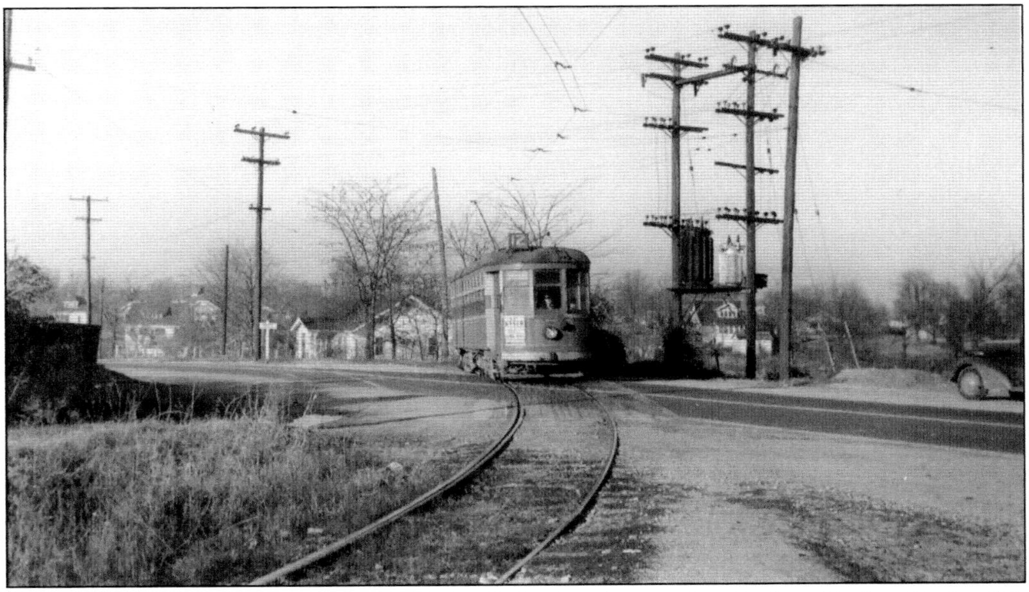

For nearly a century, the Louisville & Nashville Railroad's sprawling Radnor Yard on Nashville's south side has been a major employer for the region as well as the mid-state's largest rail hub for freight. The Nashville Railway & Light Company eventually extended its Nolensville Road line south to serve Radnor Yard after its opening in the late 1910s. The streetcar line was all street operation within Nashville, but once outside city limits, the line operated on its own dedicated right-of-way for the remainder of the trip. At the end of the Radnor line, there was a loop near the L&N roundhouse to facilitate turnaround for the return trip. An outbound TEPCO car is seen south of the Woodbine community crossing Nolensville Road near Wheeler Avenue. From here, the track turns west as it reaches the end of its run. (Nashville Public Library, Special Collections.)

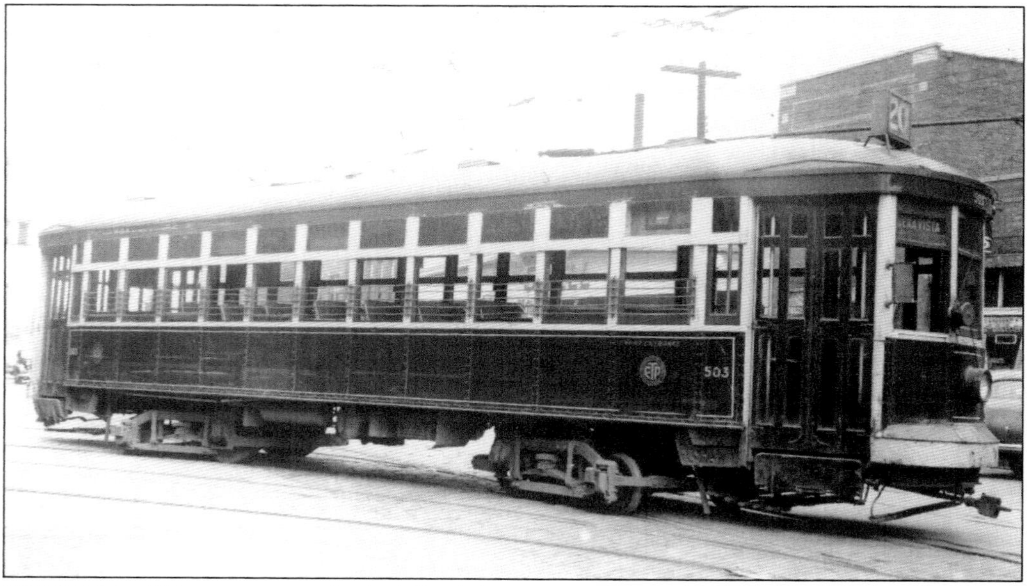

TEPCO No. 503 is seen outside the Third Avenue carbarn in preparation for its run over the Buena Vista line in the late 1930s. (David H. Steinberg collection.)

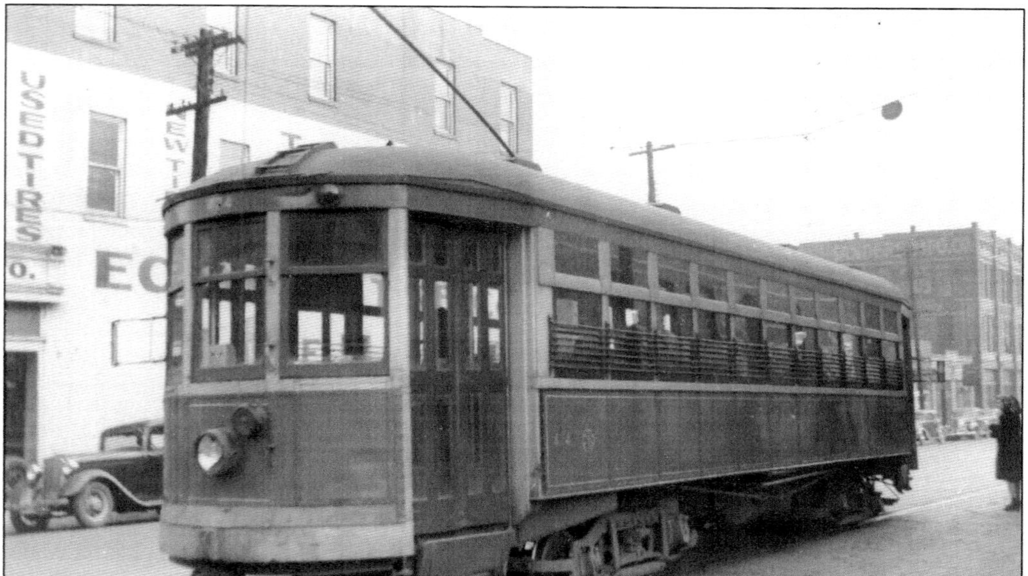

A woman at far right patiently waits to board TEPCO No. 424 as the car eases to a stop on a cold day near downtown Nashville. Unlike other streetcar systems, Nashville's street railways had few if any safety islands from which to board. This required walking to the middle of the street unprotected to board the car, often in heavy traffic. (David H. Steinberg collection.)

Six

Safety First!

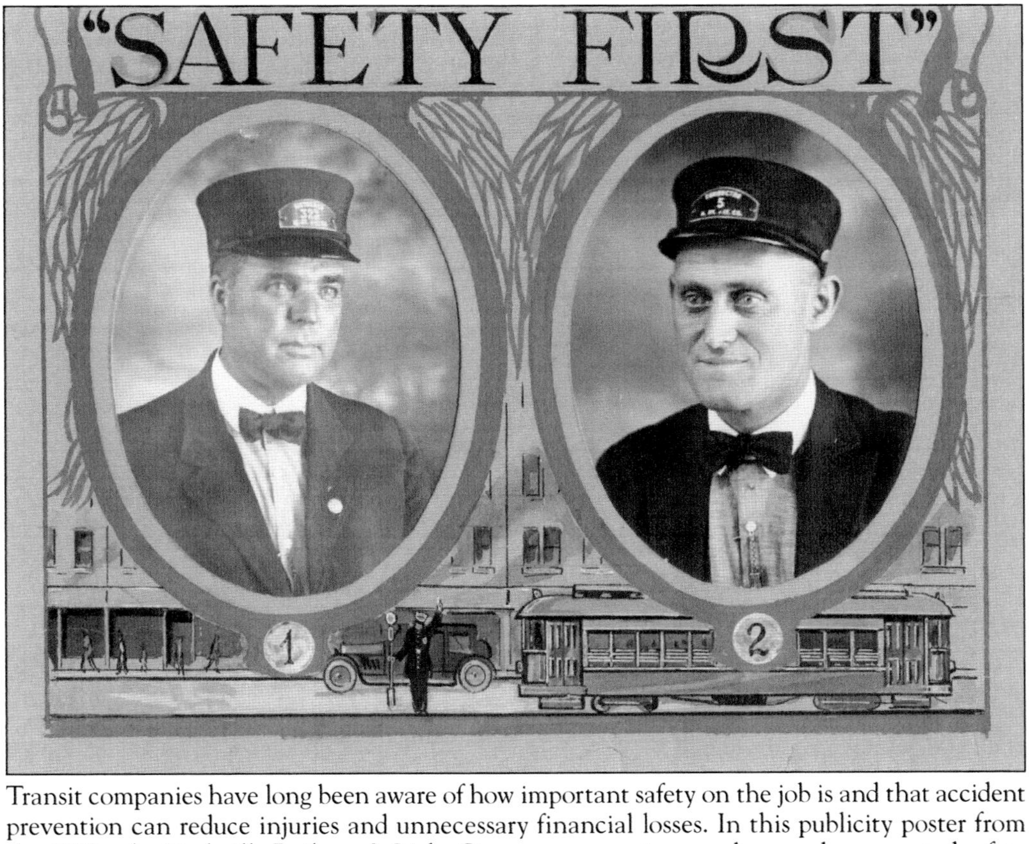

Transit companies have long been aware of how important safety on the job is and that accident prevention can reduce injuries and unnecessary financial losses. In this publicity poster from the 1920s, the Nashville Railway & Light Company recognizes employees who promoted safety the most. The winners featured in the poster are an unidentified motorman and conductor who placed first and second respectively in the contest. The concept of occupational safety was still in its infancy. It would be decades before hard hats, earplugs, and safety vests would be mandatory in dangerous job environments. (Metro Nashville Archives, MTA Collection.)

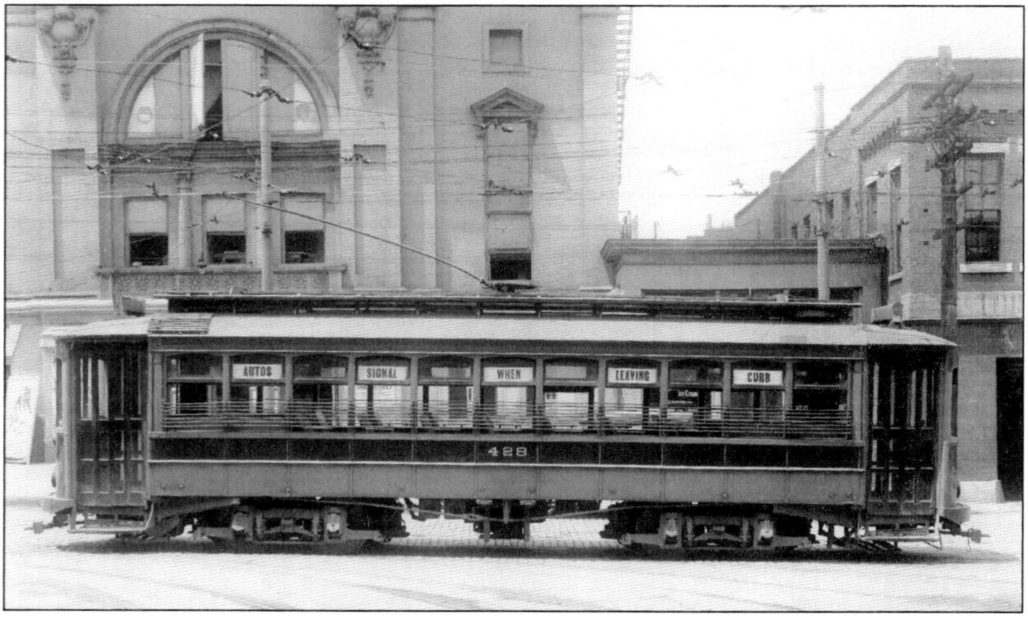

This publicity photograph staged by NR&L shows car No. 428 adorned with signs spelling out "Autos Signal When Leaving Curb" in an effort to alert motorists not to carelessly pull in front of the streetcars. The effort by the transit agency was probably in response to several previous encounters. The scene was recorded in the 1920s outside the car barn on Fourth Avenue North. The Bijou Theater is in the background. (Metro Nashville Archives, MTA Collection.)

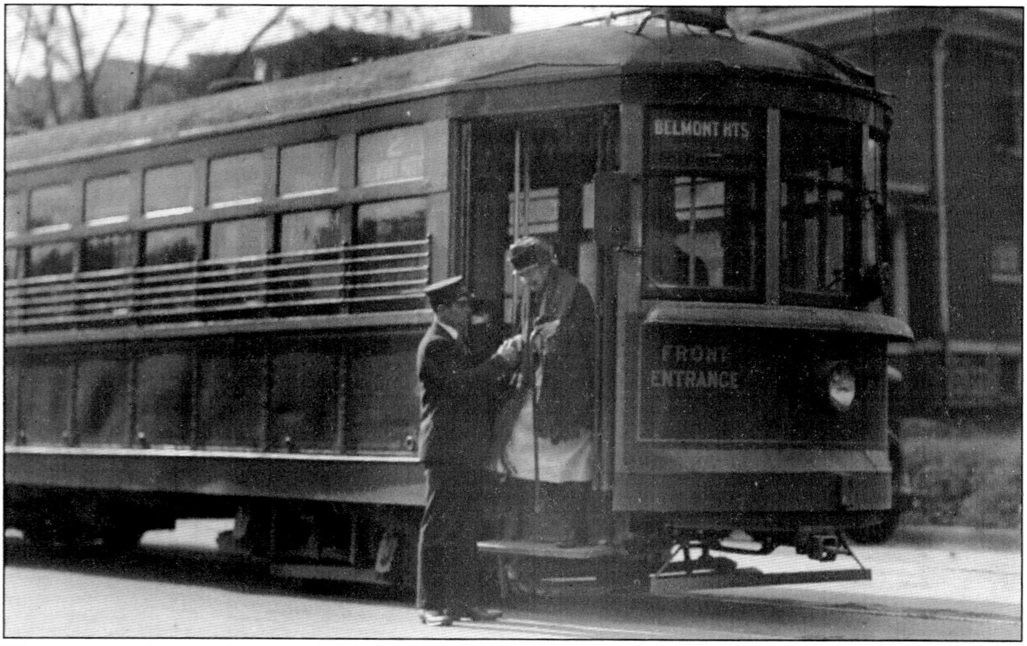

The primary duties of streetcar conductors were to collect fares and keep passengers safe. Another important responsibility was assisting the elderly and passengers with mobility problems while boarding and disembarking. Although this is a staged company photograph, it does illustrate what the job of streetcar personnel entailed. This photograph was taken in the Belmont neighborhood on Nashville's south side. (Metro Nashville Archives, MTA Collection.)

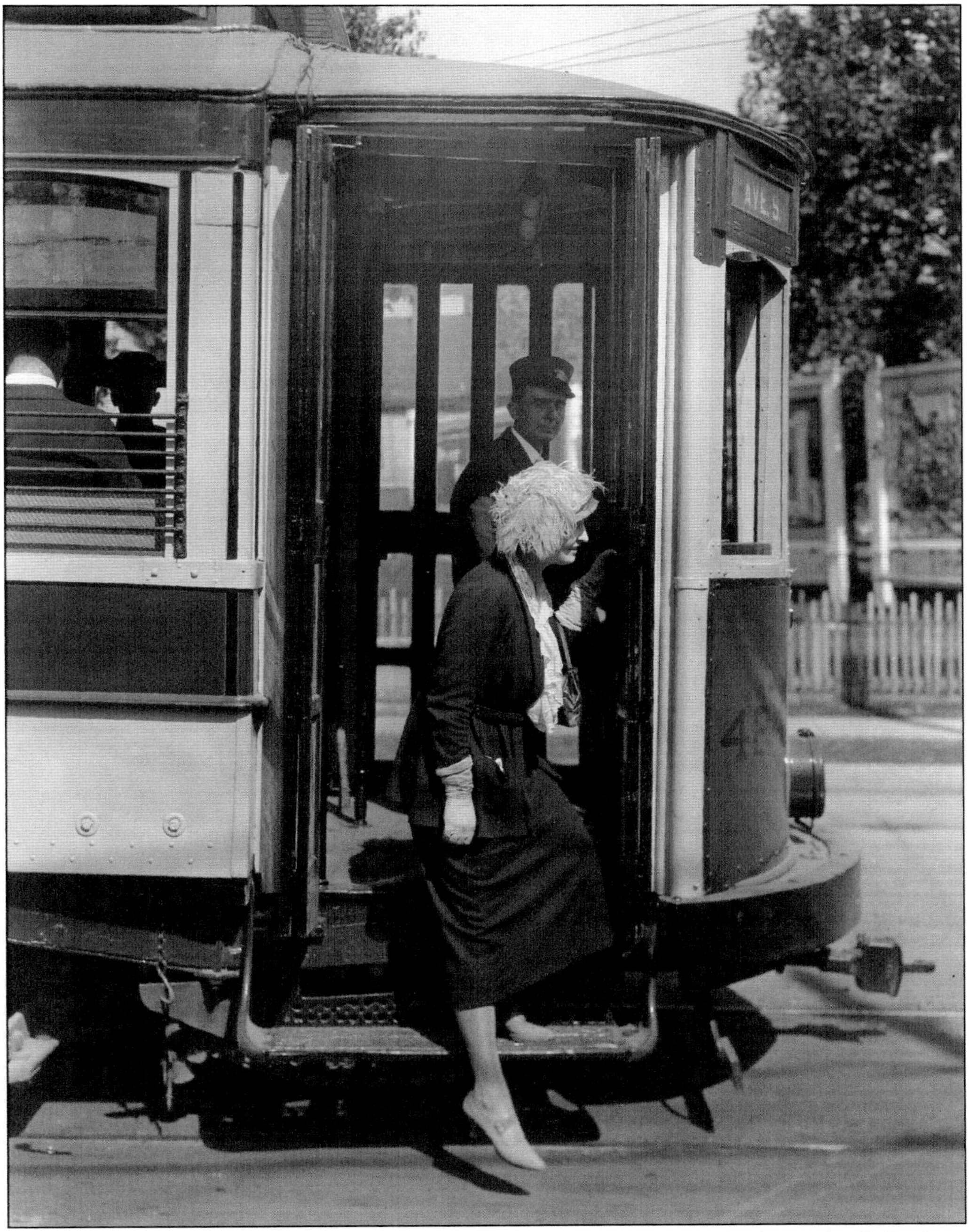

Another publicity photograph from the 1920s designed to promote safety by the Nashville Railway & Light Company depicts the correct way for a passenger to disembark from a streetcar. This photograph may have been taken for training new personnel or for safety brochures. Boarding and deboarding from streetcars typically presented the greatest risk of injury to passengers. (Metro Nashville Archives, MTA Collection.)

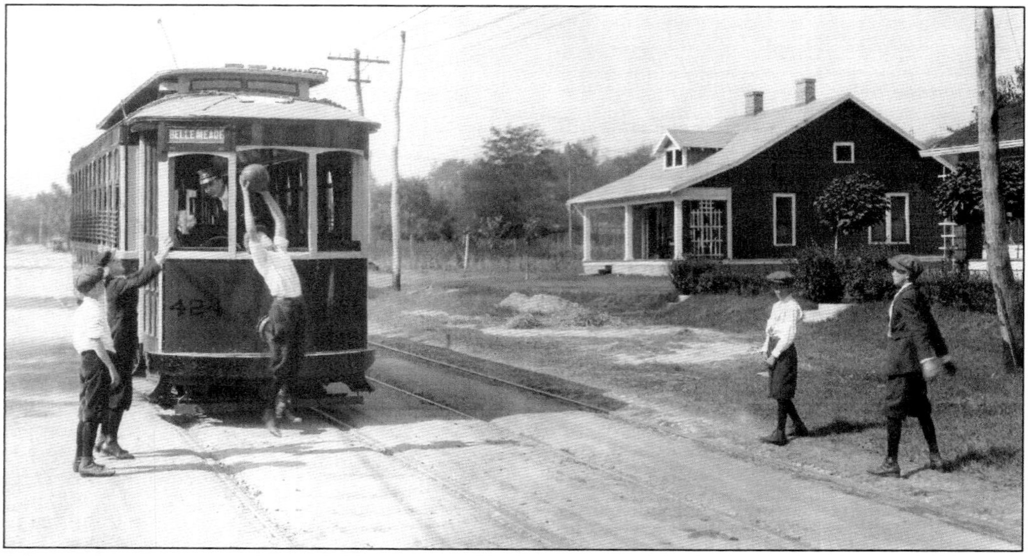

The Nashville Railway & Light Company made a series of photographs in 1921 depicting various accident scenarios that present unexpected dangers when the cars are in operation. Many incursions were caused by autos pulling in front of a streetcar suddenly while driving away from the curb without signaling. An even worse scenario involves children playing on the right-of-way or riding their bicycles on the track, as this view illustrates. This first simulated scene shows a group of youngsters playing basketball on the tracks as a car approaches from behind. Although the destination sign says Belle Meade, car No. 424 is shown on Wedgewood Avenue near the Tennessee State Fairgrounds on Nashville's south side. (Metro Nashville Archives, MTA Collection.)

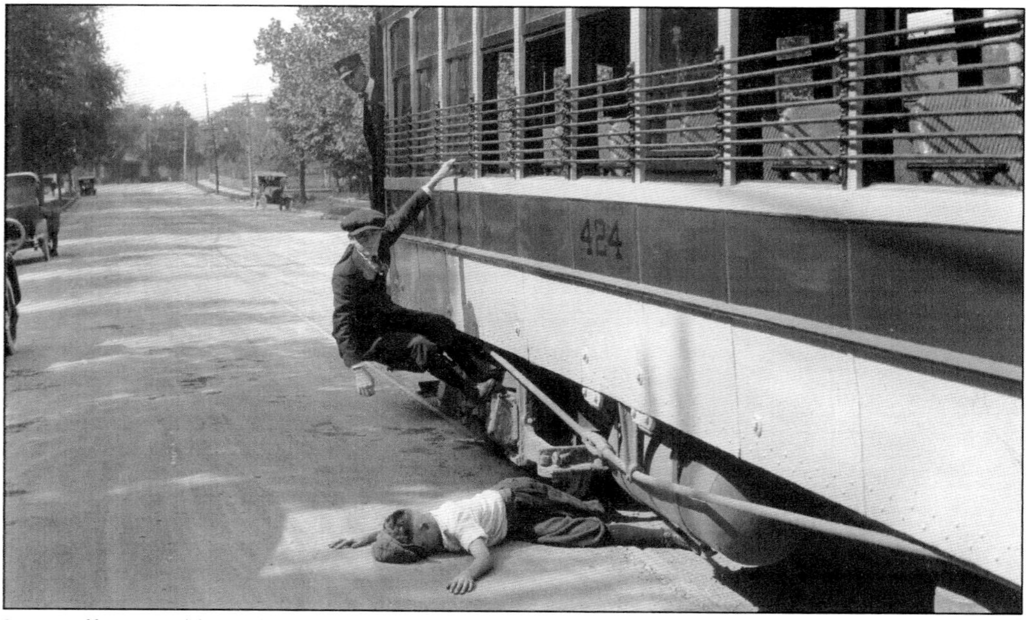

In an effort to address the continuing problem of boys hitching rides on streetcars, the NR&L created this public awareness photograph to show what can happen when horseplay turns to tragedy. In reality the car was not moving, but it still presents a powerful image. This composition uses car No. 424 as a prop on the same day and at the same general location as many of the other photographs in this chapter. (Metro Nashville Archives, MTA Collection.)

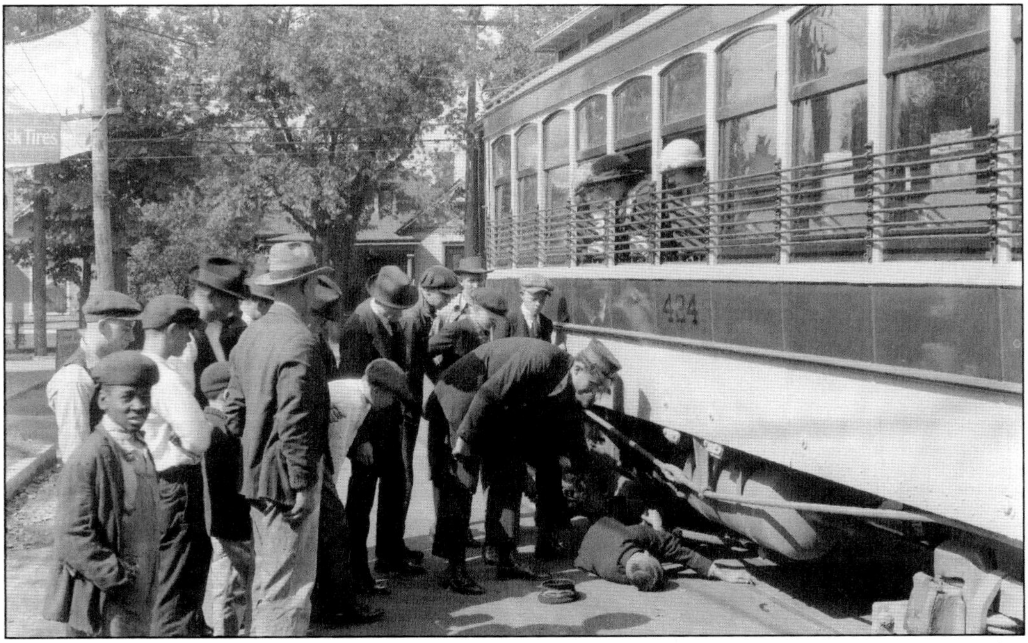

In another staged photograph, a young boy on a bicycle has just been hit by a streetcar. The conductor examines the boy as passengers and a crowd look on. The bicycle is barely visible under the car. A couple of the actors have "broken character" and can be seen looking at the camera. (Metro Nashville Archives, MTA Collection.)

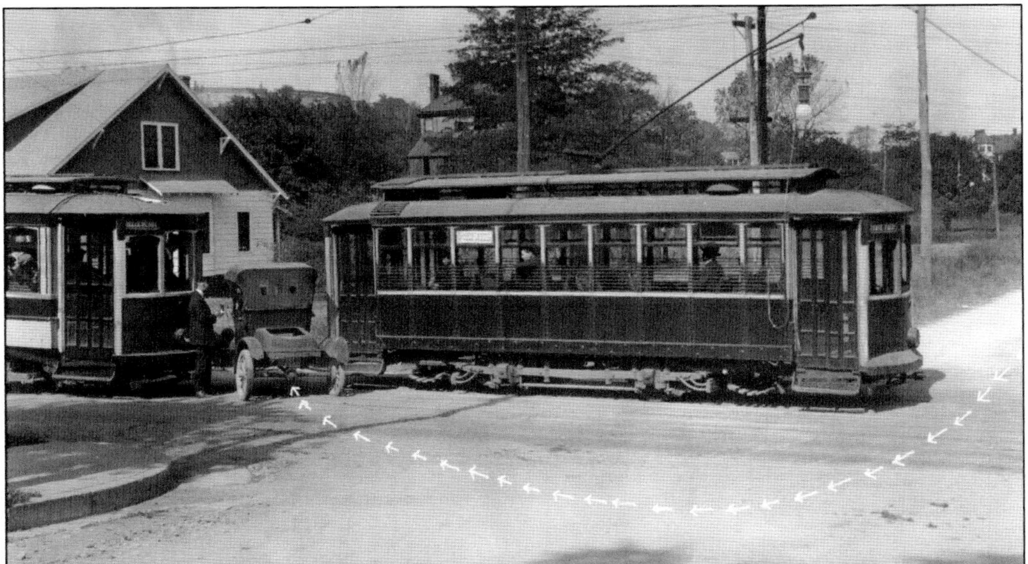

Although streetcars were normally a safe way to travel, there were occasional accidents. The incidents that did occur were usually caused by automobiles pulling in front of a streetcar suddenly. This public awareness photograph shows just such a scenario illustrating what can happen when a motorist carelessly tries to pass on a street with two tracks. As in the previous photographs, car No. 424, at left, makes an appearance. This staged scene was recorded on Wedgewood Avenue near Eighth Avenue, west of the state fairgrounds. The top of the Nashville City Reservoir can be seen in the background. (Metro Nashville Archives, MTA Collection.)

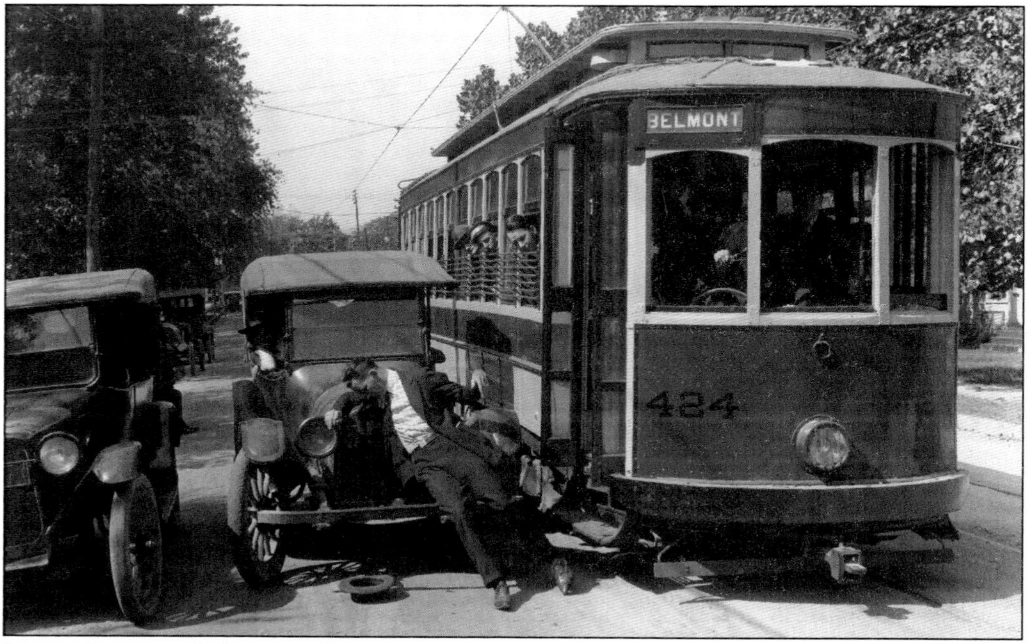

In another staged photograph using car No. 424 as a prop, taken near the Tennessee State Fairgrounds on Wedgewood Avenue, passengers peer out of their streetcar at a disembarking passenger who was hit by a reckless motorist. This image illustrates what can happen when both riders and drivers become careless. (Nashville Public Library, Special Collections.)

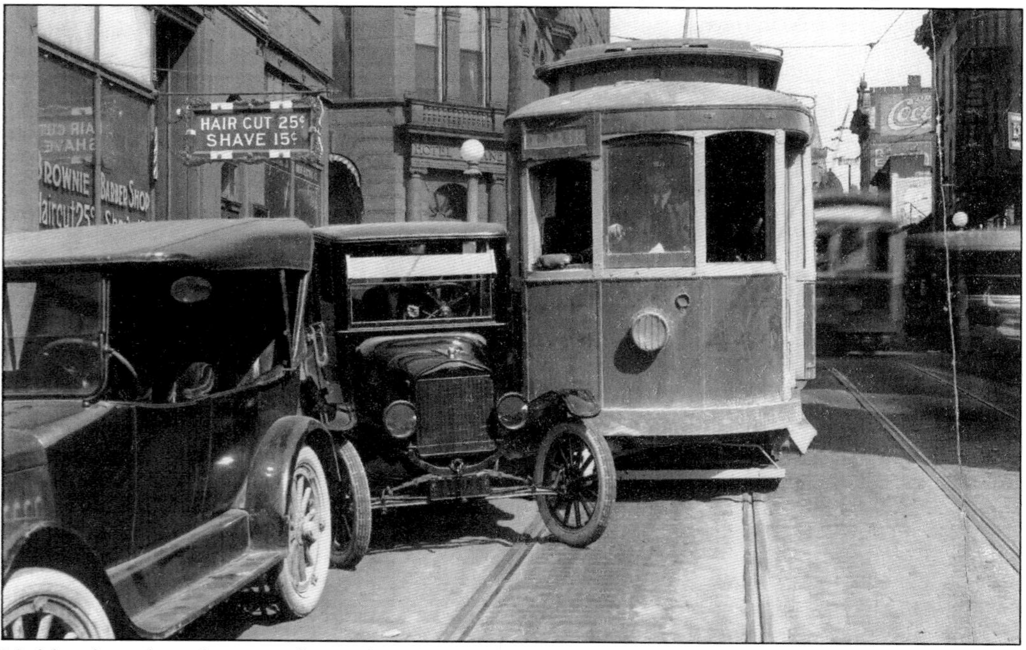

Unlike the other photographs in this chapter, this view was recorded in the heart of downtown Nashville in a more congested setting. This simulated scene illustrates that a Ford Model T is no match for a moving streetcar. The venerable Hotel Tulane, at left, confirms the location as Church Street and Eight Avenue North. The blurred streetcars in the background are an indication of the camera's long exposure, typical for 1921. (Nashville Public Library, Special Collections.)

Seven

The Pageant of Street Railway Progress

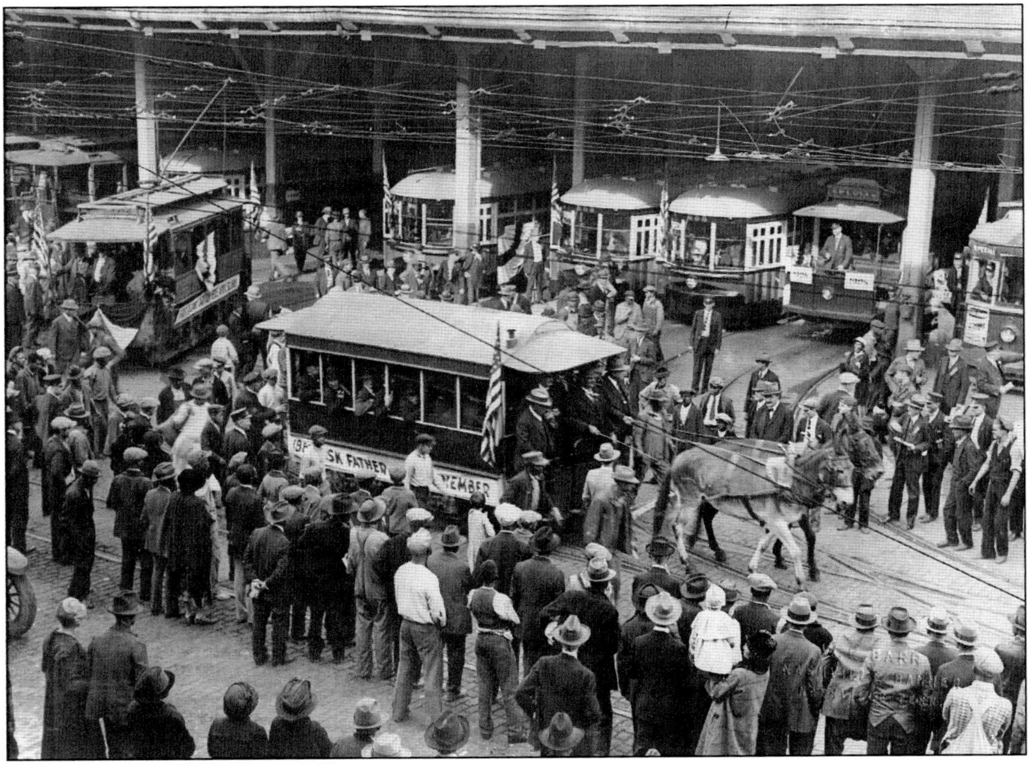

During the 1920s, Nashville had one of the best public transportation systems in the nation in terms of safety and efficiency. The streetcars of the Nashville Railway & Light Company were still profitable for the firm, while automobiles were still too pricey for average Americans. A most memorable day for Nashvillians from that era occurred on October 29, 1926, when the Pageant of Street Railway Progress was held. The event celebrated 60 years of streetcar service in the city, showcasing the various types of streetcars going back to 1866. More importantly, however, the street railway company used the occasion to inaugurate 10 new streetcars, ushering in a new era of transit to the public. Here, various cars leave the carbarn traveling south on Fourth Avenue as the parade begins. The line of cars comprised various types of equipment dating from an 1866 mule-drawn car to the 10 new "Noiseless" electric cars delivered days earlier. It was a banner day for public transportation in Nashville! (Nashville Public Library, Special Collections.)

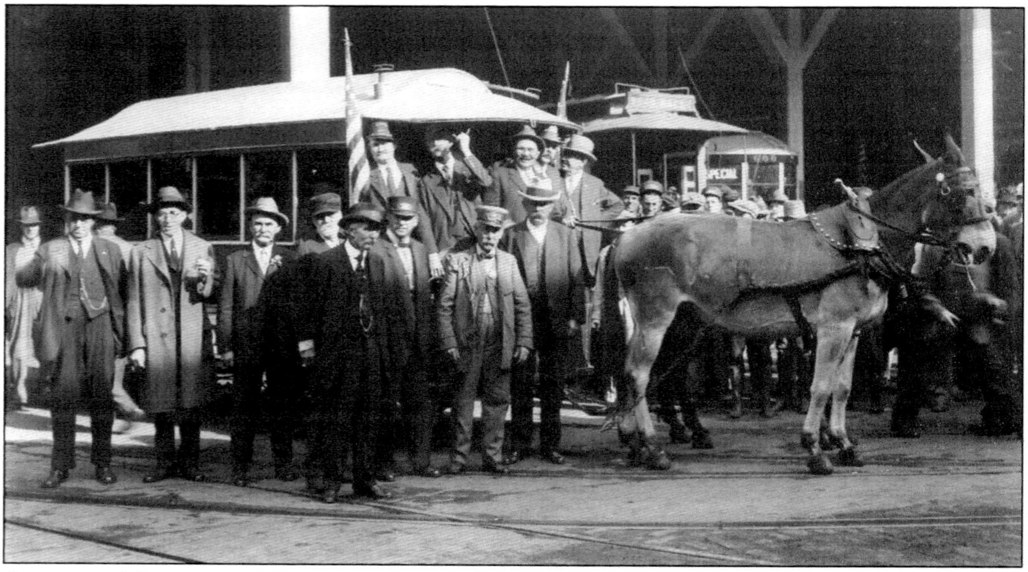

A group of former streetcar motormen and conductors from the Nashville Railway & Light Company and predecessor lines pose for photographers at the carbarn before the commencement of the parade on October 29, 1926. The veteran car men were guests of honor this day; most of those shown had worked the horse or mule-drawn streetcars from the 1860s until electrification of the system was completed 30 years later. The moment was one of nostalgia for many but also signified a new era with the inauguration of 10 modern cars for Nashville. The old timers, a few dressed in their old uniforms, rode at the front of the procession in the vintage car, followed by other cars from the previous 60 years. The 10 new cars brought up the rear. (Nashville Public Library, Special Collections.)

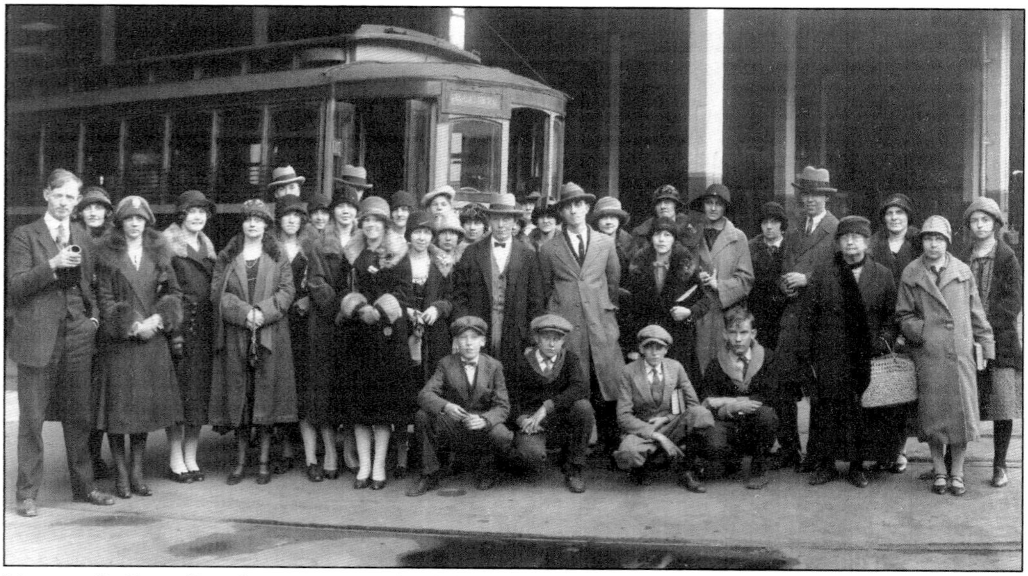

Using a Gallatin Road streetcar as a backdrop, Nashville Railway & Light Company employees and their families pose for a formal company photograph at the carbarn on Fourth Avenue North shortly before the celebration and parade began on a chilly October 29, 1926. This view clearly illustrates the pride that employees had in the company they worked for. (Nashville Public Library, Special Collections.)

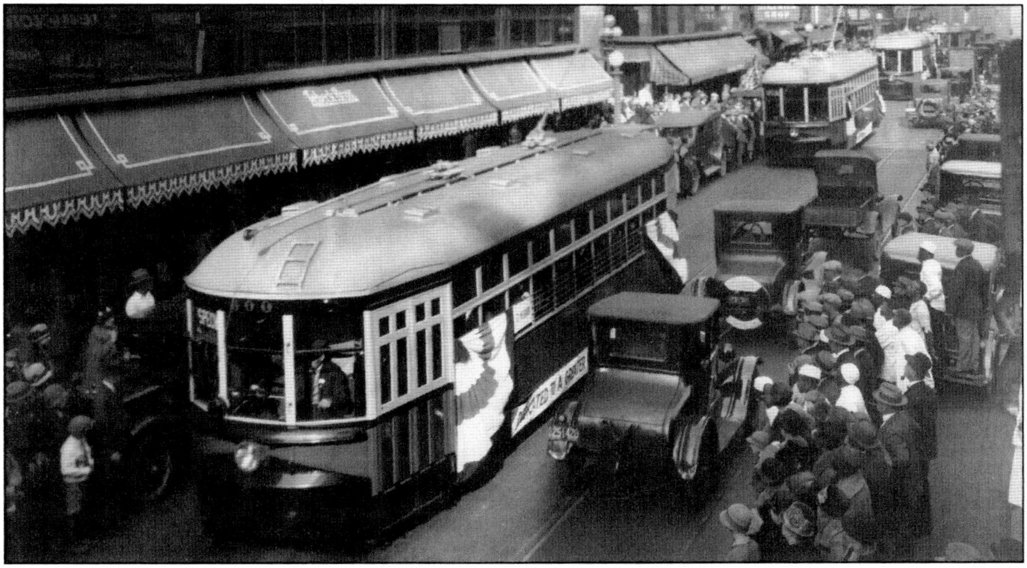

A procession of 15 streetcars trundle down Church Street through the heart of downtown on a brisk fall day as part of the Pageant of Transportation Progress. The event marked the 60th anniversary of streetcar service in Nashville but also served as the public inauguration for 10 new cars purchased from the Light Weight Noiseless Streetcar Company. The St. Paul, Minnesota, car builder had a rather short existence from 1924 to 1927. The modern cars shown were the last new equipment purchase for the Nashville Railway & Light Company. All of these cars bear the names of notable Tennesseans. The closest car in this scene, *President Andrew Jackson*, carried city leaders and dignitaries as its first passengers, including Nashville mayor Hillary E. Howse and members of the chamber of commerce, state railroad commission, board of education, and other agencies. (Nashville Public Library, Special Collections.)

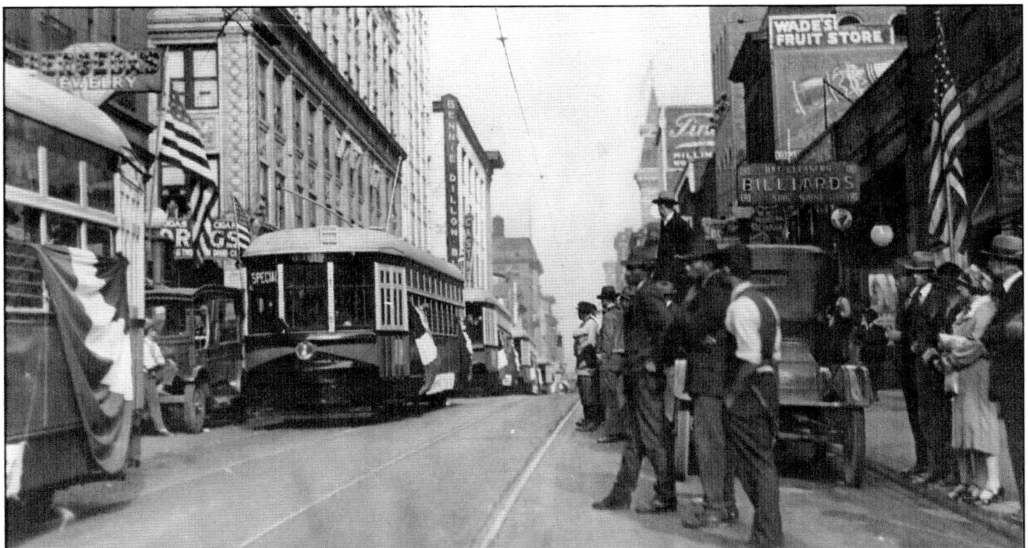

In a scene recorded moments after the previous photograph, people crowd Church Street to get a glimpse of the procession of new streetcars headed west for Nashville's Centennial Park. The three buildings to the left—the Doctors, Bennie Dillon, and Caster Knott Buildings—are the only buildings from this photograph that survive today. (Nashville Public Library, Special Collections.)

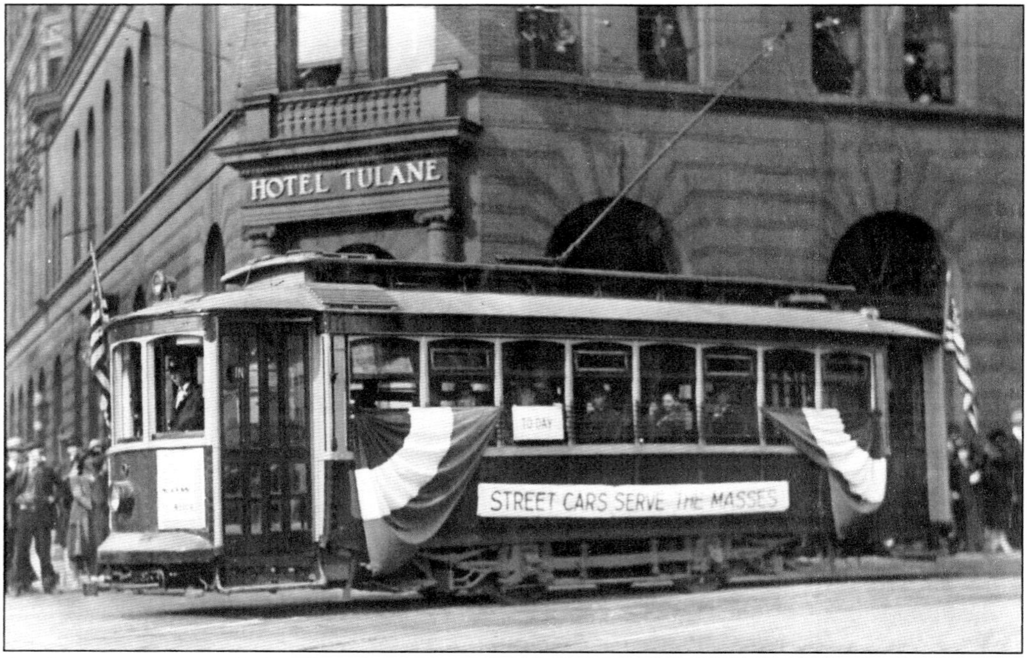

As the streetcar parade heads west on Church Street, an older single-truck Brill car passes the stately Hotel Tulane as it turns south onto Eighth Avenue, where it will follow the other 14 streetcars down Broadway and West End Avenue to Centennial Park. Once the procession returned downtown, the cars were open for public display on Eighth Avenue. (Nashville Public Library, Special Collections.)

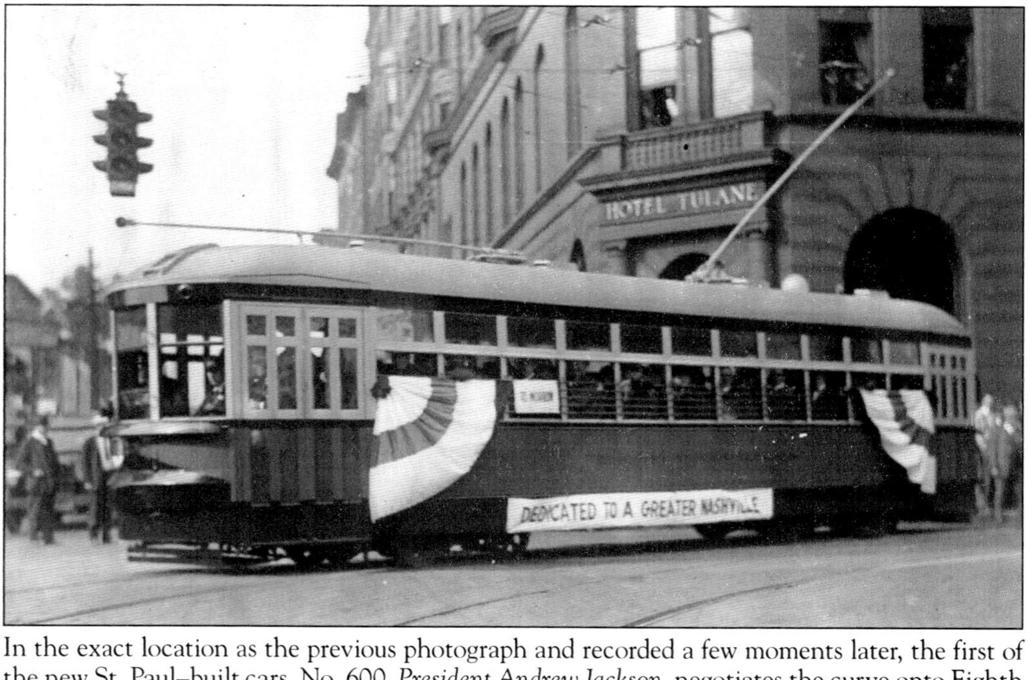

In the exact location as the previous photograph and recorded a few moments later, the first of the new St. Paul–built cars, No. 600, *President Andrew Jackson*, negotiates the curve onto Eighth Avenue from Church Street with nine of its cousins following in its path. (Nashville Public Library, Special Collections.)

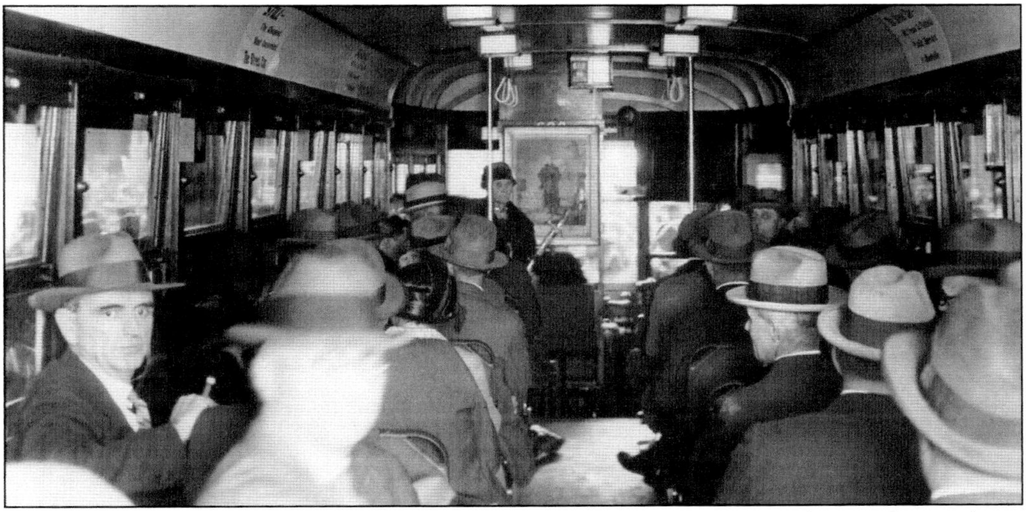

The procession of the city's newest streetcars was led by car No. 600, *President Andrew Jackson*, which gave Nashville dignitaries their first opportunity to enjoy modern public transit. Nashville Railway & Light Company vice president and manager J.P.W. Brown acted as host of the car for its inaugural run. This rare interior photograph shows the dignitaries who were on board that day. These included Nashville mayor Hillary Howse, seen toward the front of the car wearing the light hat. Standing next to the mayor is Bettie M. Donelson, president of the Andrew Jackson Society, holding the sword presented to Jackson by the State of Tennessee in commemoration of the Battle of New Orleans. Posted conspicuously next to Donelson is a picture of "Old Hickory" himself, one of several personal articles of Jackson memorabilia owned by Donelson that once belonged to the Tennessee president. (Nashville Public Library, Special Collections.)

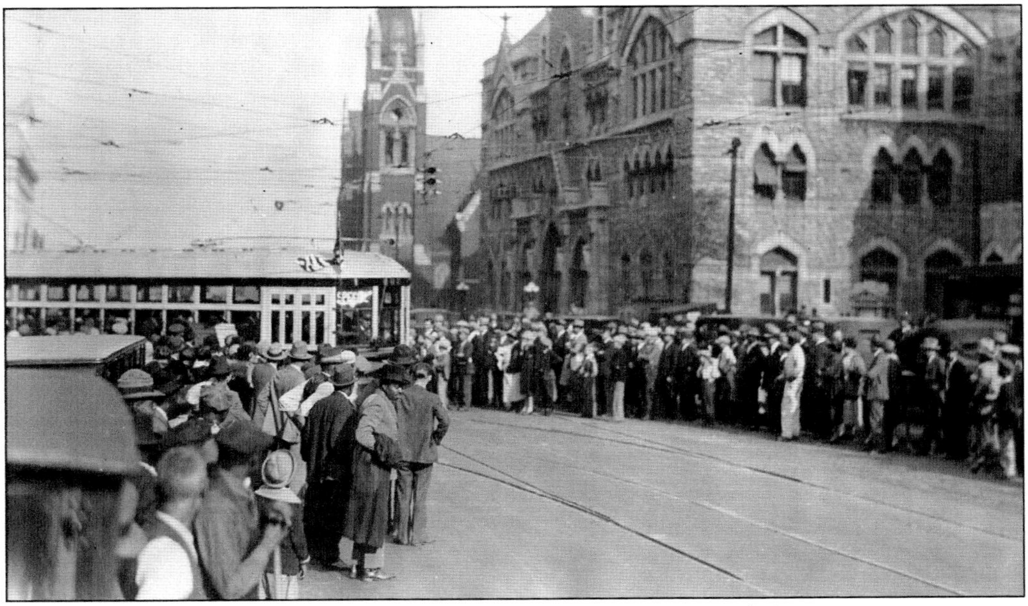

Large crowds line both sides of the parade route as car No. 607, *Samuel Houston*, turns west onto Broadway from Eighth Avenue on its way to Centennial Park, the final destination. Nashville's First Baptist Church and federal customs house–post office can be seen in the background. The church steeple and Victorian Gothic–style federal building, both dating from the 1880s, survive today. (Nashville Public Library, Special Collections.)

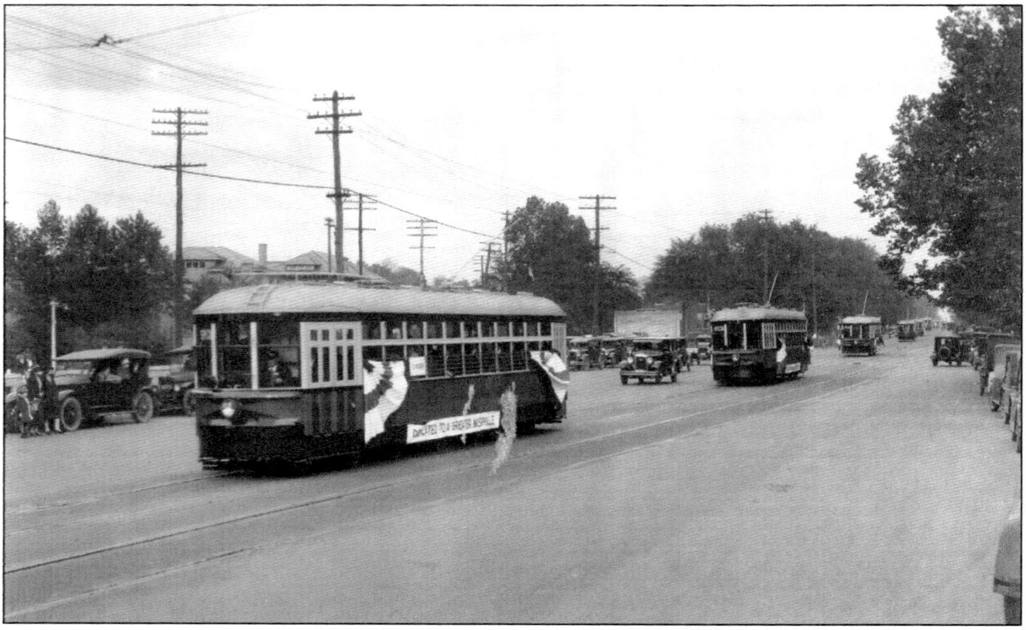

The 10 new streetcars, constructed by the Light Weight Noiseless Streetcar Company, proceed down West End Avenue near Vanderbilt University on October 29, 1926. Mayor Hillary Howse and other city officials are riding in the lead car. A few blocks later, the entourage of streetcars reversed directions at Centennial Park, returning to downtown, where the equipment was open for public display. (Nashville Public Library, Special Collections.)

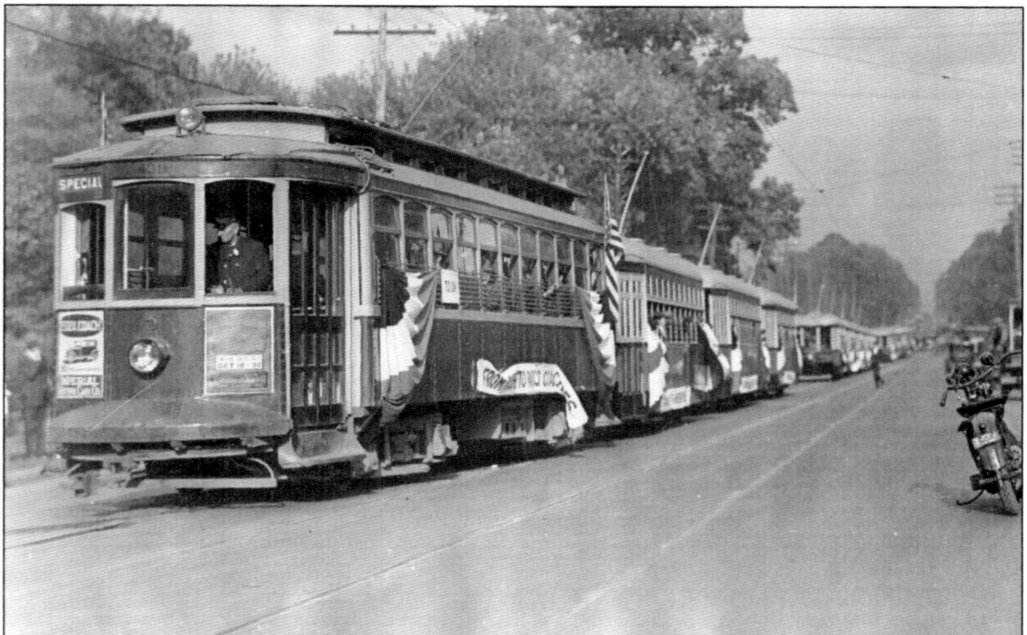

The long line of streetcars from the Pageant of Transportation Progress parade has stopped in front of Nashville's Centennial Park on West End Avenue as the motorman in car No. 439 prepares to move to the opposite end for the return trip downtown. (Nashville Public Library, Special Collections.)

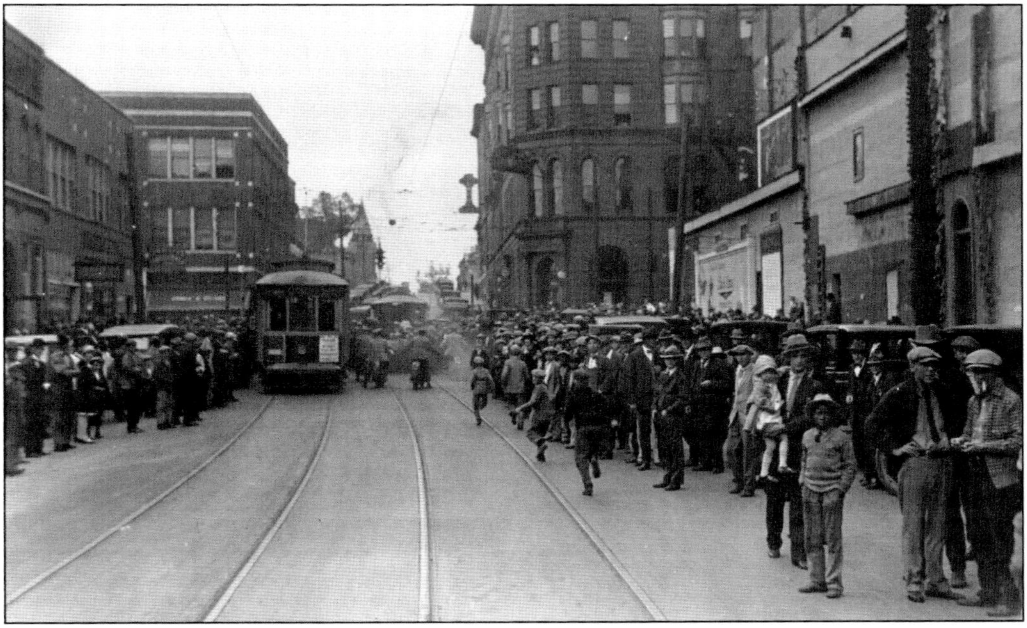

People line both sides of the street, eagerly awaiting the arrival of the parade of streetcars as they return from their tour across the city. This view shows the motorman's point of view from the front of the streetcar as it travels north toward its destination at Eighth Avenue and Church Street. The Hotel Tulane can be seen at right. (Nashville Public Library, Special Collections.)

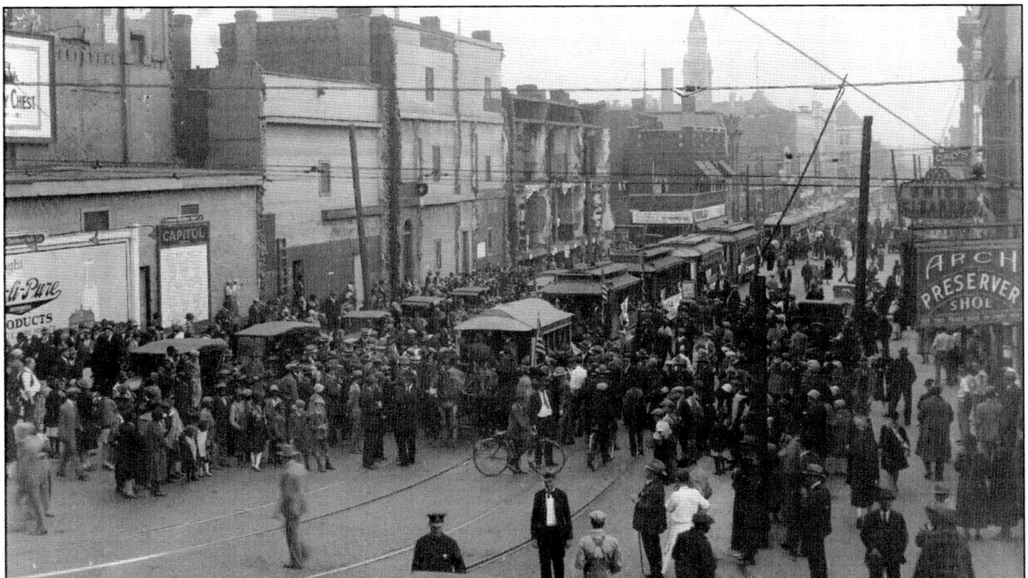

After the streetcar tour across town concluded, all 15 cars spanning the history of public transportation in Nashville from 1866 to the present were assembled for public display. In this view looking south down Eighth Avenue, the street has been closed to vehicular traffic between Church Street and Broadway for this historic occasion. Many residents were on hand for the occasion, immediately surrounding the rolling stock and wanting to get a closer look at both the vintage mule-drawn car and the 10 state-of-the-art parlor cars. In the distance, the tower of Nashville's federal customs house can be seen through the hazy sky. (Nashville Public Library, Special Collections.)

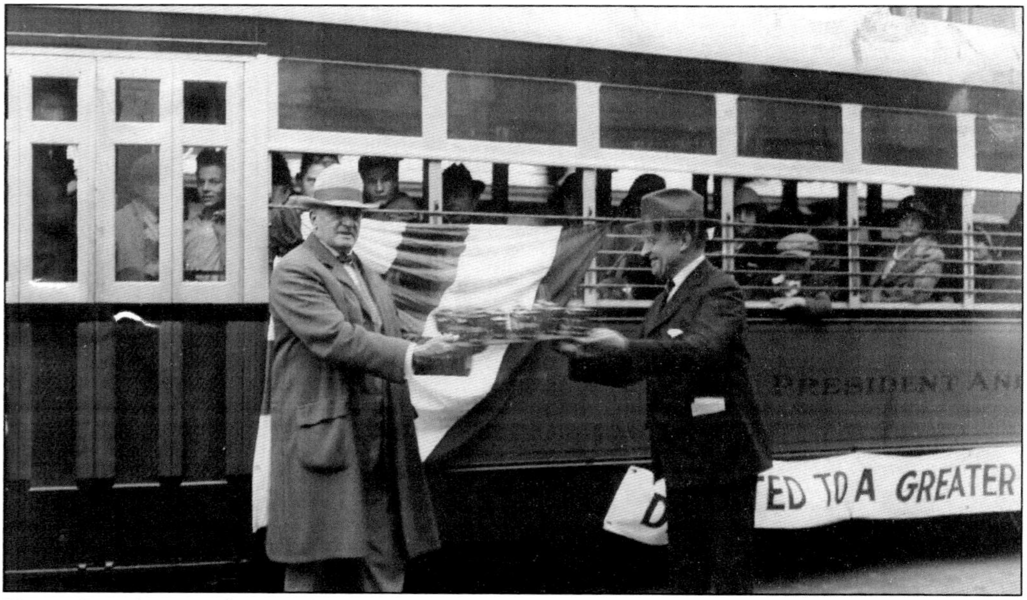

Using *President Andrew Jackson* as a backdrop, Mayor Howse, at left, accepts 10 miniature streetcars from J.P.W. Brown, vice president and general manager of the Nashville Railway & Light Company, symbolizing their exchange from the hands of the company to the service of the people of Nashville. The streetcar, one of a group of 10, had just completed its inaugural trip earlier that day as part of the Pageant of Transportation celebration. (Nashville Public Library, Special Collections.)

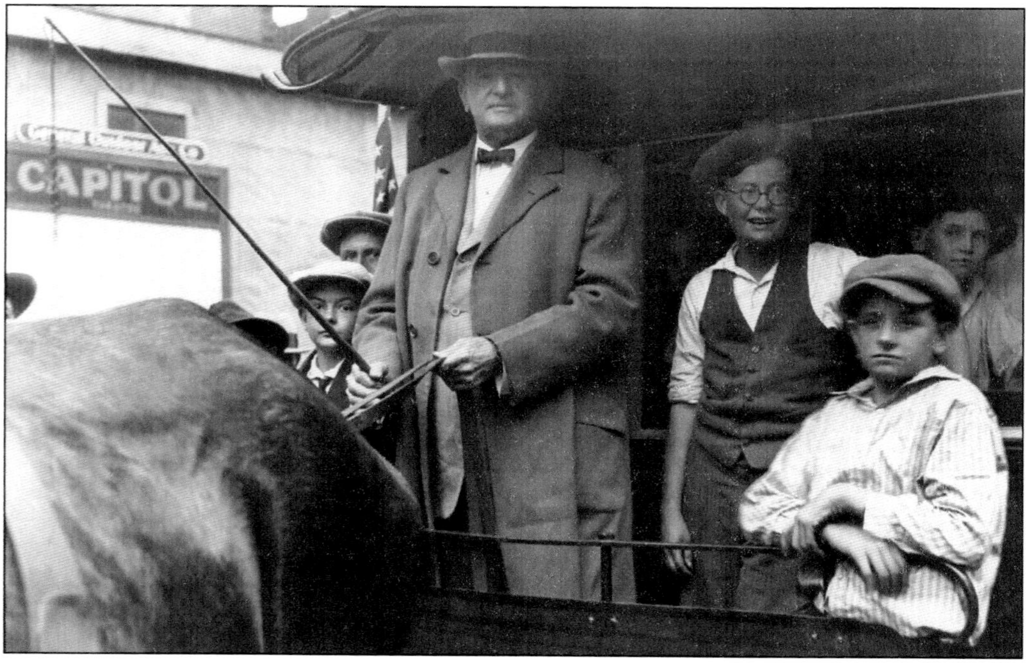

Posing for photographers, Mayor Howse takes the reins of the 60-year-old mule car, surrounded by curious young boys exploring the vintage streetcar. Afterward, Mayor Howse took time to inspect the 10 new cars on display on Eighth Avenue between Church Street and Broadway. (Nashville Public Library, Special Collections.)

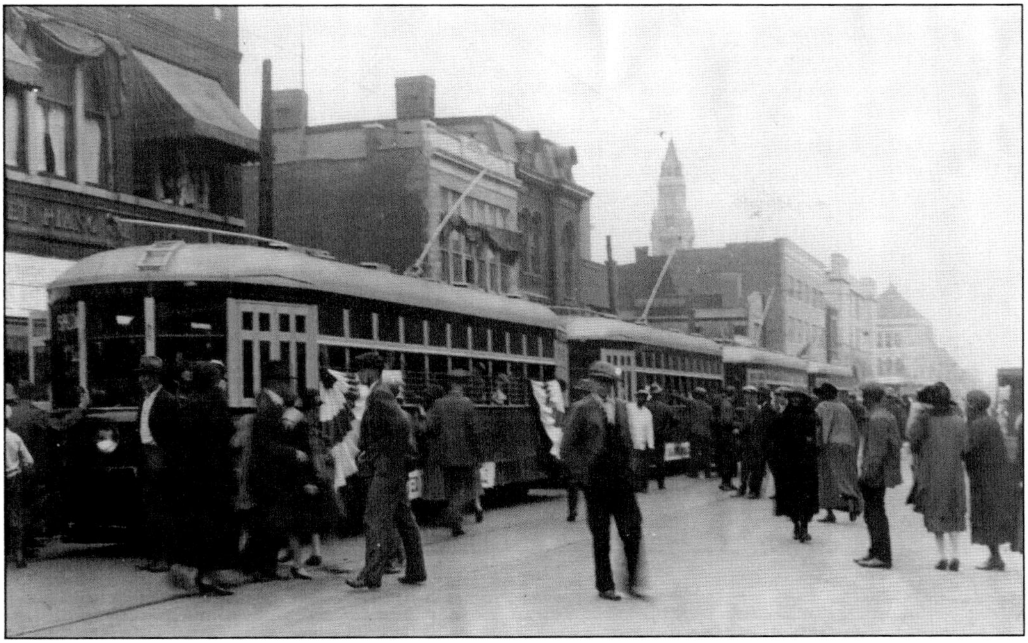

For several hours, Eighth Avenue was closed to vehicular traffic between Church Street and Broadway, giving the public an opportunity to inspect the variety of equipment on display by the Nashville Railway & Light Company during an overcast October 29, 1926. Hume-Fogg High School and the federal customs house can be seen in the distance. (Nashville Public Library, Special Collections.)

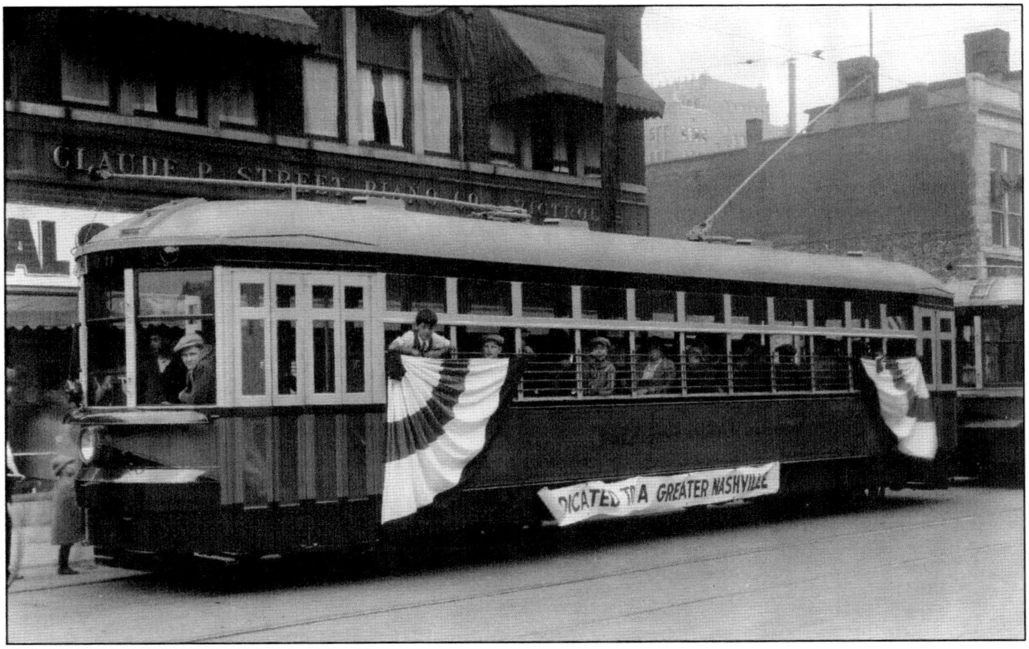

The day had been an exciting one for the city, ushering in a new era of transportation and marking the zenith of Nashville's streetcar era. The St. Paul–built cars would prove to be the last new cars built for the system. Shortly after No. 600 returned from the inaugural run and opened for public tours, youngsters wasted no time getting on board, trying out the seats and mugging for the photographer. (Nashville Public Library, Special Collections.)

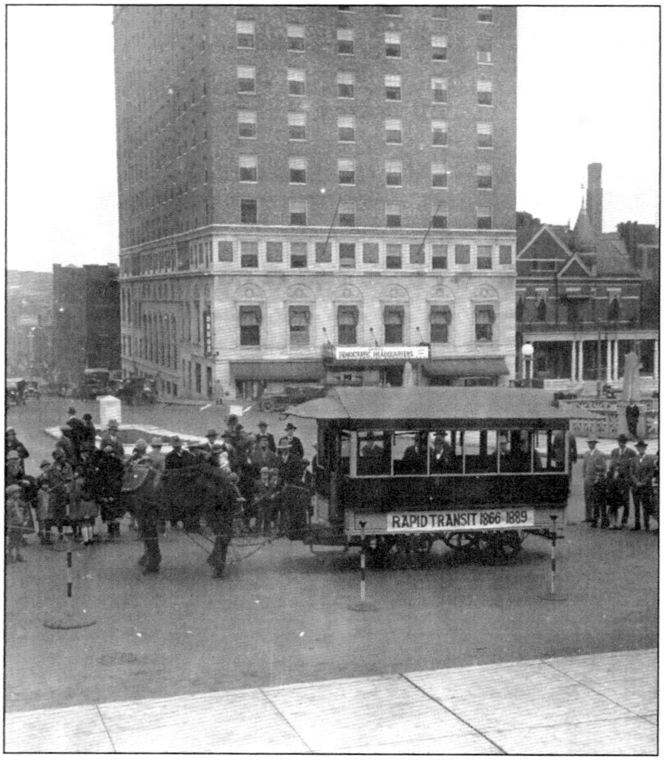

Due to the unexpected popularity of the historic mule-drawn streetcar during the display, the NR&L arranged to have Nashville's earliest form of public transportation exhibited an additional day for the benefit of schoolchildren who were unable to see it in Friday's parade. Several Nashville newspapers ran ads on Sunday, October 31, 1926, notifying families who missed the relic two days earlier. The mule car was exhibited in Memorial Square at Deaderick Street and Capitol Boulevard for most of the day. Here, it has just been moved into position. Since there are no tracks at this location, it is not known how the vehicle was moved there from the carbarn. (Nashville Public Library, Special Collections.)

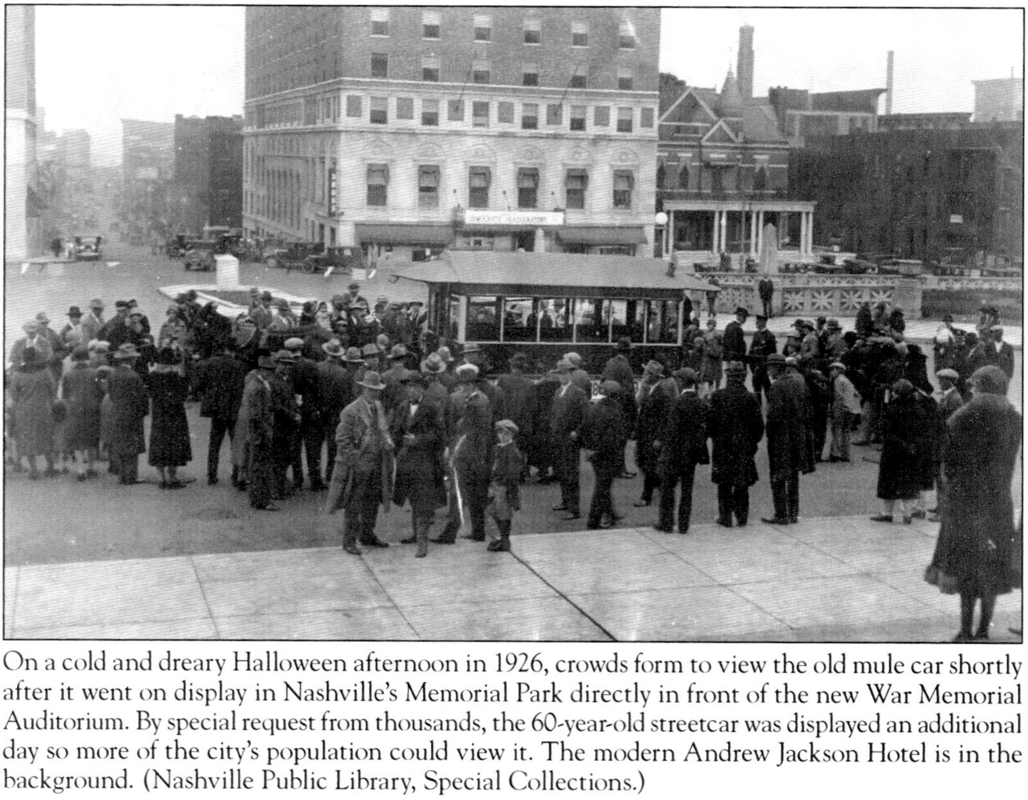

On a cold and dreary Halloween afternoon in 1926, crowds form to view the old mule car shortly after it went on display in Nashville's Memorial Park directly in front of the new War Memorial Auditorium. By special request from thousands, the 60-year-old streetcar was displayed an additional day so more of the city's population could view it. The modern Andrew Jackson Hotel is in the background. (Nashville Public Library, Special Collections.)

Eight

Nashville's Interurban Railways

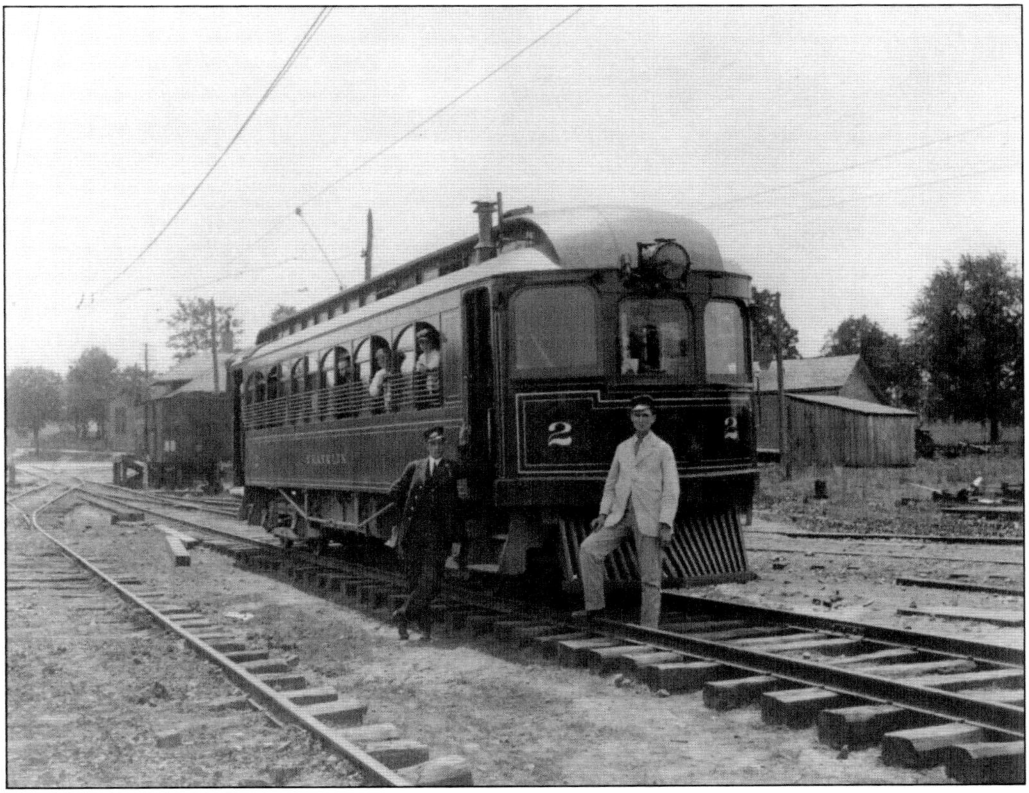

The Nashville-Franklin Interurban Railway (NFI) was one of two electric interurban railways linking Nashville with communities to the north and south during the early 20th century. The company began regular service on May 1, 1909, connecting Franklin with Tennessee's capital. The cars of the NFI were always well patronized even until the end of operation in 1941. At that time, Nashville's street railways, whose cars the interurban used from city limits to the downtown Transfer Station, converted to buses, leaving the popular service landlocked. The company continued its commuter operation with buses until the late 1960s. In this scene, the conductor, motorman, and passengers pose with car No. 2 for a portrait at the company's yard in Franklin, Tennessee, soon after operations commenced. The track continued two blocks south to its terminus, where it looped around Franklin's square. The interurban railway exchanged passengers and freight with the Middle Tennessee Railroad, whose depot can be seen in the background. (James D. Le Croy collection.)

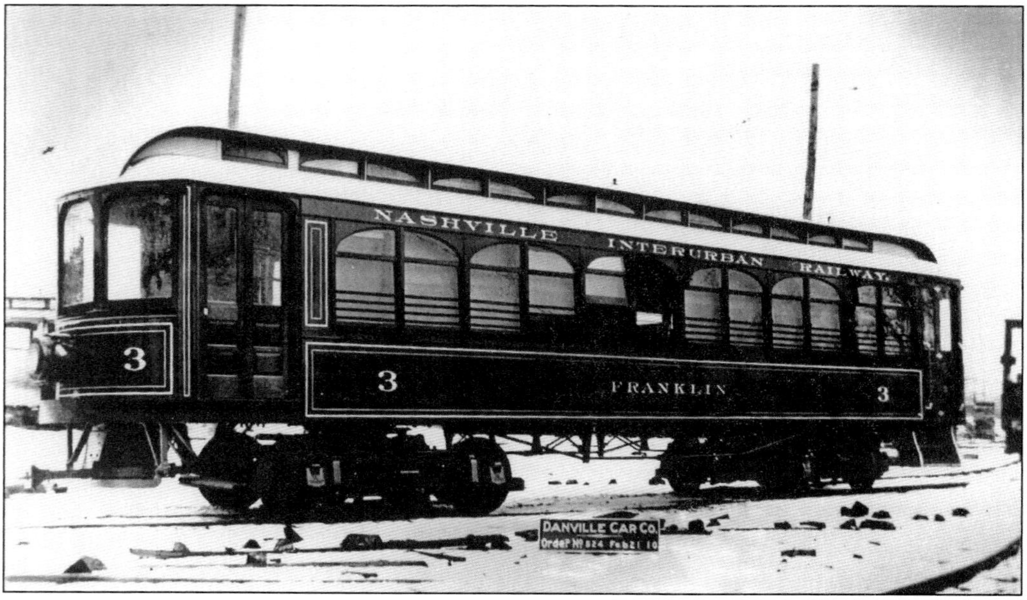

Several cars that operated over the Nashville-Franklin Interurban Railway were built by the Danville Car Company and were identical in appearance. This builder's photograph shows car No. 3 after emerging from the Illinois facility on February 21, 1910. (James D. Le Croy collection.)

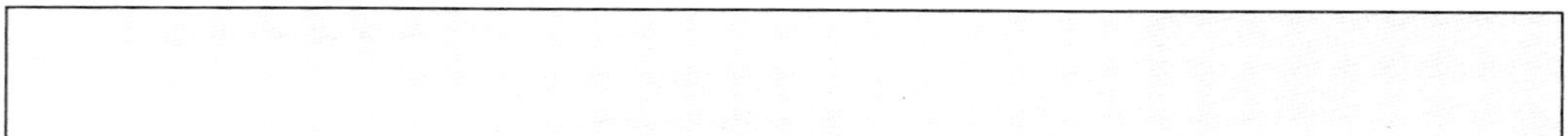

In addition to carrying passengers, the NFI also had a successful freight operation between Franklin, where it interchanged cars with the Middle Tennessee Railroad, and the outskirts of Nashville, connecting with the Tennessee Central Railway. The locomotive shown in this builder's photograph, No. 200, was built by General Electric Company and American Locomotive Company at Schenectady, New York, in February 1910 to haul freight for the railway. (James D. Le Croy collection.)

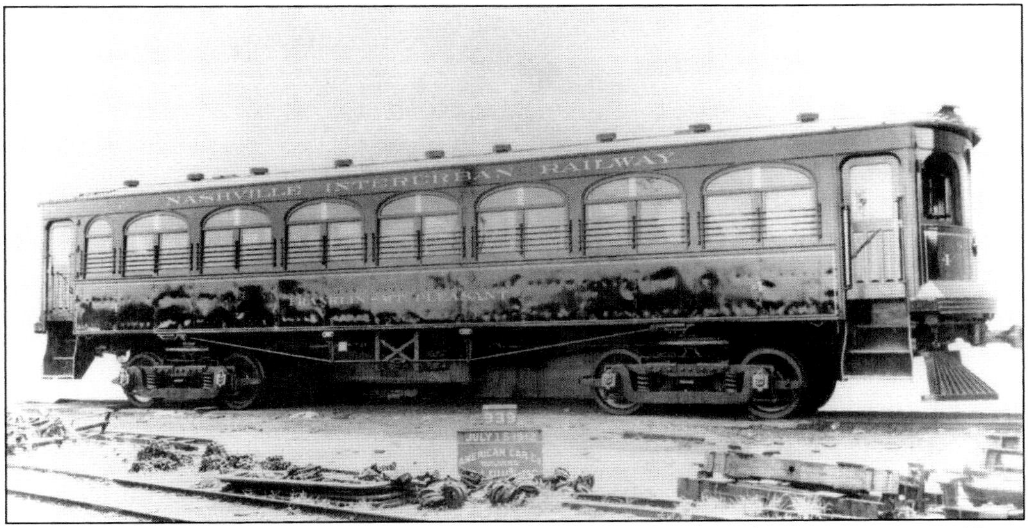

Looking very similar to the Danville-constructed cars but having a larger capacity, car No. 4 was built by the American Car Company of St. Louis in 1912. The lettering under the windows, "Franklin–Mt. Pleasant," indicates that this car most likely saw service on the Middle Tennessee Railroad, which operated between those cities until the 1920s, when the road was operated by the Nashville-Franklin Interurban Railway. (James D. Le Croy collection.)

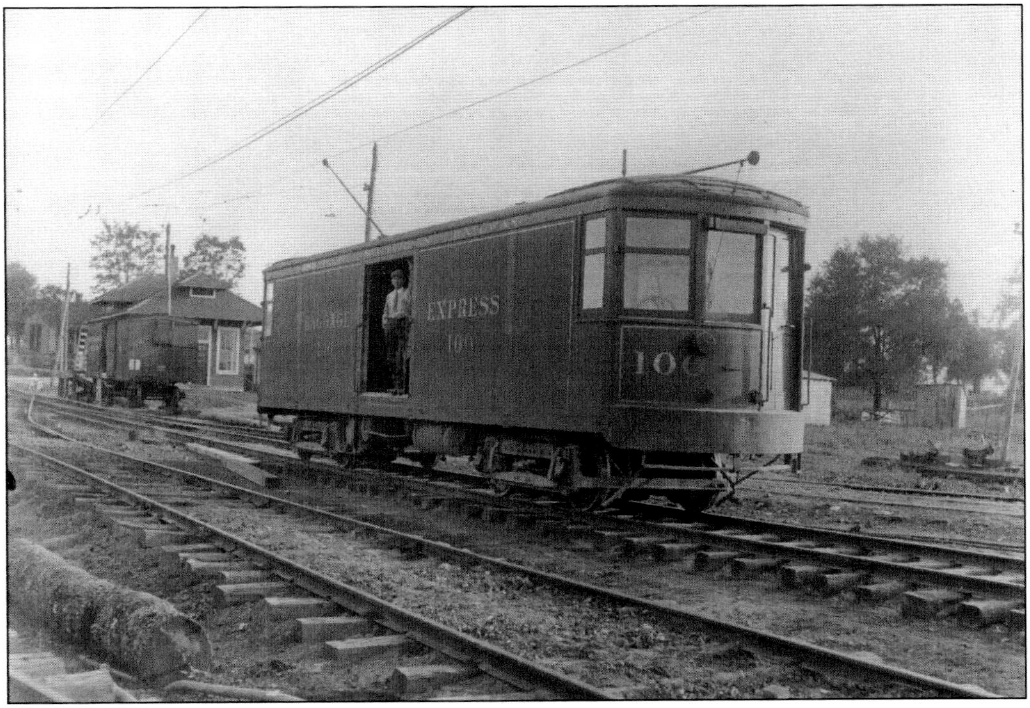

The NFI introduced freight and express service shortly after inaugurating its passenger service in 1909. Baggage express car No. 100 was built by the Danville Car Company in 1908 and operated independently of the passenger coaches, picking up and dropping off supplies to merchants and farmers along the way during an era before trucks and paved roads. An unidentified railway employee poses in the doorway at the Franklin yard. The Middle Tennessee Railroad depot can be seen in the background. (James D. Le Croy collection.)

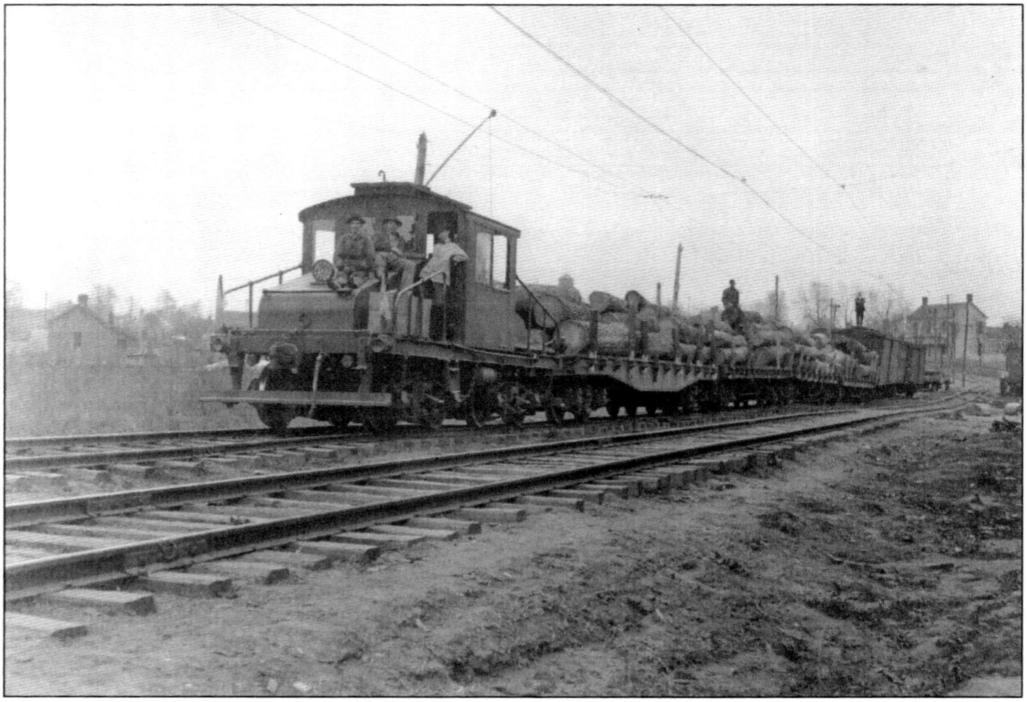

A freight train crew poses for the photographer at Franklin before heading north to Nashville, where the cars will be dropped off at the Tennessee Central Railway interchange. On this day, No. 200 is pulling four cars of lumber and two boxcars. (James D. Le Croy collection.)

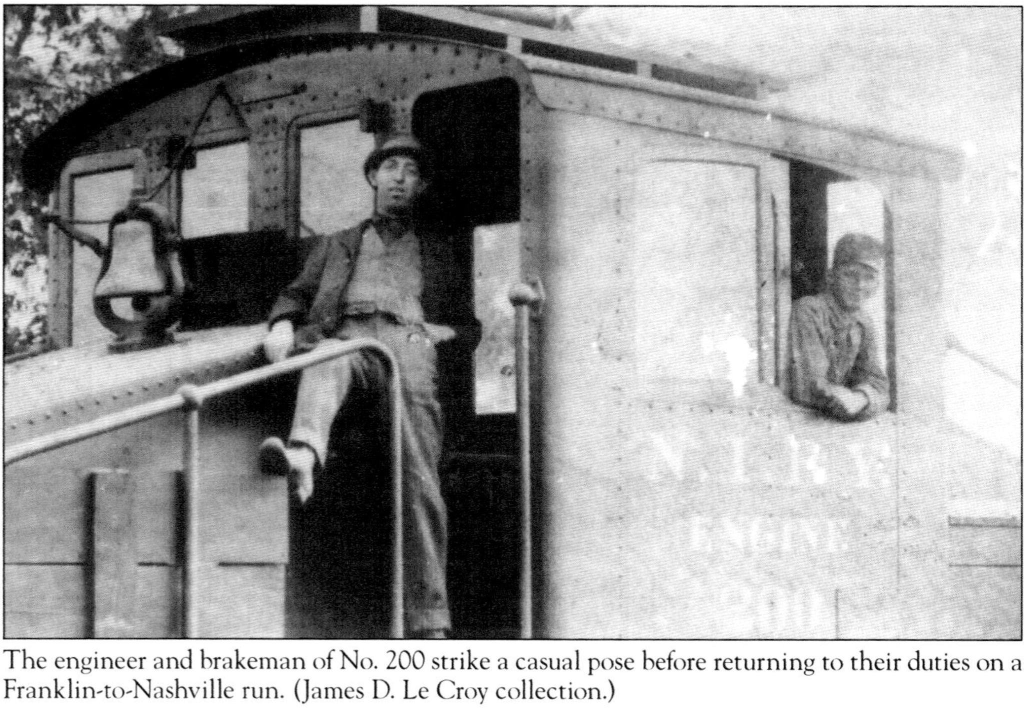

The engineer and brakeman of No. 200 strike a casual pose before returning to their duties on a Franklin-to-Nashville run. (James D. Le Croy collection.)

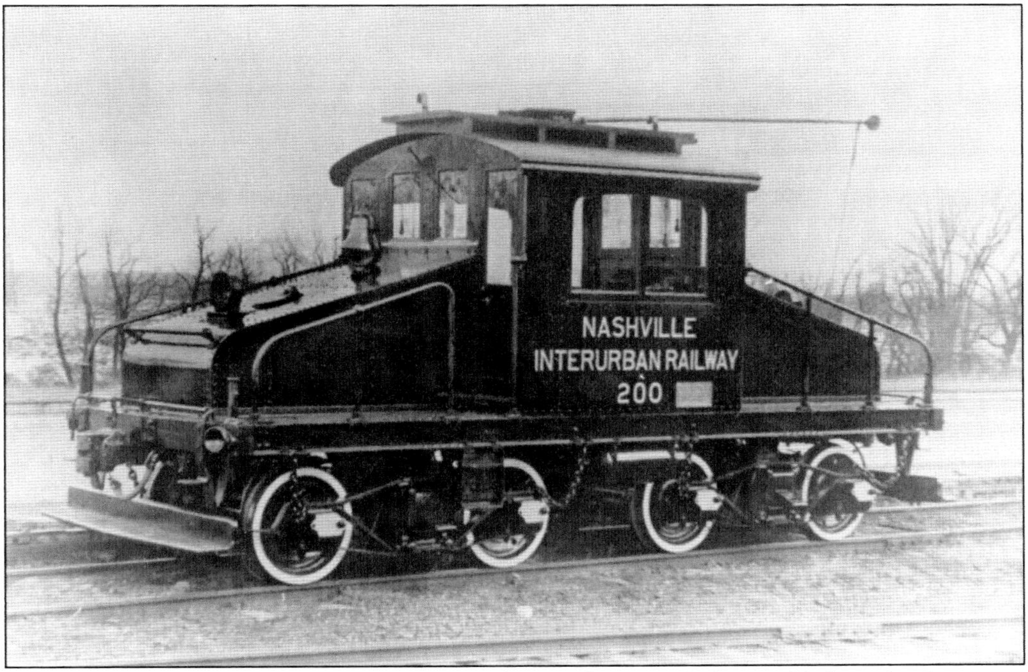

Another view shows Nashville-Franklin Interurban Railway No. 200, most likely at the American Locomotive Company at Schenectady, New York, before the car was shipped to Tennessee in 1910. It was common practice for manufacturers to photograph locomotives before delivering them to the buyer. (James D. Le Croy collection.)

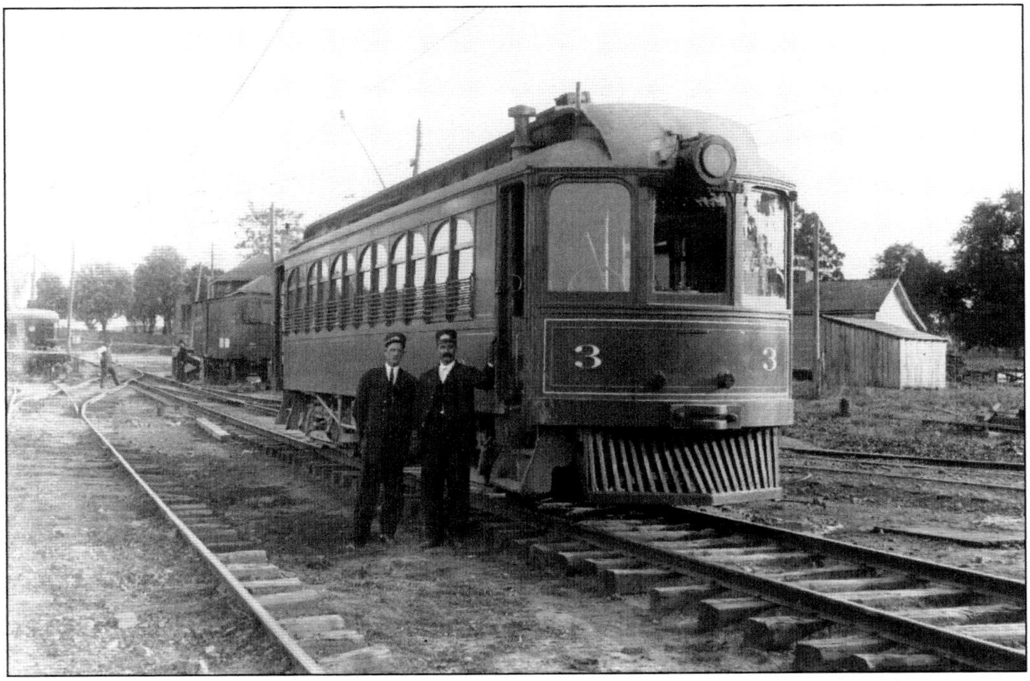

Danville Car Company No. 3, built in 1909, is seen again with the motorman and conductor posing next to the car at the company's yard in Franklin. This car was typical of the passenger equipment for the Franklin line until newer cars were ordered 10 years later. (James D. Le Croy collection.)

Columbia Motor Bus Co.

IN CONNECTION WITH

Nashville Interurban Railway

Daily and Sunday. Schedule in Effect November 1, 1921

GOING SOUTH	a.m.	p.m.	p.m.	GOING NORTH	a.m.	p.m.	p.m.
Lv. Nashville	8:00	1:00	5:00	Lv. Columbia	7:45	1:45	4:45
Ar. Franklin	9:00	2:00	6:00	Ar. Spring Hill	8:20	2:20	5:20
Lv. Franklin	9:00	3:00	6:00	Ar. Franklin	9:00	3:00	6:00
Ar. Spring Hill	9:35	3:35	6:35	Lv. Franklin	9:00	3:00	6:00
Ar. Columbia	10:15	4:15	7:15	Ar. Nashville	10:00	4:00	7:00

STOPS AT ALL INTERMEDIATE POINTS.

Leaving Nashville, passengers take Nashville Interurban Railway cars at Transfer Station, or at any stop on the line. Up-to-date motor busses, enclosed and heated, make close connections at Franklin for Spring Hill, Columbia and intermediate points, stopping to take or leave passengers at any point on the route.

Passengers leave from and arrive at the business centers at Nashville, Franklin, Spring Hill and Columbia, saving taxi fares to and from railroad stations.

Arriving at Nashville, passengers may transfer to any city street car line without additional cost.

FARES---Including War Tax

From NASHVILLE		From FRANKLIN		From COLUMBIA	
To FRANKLIN—		To NASHVILLE—		To NASHVILLE—	
One Way	$0.75	One Way	$0.75	One Way	$1.75
Round Trip	1.25	Round Trip	1.25	Round Trip	3.25
To SPRING HILL—		To SPRING HILL—		To FRANKLIN—	
One Way	$1.25	One Way	$0.50	One Way	1.00
Round Trip	2.25	Round Trip	1.00	Round Trip	2.00
To COLUMBIA—		To COLUMBIA—		To SPRING HILL—	
One Way	$1.75	One Way	$1.00	One Way	$0.50
Round Trip	3.25	Round Trip	2.00	Round Trip	1.00

Subject to Change Without Notice.

533 Broadway, Nashville, Tenn.
Telephone Main 1464.

J. H. CARPENTER, President.

In addition to providing frequent service between Nashville and Franklin, for many years, the Nashville-Franklin Interurban Railway made convenient connections with the Columbia Motor Bus Company at the latter city. Although this required changing from the interurban to a bus, it gave passengers the option to travel farther south to Spring Hill and Columbia. This arrangement also provided direct competition with the Louisville & Nashville Railroad's faster passenger trains, which ran parallel to this route and served the same communities. The interurban-bus route was slower but had the advantage of stopping virtually anywhere a passenger chose to board or disembark, served the center of each town, and offered lower fares. (David H. Steinberg collection.)

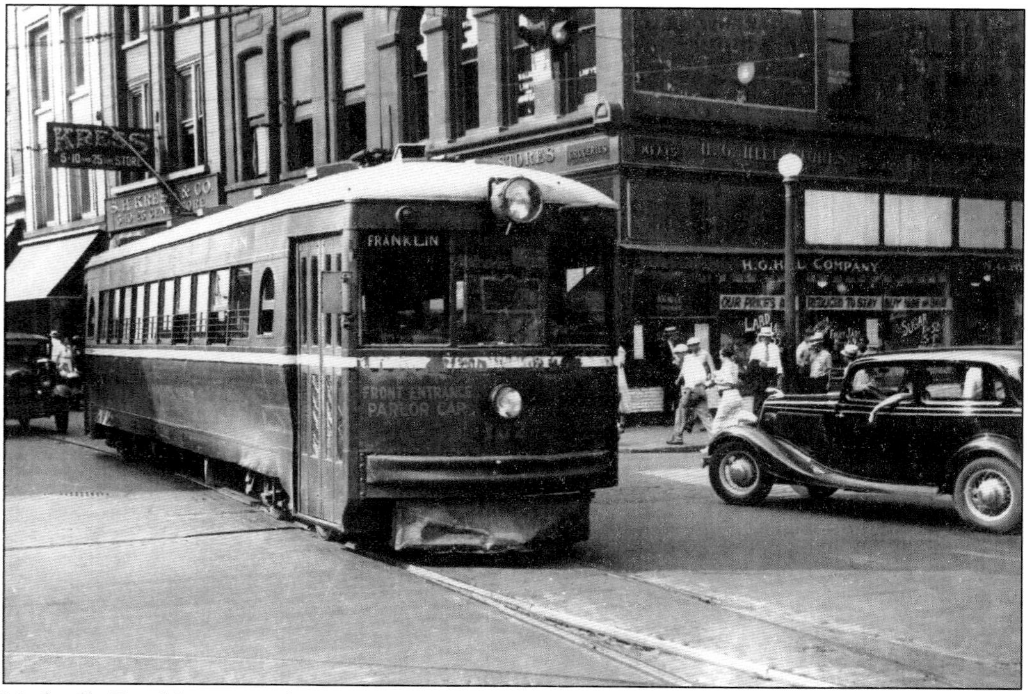

Nashville-Franklin Interurban Railway car No. 102 heads northbound on Third Avenue crossing Deaderick Street as it nears the end of its run during the late 1930s. Both the Franklin and Gallatin interurban cars operated over the Tennessee Electric Power Company rails within city limits to access Nashville's Transfer Station. (James D. Le Croy collection.)

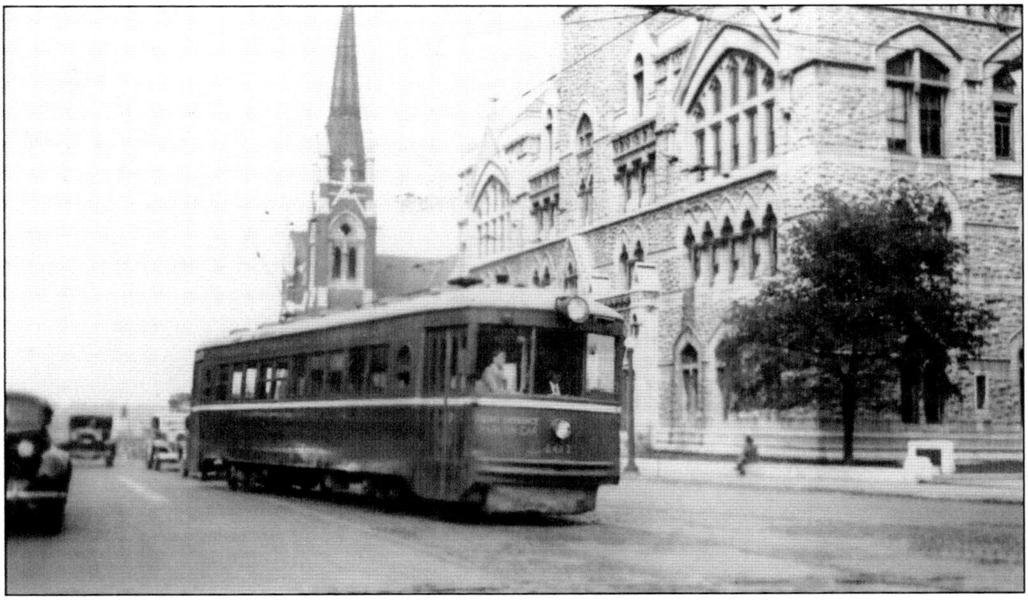

NFI No. 101 negotiates the curve as it turns south onto Eighth Avenue from Broadway. Once the car reaches the Nashville city limit, the track leaves the street, moving onto a dedicated right-of-way for the remainder of the journey to Franklin. The First Baptist Church and customs house can be seen in the background. (James D. Le Croy collection.)

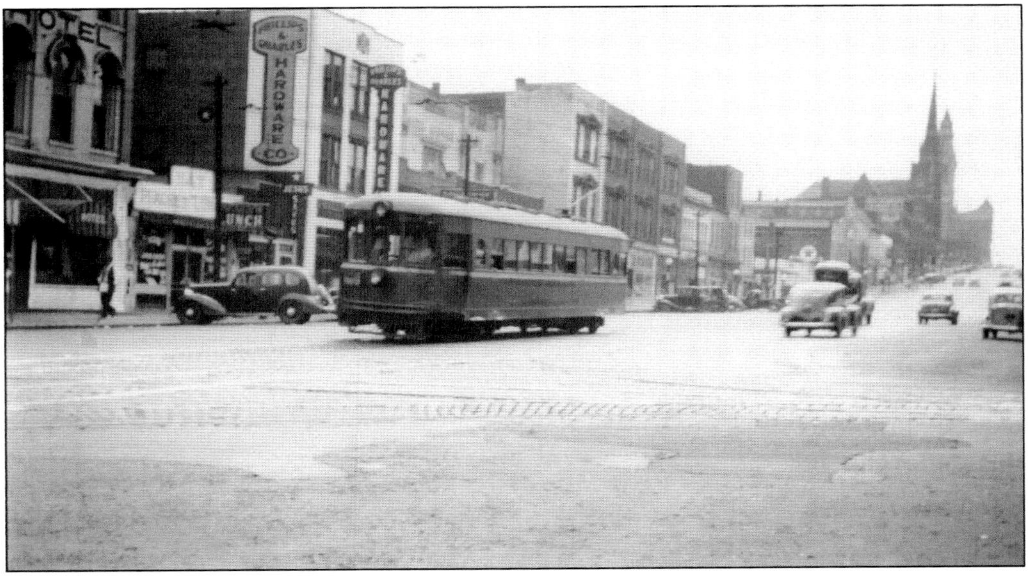

An inbound Cincinnati-built curved-side car from Franklin trundles east down Broadway near Fourth Avenue around 1940. The towers of the First Baptist Church and federal customs house can be seen in the distance. (James D. Le Croy collection.)

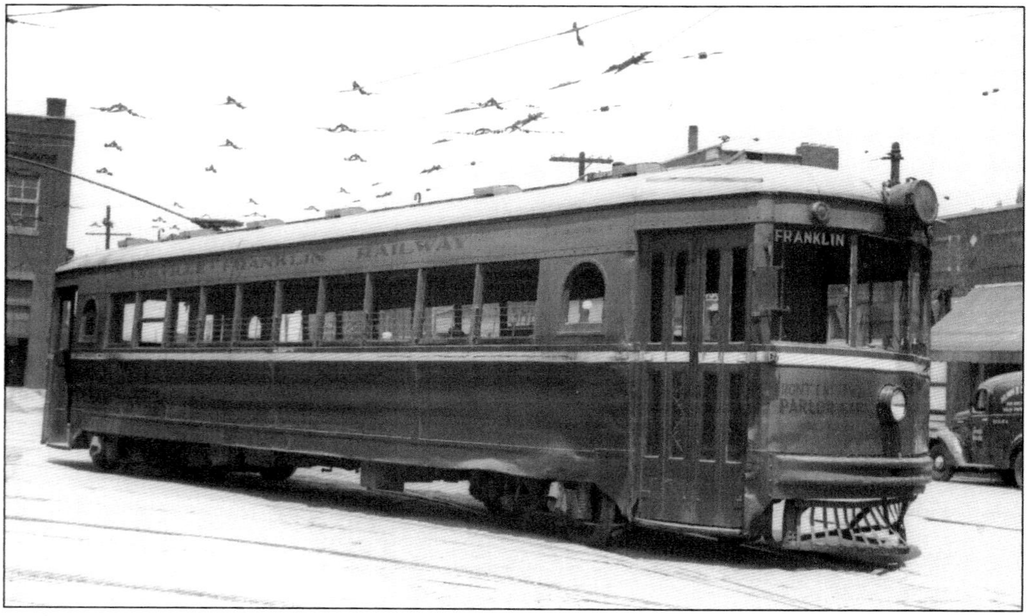

Nashville-Franklin Interurban car No. 103 was one of four curved-side lightweight cars built by the Cincinnati Car Company for the interurban. Seen in the late 1930s, the car has just been staged in front of TEPCO's carbarn on Third Avenue. Shortly, the motorman will board and ferry the car one block south to Nashville's Transfer Station to pick up passengers for the next run to Franklin. (James D. Le Croy collection.)

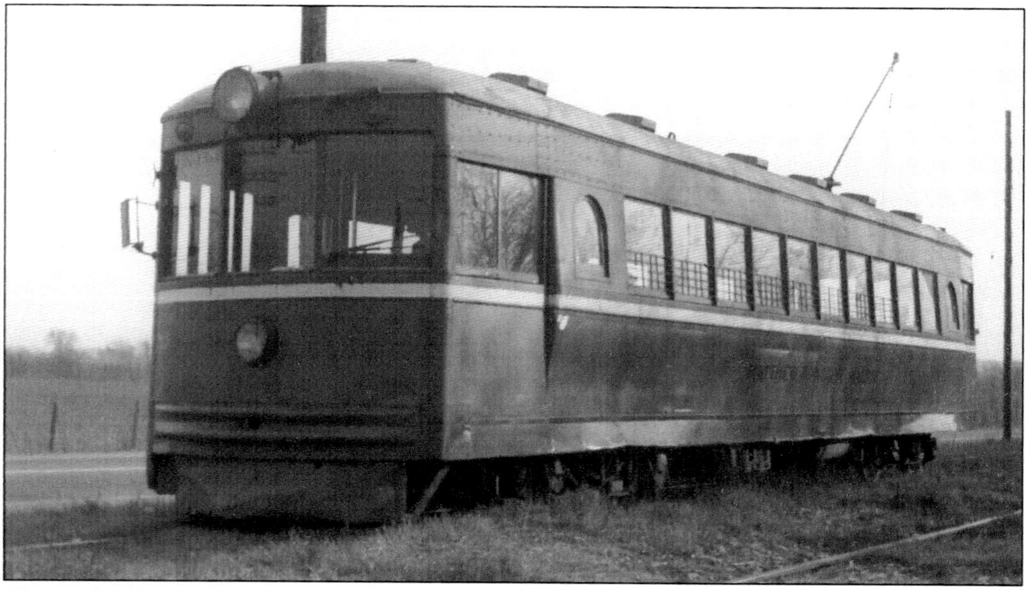

The Nashville-Franklin Interurban Railway was single-tracked for most of the length between its namesake cities except for the northernmost section. Within the city of Nashville, the interurban had trackage rights over Nashville's street railways, which were double-tracked the entire way. On the remainder of the line, sidings were strategically placed, allowing opposing cars to pass without problem. Here, southbound car No. 102 waits patiently on a siding about three miles south of Brentwood to allow a Nashville-bound train to pass during a winter day in early 1940. (James D. Le Croy collection.)

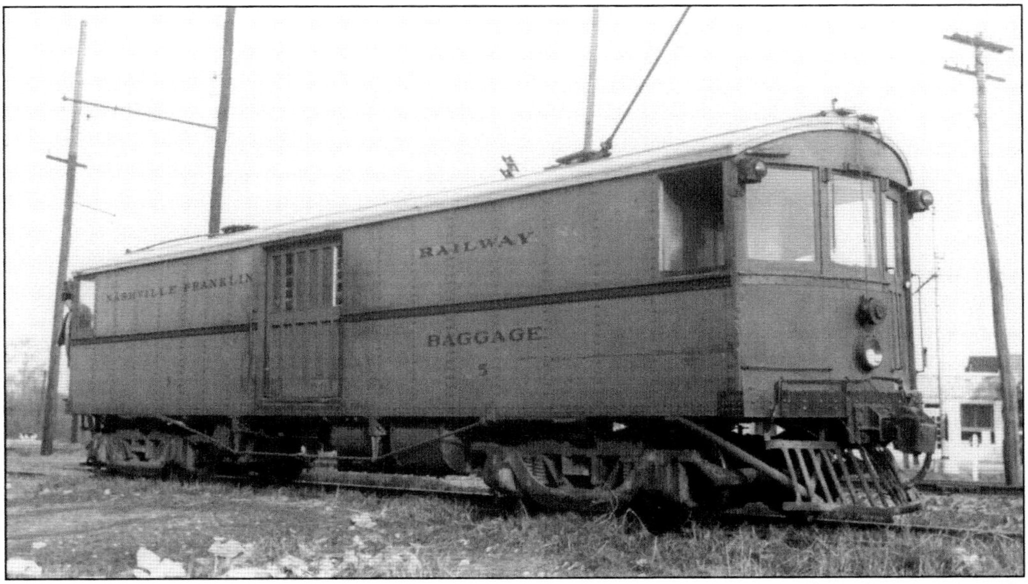

NFI baggage express car No. 5 was built by the Southern Car Company of High Point, North Carolina, in 1916. The car was purchased by the railway to handle baggage and express traffic between Nashville and Franklin and ran independently of the passenger service. The motorman is seen standing in the cab in the Franklin yard. (James D. Le Croy collection.)

NASHVILLE-FRANKLIN RAILWAY

R. R. JOHNSON, President and General Manager, Franklin, Tenn.
L. B. HOWARD, Secretary and Treasurer, Nashville, Tenn.
J. W. GRIMES, Asst. Secretary and Treasurer, Franklin, Tenn.
R. E. JONES, General Freight and Passenger Agt., Nashville, Tenn.
J. M. COLEMAN, Master Mechanic, Franklin, Tenn.
(Miles owned 16,8.)

DAILY PASSENGER SCHEDULE. *March*, 1937.

Carload and less than carload freight interchanged with the Tennessee Central Railway Company at Nashville, Tenn.

No.	Leave NASHVILLE	Arrive FRANKLIN	Leave FRANKLIN	Arrive NASHVILLE	No.
63	†6 55 A M	†8 00 A M	†6 00 A M	†6 55 A M	62
65	7 55 A M	9 00 A M	7 00 A M	7 55 A M	64
67	8 55 A M	10 00 A M	8 00 A M	8 55 A M	66
69	9 55 A M	11 00 A M	9 00 A M	9 55 A M	68
71	11 55 A M	1 00 P M	10 00 A M	10 55 A M	70
73	12 55 P M	2 00 P M	12 00 Noon	12 55 P M	72
89	*k*1 55 P M	*k*3 00 P M	1 00 P M	1 55 P M	74
75	2 55 P M	4 00 P M	*k*2 00 P M	*k*2 55 P M	88
77	4 00 P M	5 00 P M	3 00 P M	4 00 P M	76
79	5 00 P M	6 00 P M	4 00 P M	5 00 P M	78
81	6 00 P M	7 00 P M	5 00 P M	6 00 P M	80
83	7 00 P M	8 00 P M	6 00 P M	7 00 P M	82
85	9 30 P M	10 30 P M	7 00 P M	8 00 P M	84
87	11 30 P M	12 30 A M	10 30 P M	11 30 P M	86

Trains marked † run daily, except Sunday; *k* Saturday only.

This Nashville-Franklin Interurban timetable from 1937 illustrates the frequency with which the cars ran between the two cities, also mentioning the carrier's freight service. (Author's collection.)

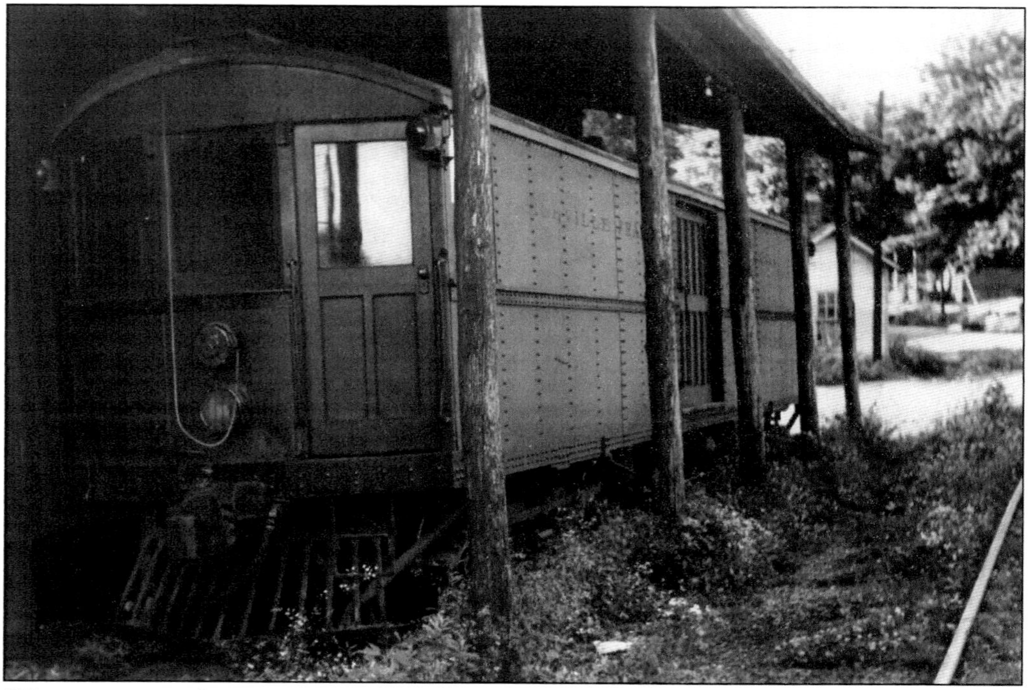

When not in use, baggage express car No. 5 was stored in a simple open shelter in the railway's yard two blocks from Franklin's square. This photograph was taken around 1940. (James D. Le Croy collection.)

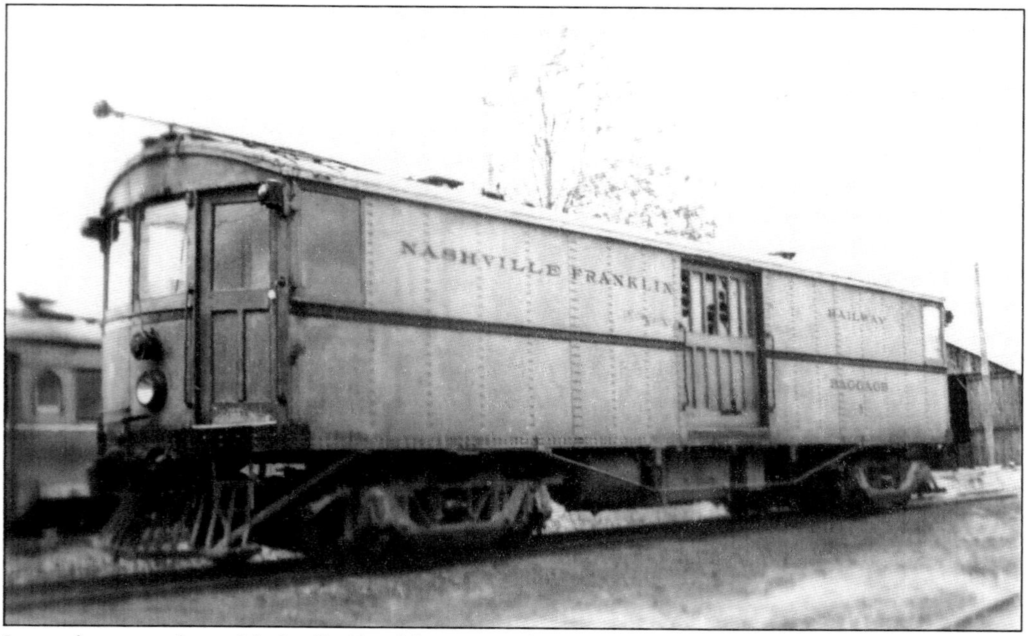

Just a few years later, Nashville-Franklin Interurban No. 5 is seen stored and neglected at the Franklin yard. The baggage express car was likely out of service at this time and headed to the scrap yard. (James D. Le Croy collection.)

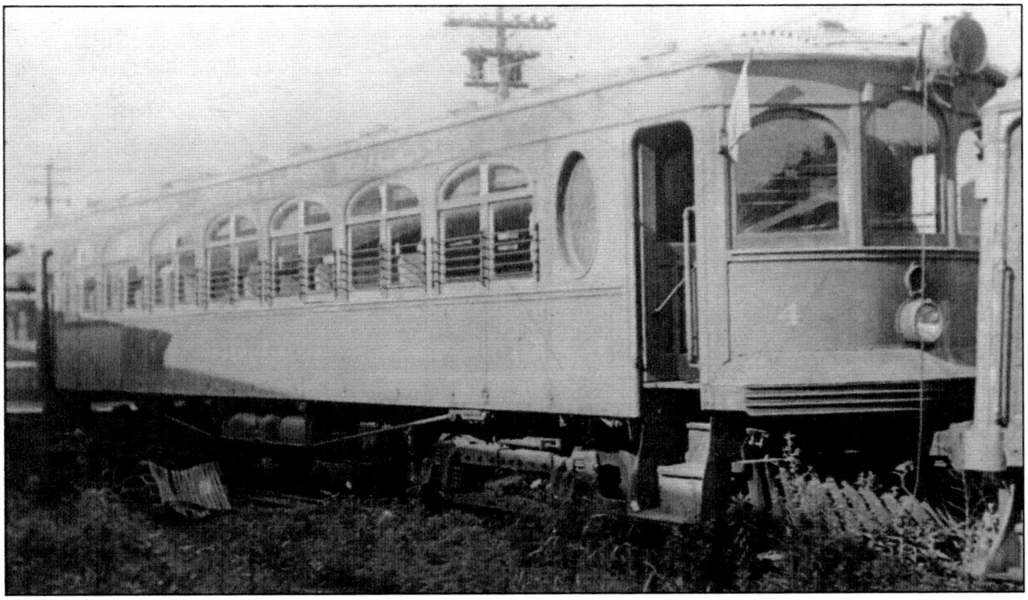

Car No. 4 is seen at the railway's Franklin yard around the same time as the previous photograph. In a few years, the interurban railway would end passenger rail service, converting to buses. Freight service would also be discontinued shortly after. (James D. Le Croy collection.)

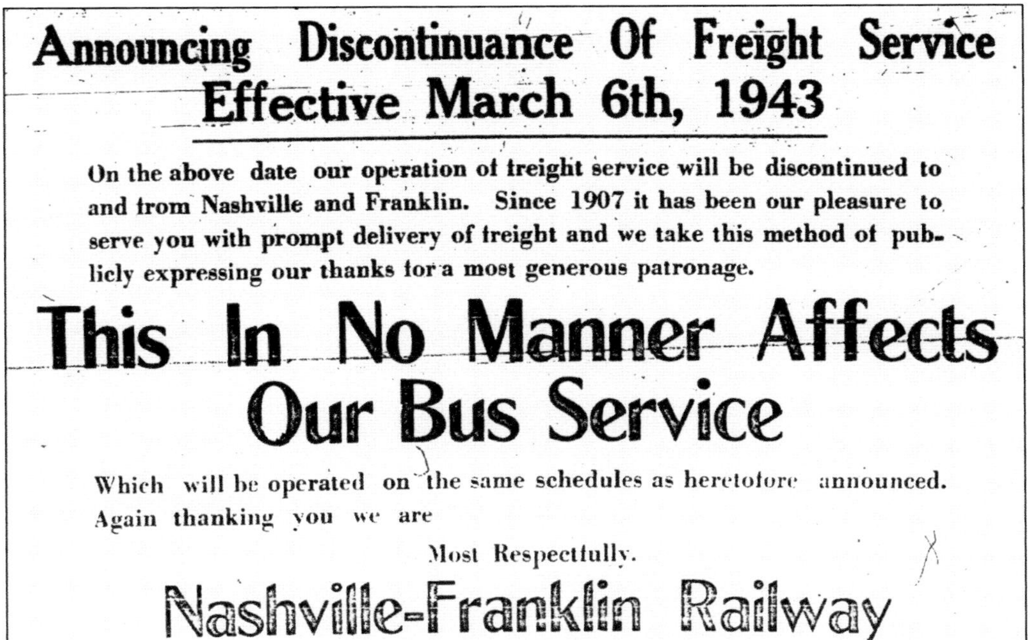

Announcing Discontinuance Of Freight Service Effective March 6th, 1943

On the above date our operation of freight service will be discontinued to and from Nashville and Franklin. Since 1907 it has been our pleasure to serve you with prompt delivery of freight and we take this method of publicly expressing our thanks for a most generous patronage.

This In No Manner Affects Our Bus Service

Which will be operated on the same schedules as heretofore announced. Again thanking you we are

Most Respectfully.

Nashville-Franklin Railway

After more than 35 years, the Nashville-Franklin Interurban Railway ceased its freight operations on March 6, 1943. Soon after, the trolley wire came down and the track was removed and sold for scrap. Much of the right-of-way that ran parallel to major highways such as US 31 was purchased for future road widening projects. The railway company had been forced to convert its passenger service to buses in 1941 after Nashville's street railways ceased operation. It eventually changed its name to Franklin Interurban and continued to run a successful bus commuter operation until the late 1960s. (David H. Steinberg collection.)

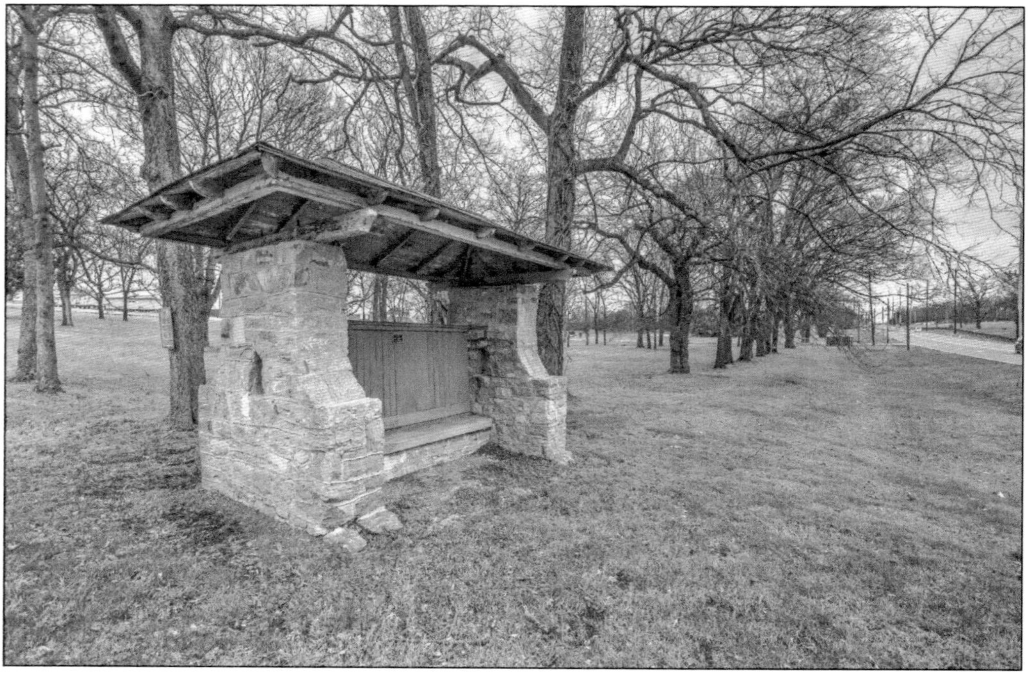

Only a few structures survive from the Nashville-Franklin Interurban Railway. The restored interurban shelter in the Oak Hill community above dates from 1909 and is typical of the style of stations along the NFI. A few miles farther south, near Brentwood, a similar structure pictured below is preserved. (Both, Bryan Turner.)

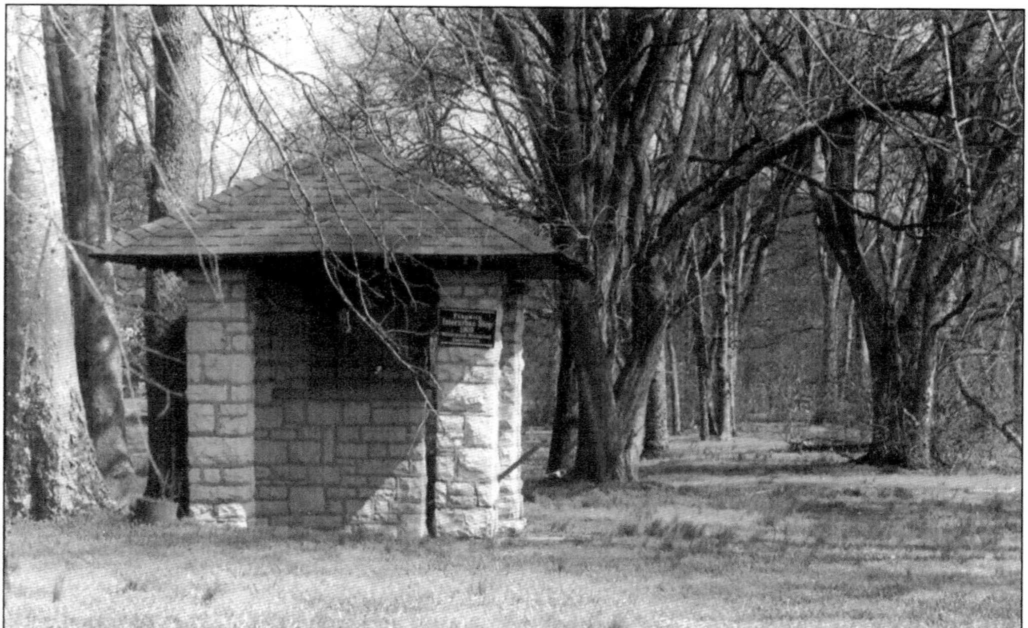

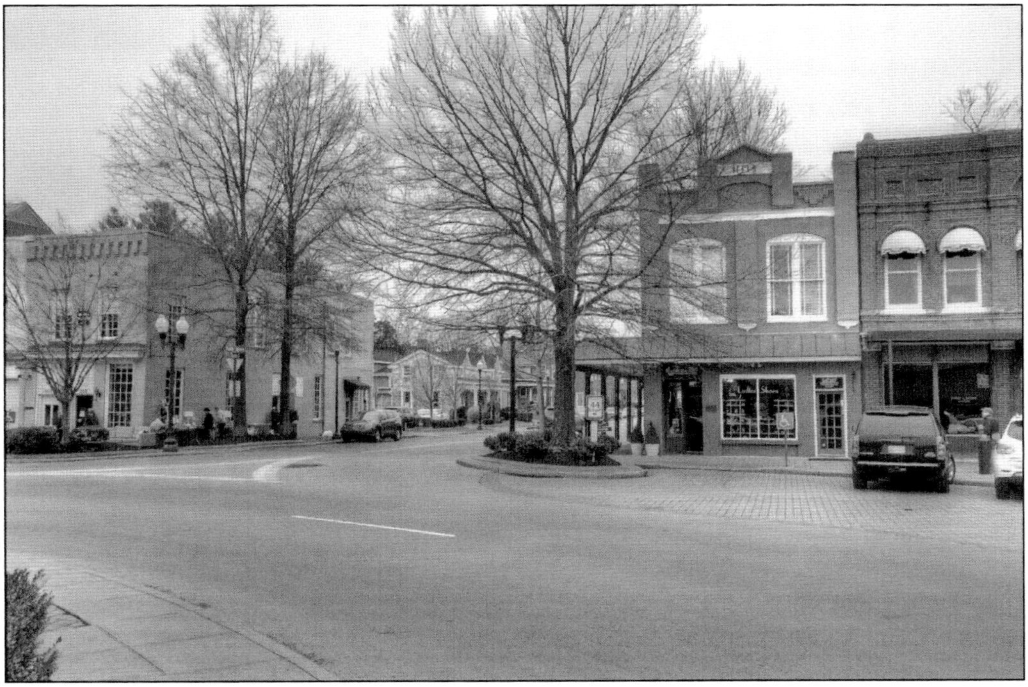

The south terminus for the Nashville-Franklin Interurban was Franklin's square, where the railway track made a loop to reverse directions. The 1895 building on the right above housed the ticket office and waiting room. (Both, Bryan Turner.)

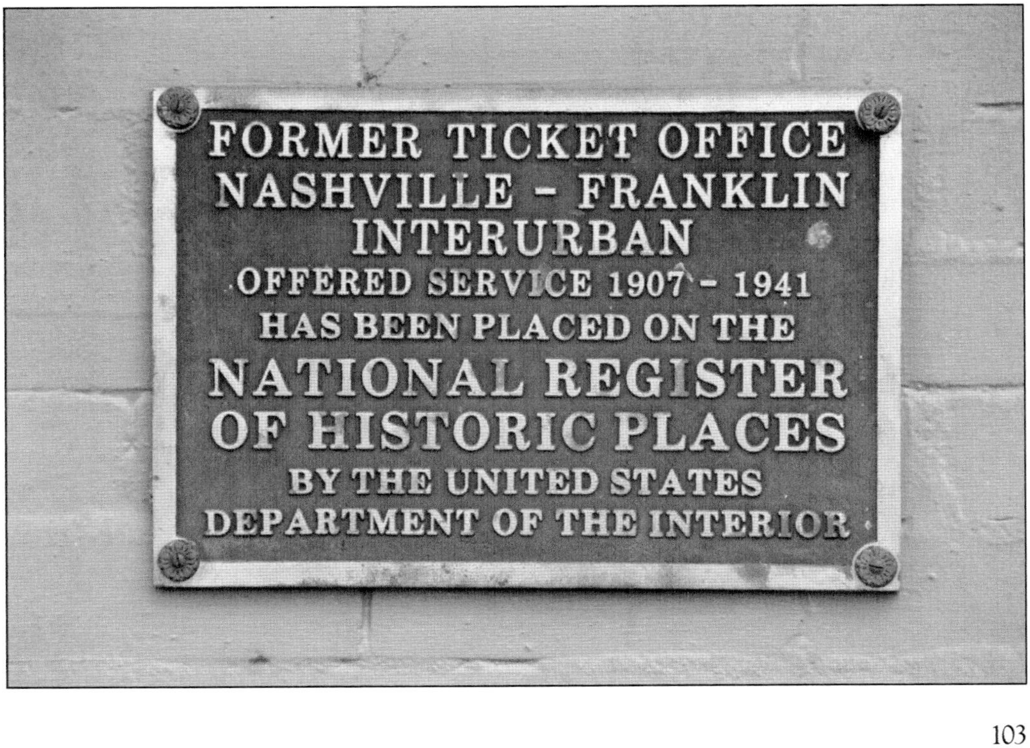

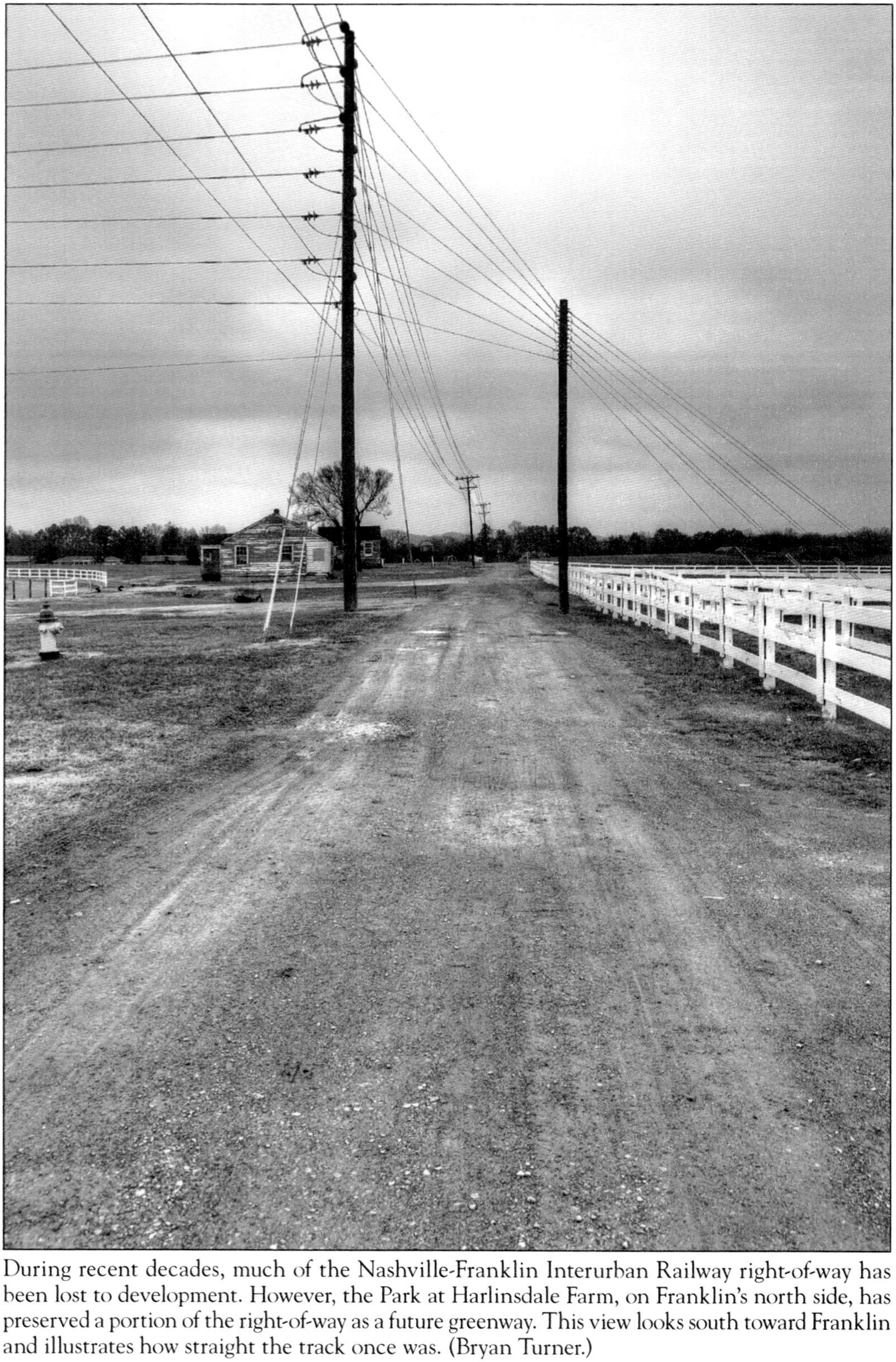

During recent decades, much of the Nashville-Franklin Interurban Railway right-of-way has been lost to development. However, the Park at Harlinsdale Farm, on Franklin's north side, has preserved a portion of the right-of-way as a future greenway. This view looks south toward Franklin and illustrates how straight the track once was. (Bryan Turner.)

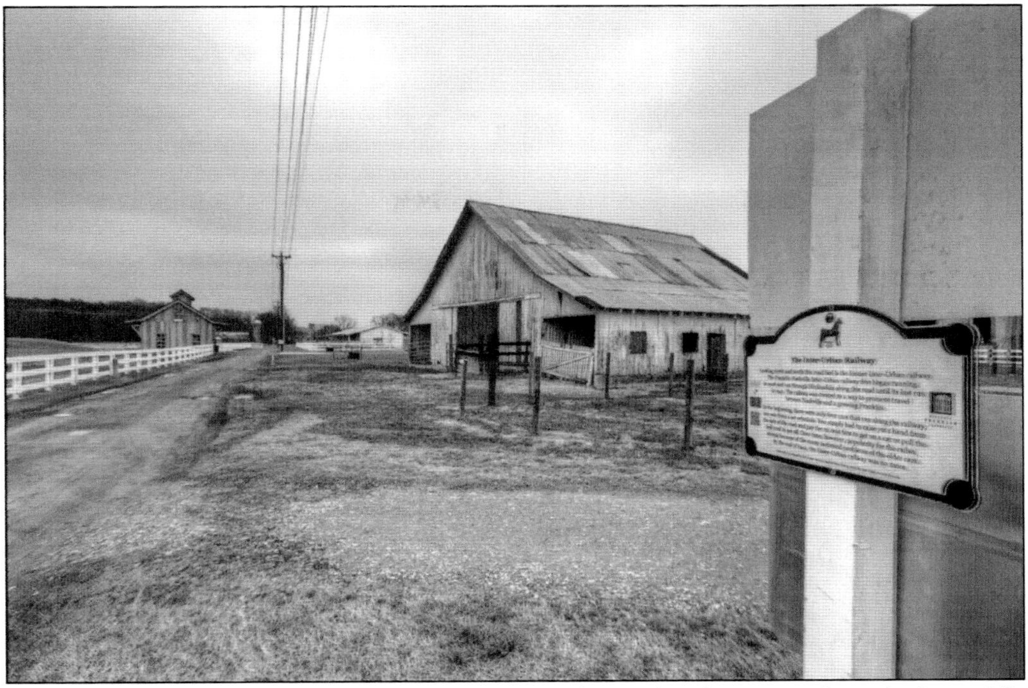

Looking in the opposite direction, the former interurban right-of-way goes through the middle of the Park at Harlinsdale Farm. While many of the rustic structures are historic, the building at left resembling an old railroad depot appears to be newer. (Bryan Turner.)

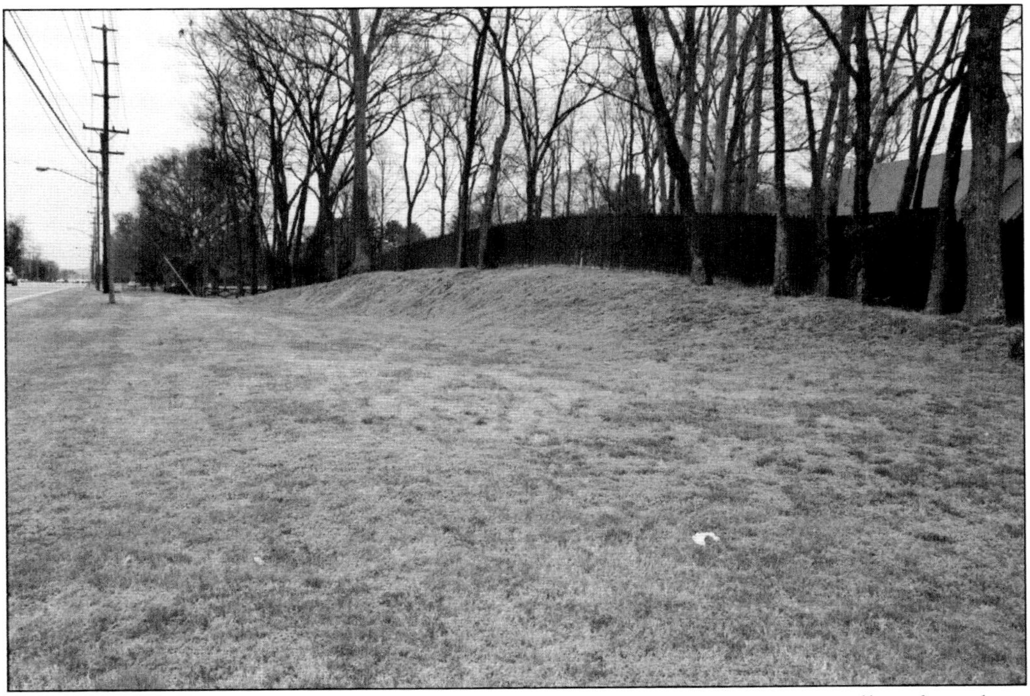

Even 75 years after the interurban railway's abandonment, the right-of-way is still evident along Franklin Road in the community of Oak Hill, just south of Nashville. (Bryan Turner.)

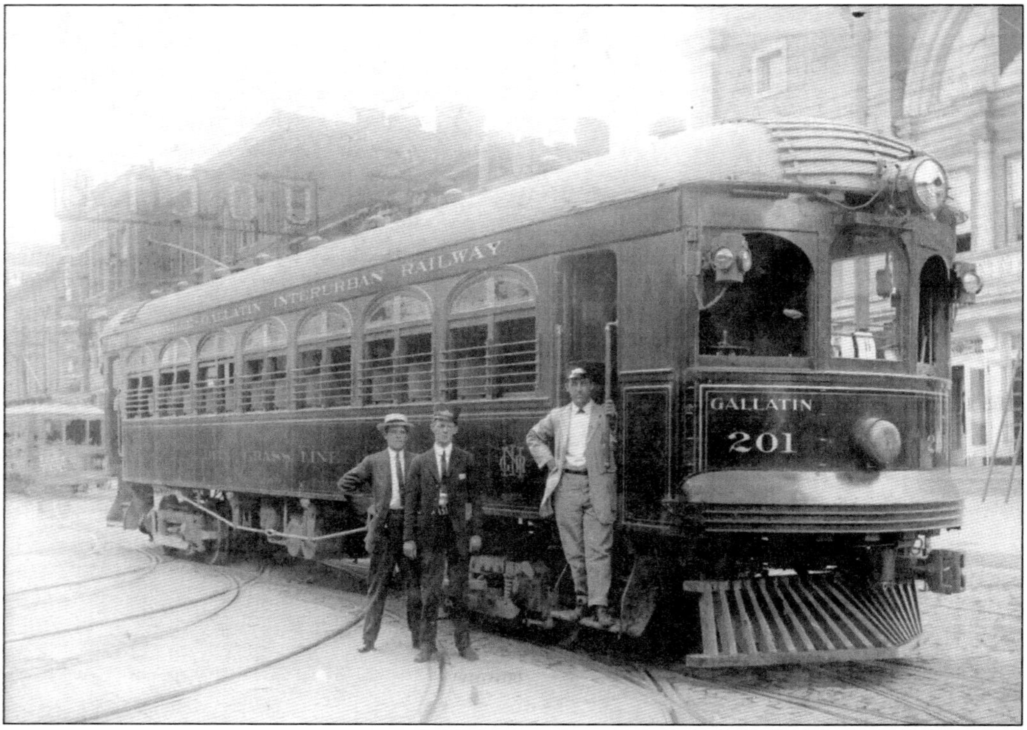

The passenger schedules for the Nashville-Gallatin Interurban Railway were protected by Car Nos. 201 through 204, built by the American Car Company in 1912. Before starting out on their run, three men pose with car No. 201 in front of the carbarn on Fourth Avenue in Nashville. The conductor is in the middle, and motorman Jesse James Jennings stands on the steps. The elegant Bijou Theater can be seen in the background. (James D. Le Croy collection.)

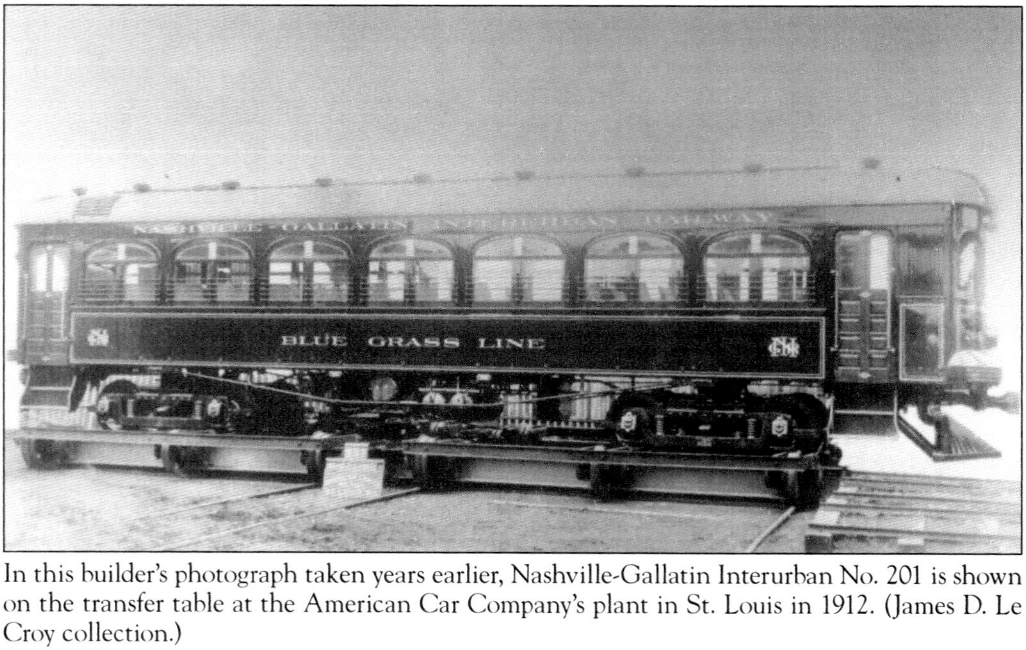

In this builder's photograph taken years earlier, Nashville-Gallatin Interurban No. 201 is shown on the transfer table at the American Car Company's plant in St. Louis in 1912. (James D. Le Croy collection.)

NASHVILLE-GALLATIN

Interurban Railway

THE BLUE GRASS LINE

The Nashville-Gallatin Interurban Railway maintains a private telephone line between Nashville and Gallatin, to be used for the convenience of the Gallatin merchants. A merchant when in need of goods in a hurry can phone to our agent at Gallatin who will phone the order to Nashville and the Nashville office will relay the message to the merchants in Nashville. We make no charge for the transmission of such messages, but do ask the merchant to whom the message is sent to ship the goods via The Nashville-Gallatin Interurban Railway.

Every Passenger Car Carries Express

On January 1st we will install delivery service of express packages in Gallatin as far as Frank Seave Fruit Company on East Main Street, around the Public Square and the Gallatin Buggy & Implement Company on Water Street. We have two freight trains out of Nashville and Gallatin daily giving to the merchant a service second to none.

Our Service Is Clean, Fast, Safe, Realiable

Use the Nashville-Gallatin Interurban Railway — The Blue Grass Route — for

PASSENGER FREIGHT EXPRESS

This early advertisement promoting the Nashville-Gallatin Interurban Railway mentions the company's passenger, freight, and express business. (David H. Steinberg collection.)

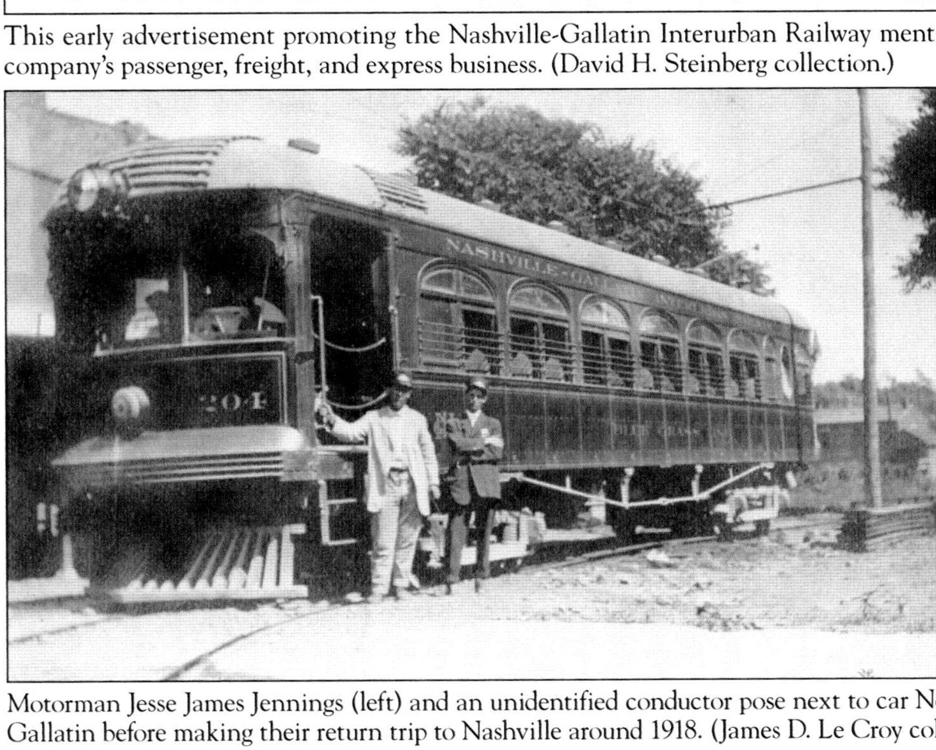

Motorman Jesse James Jennings (left) and an unidentified conductor pose next to car No. 204 at Gallatin before making their return trip to Nashville around 1918. (James D. Le Croy collection.)

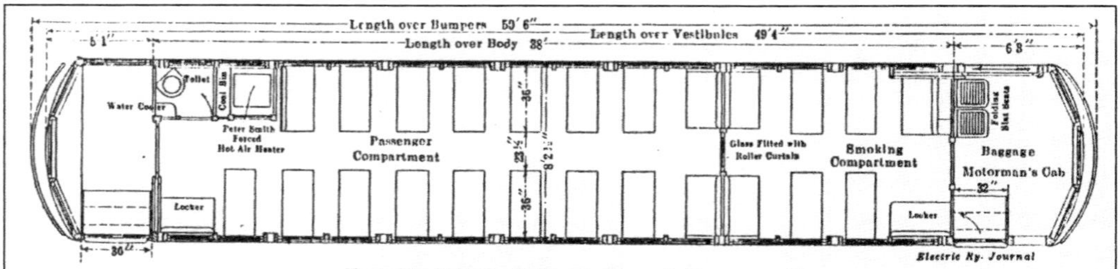

Nashville-Gallatin Railway—Plan of Passenger Car

Most interurban railway car interiors had similar designs regardless of the car builder. Many contained a smoking section, lavatory, water cooler, and space to handle baggage and mail. Because of the design, many cars could only operate in one direction, requiring turning the vehicle at the end of the run. (David H. Steinberg collection.)

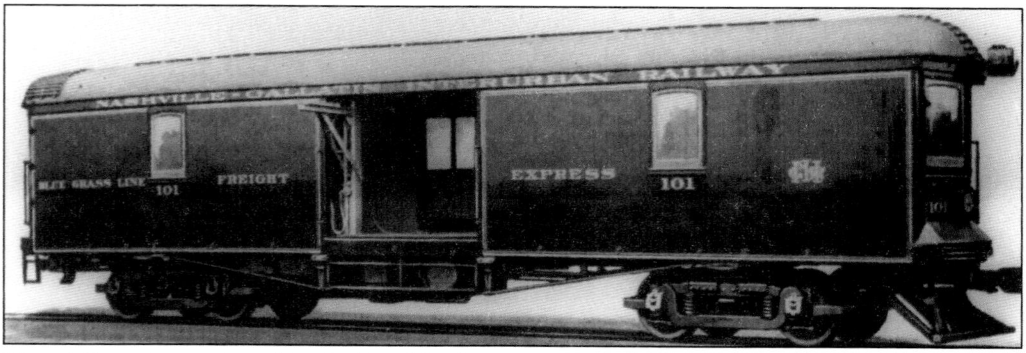

The Gallatin interurban, like the Franklin line, operated a freight and express service in addition to its frequent passenger service, serving farmers and merchants along its line. Car No. 101 is believed to be the only car of this type to operate over the Nashville-Gallatin Interurban. The interurban track closely paralleled the Louisville & Nashville Railroad line between Gallatin, Hendersonville, and Nashville, creating a spirited competition between the two rivals. (James D. Le Croy collection.)

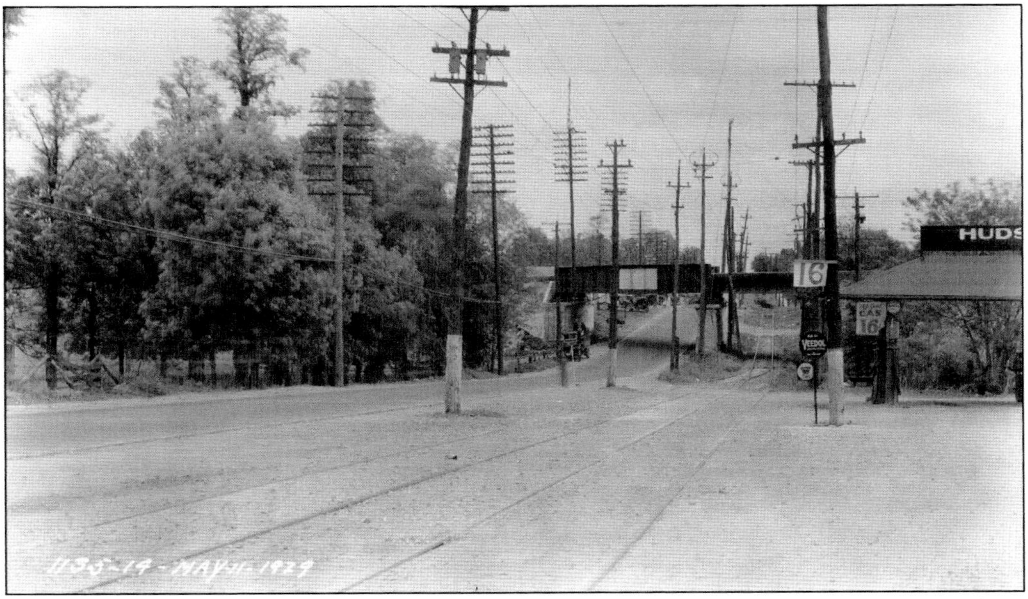

This 1929 scene looking north along Gallatin Road in the Inglewood community illustrates how the Nashville-Gallatin Interurban operated over a dedicated right-of-way for much of the way between the two cities. The railroad overpass, owned by the Louisville & Nashville Railroad, spans both the highway and electric railroad. Most of Nashville's major railroads were grade-separated from the street railways and interurban lines for safety reasons. (Nashville Public Library, Special Collections.)

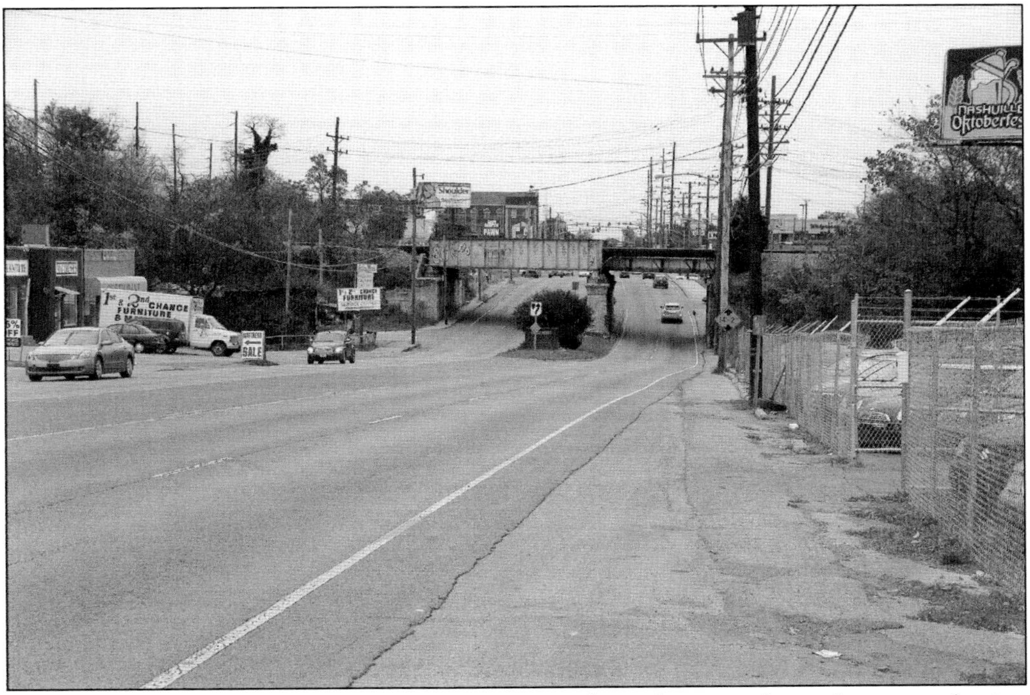

Standing at the same Gallatin Road location 85 years later, the interurban is long gone, having been replaced by the northbound lanes of Gallatin Road. The railroad overpass, now a part of CSX Transportation, remains as busy as it was decades ago. (Bryan Turner.)

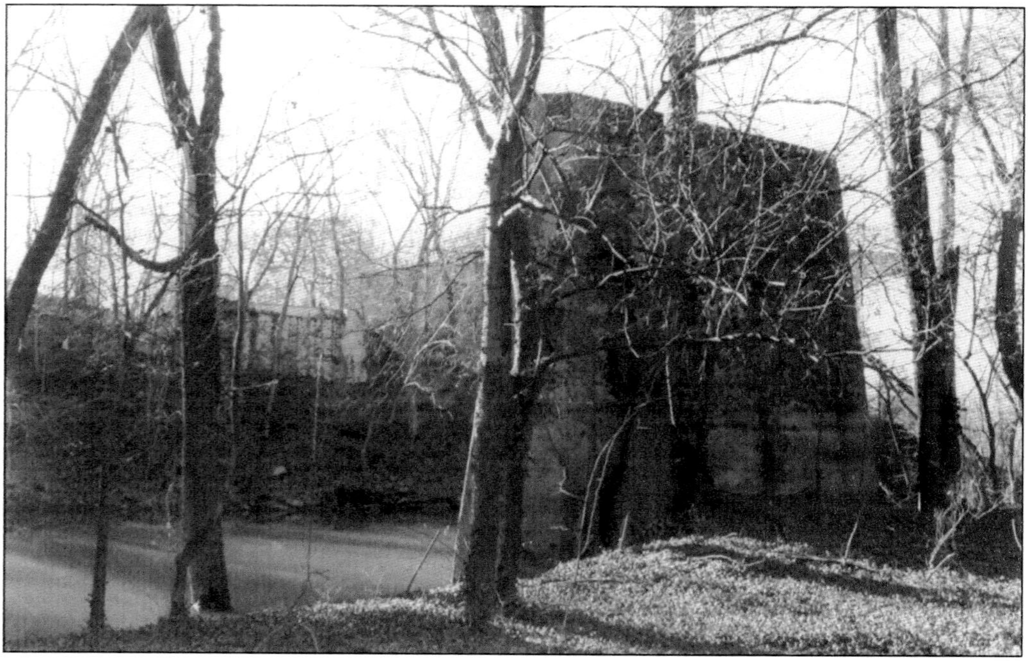

Since the shutdown of the Nashville-Gallatin Interurban Railway in 1932, there is little physical evidence remaining to prove that the company ever existed. However, during cold weather when the trees are bare, it is possible to see a bridge abutment and pier where the railway crossed Mansker Creek just south of Hendersonville. These remnants of another era serve as reminders of how people once traveled for work and pleasure. (Both, author's collection.)

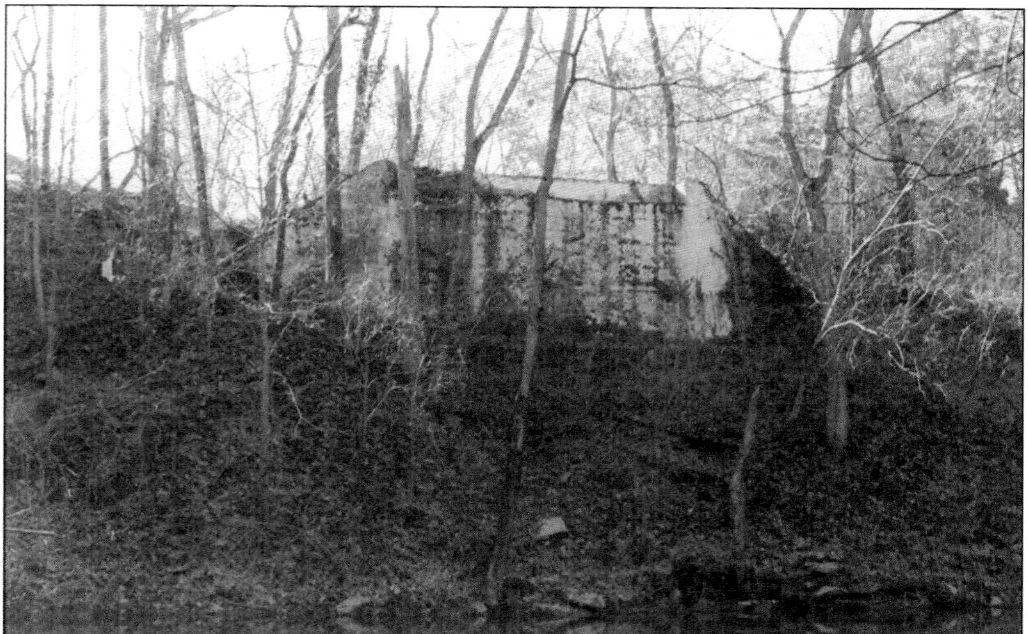

Nine

The End of an Era

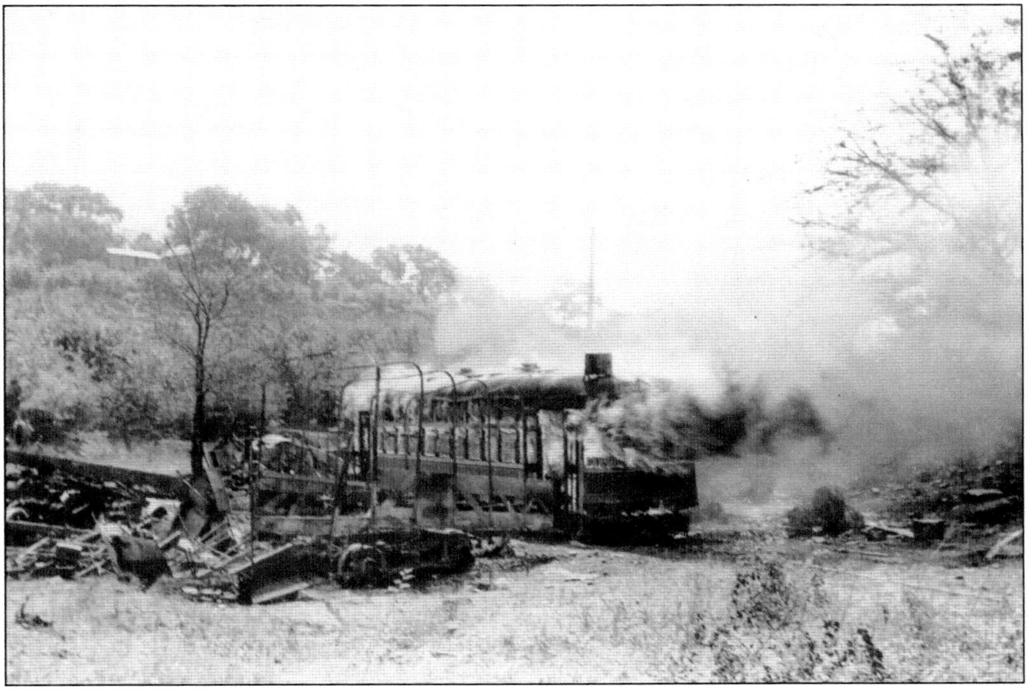

After the last of Nashville's street railways were taken out of service in early 1941, little time was wasted in disposing of the cars. In those days, it was common practice to move the derelict vehicles to a remote location, douse the wooden cars with kerosene, and set everything on fire. Once the blaze had burned itself out, only the steel wheels and frame remained, making it easier to haul away the remains. With streetcar systems across the country being converted to bus operations during the 1940s and 1950s, there was little demand for the cars or even cannibalized parts. As flames consume what was once the primary means of transportation for Nashvillians, burned-out hulks that met a similar fate earlier in the day can be seen at left. It was the end of an era. (Nashville Public Library, Special Collections.)

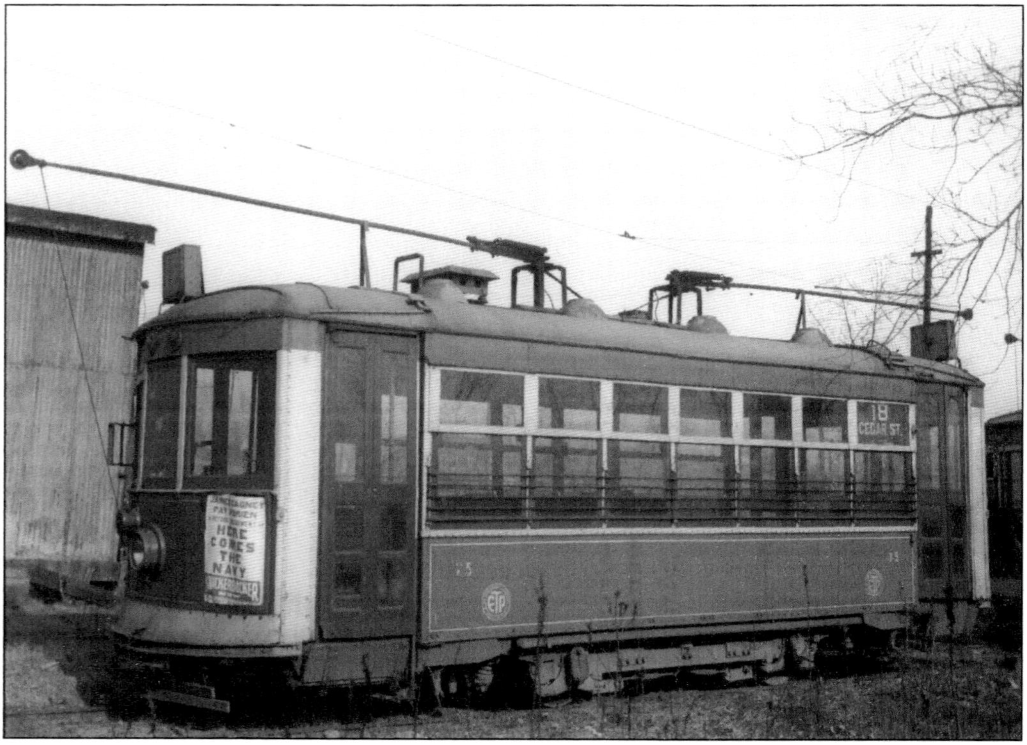

By the early 1940s, when most of Nashville's street railway lines had already been converted to bus operation, the old electric cars were quickly moved to a salvage yard near downtown where the vehicles were cut up into pieces for scrap. (Both, David H. Steinberg collection.)

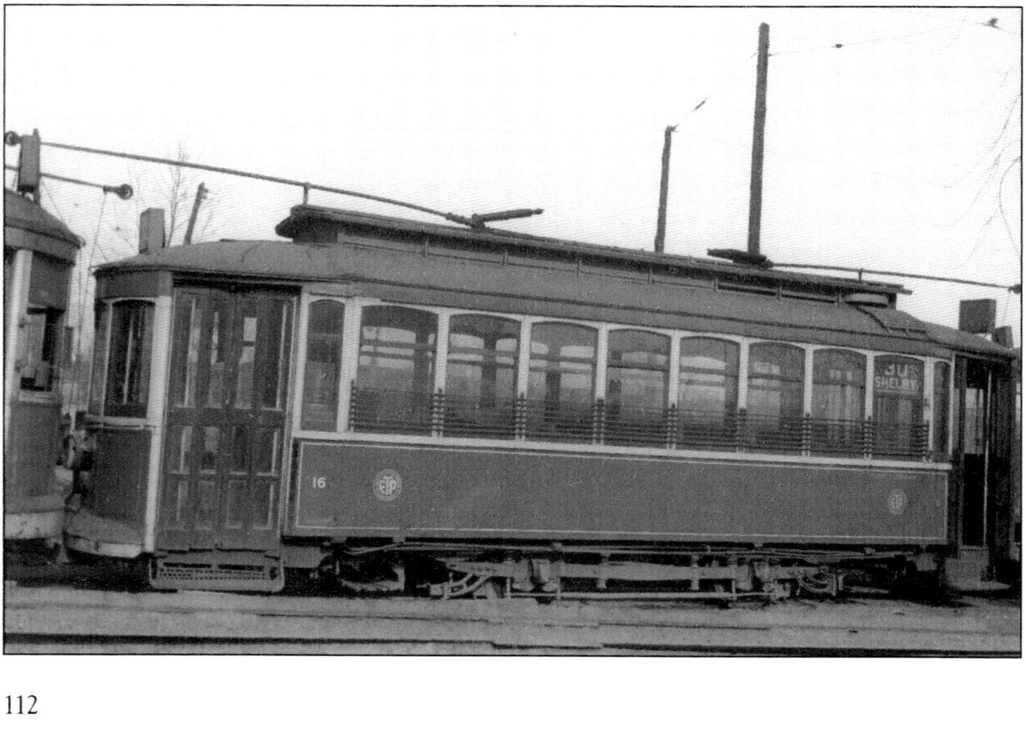

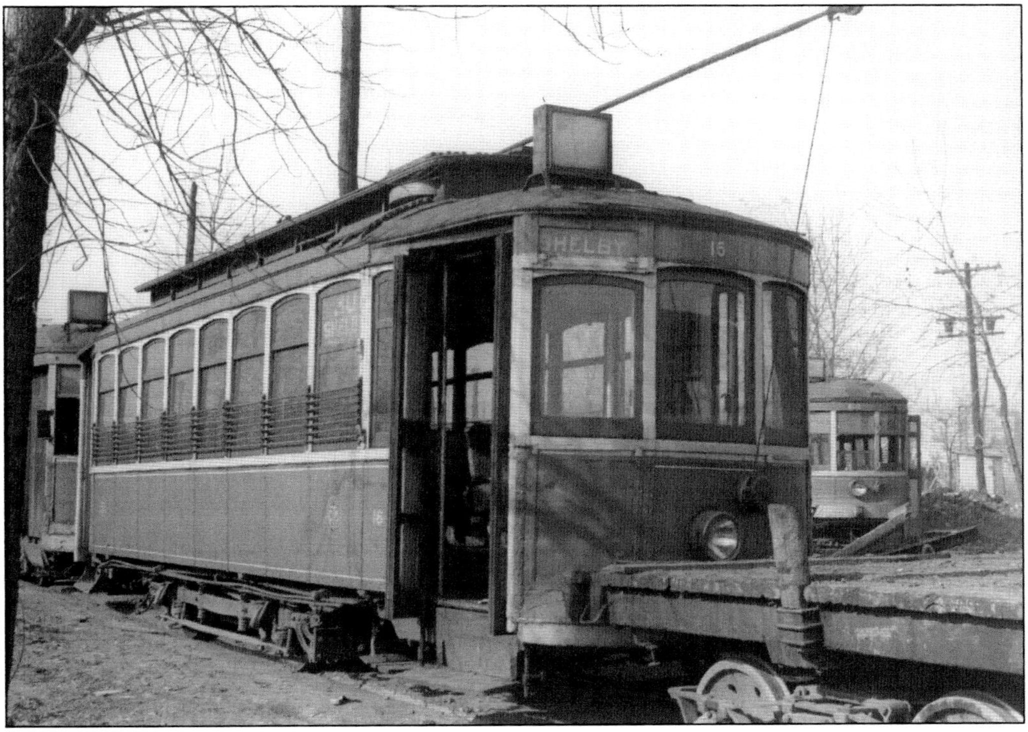

Derelict cars of the former Tennessee Electric Power Company are gathered in a salvage yard near downtown Nashville during the winter of 1941. In a matter of days, the cars will be cut up for scrap. Below, salvage workers have already begun the task of dismantling car No. 405. The Shelby Street Bridge can be seen in the background at far left. (Both, David H. Steinberg collection.)

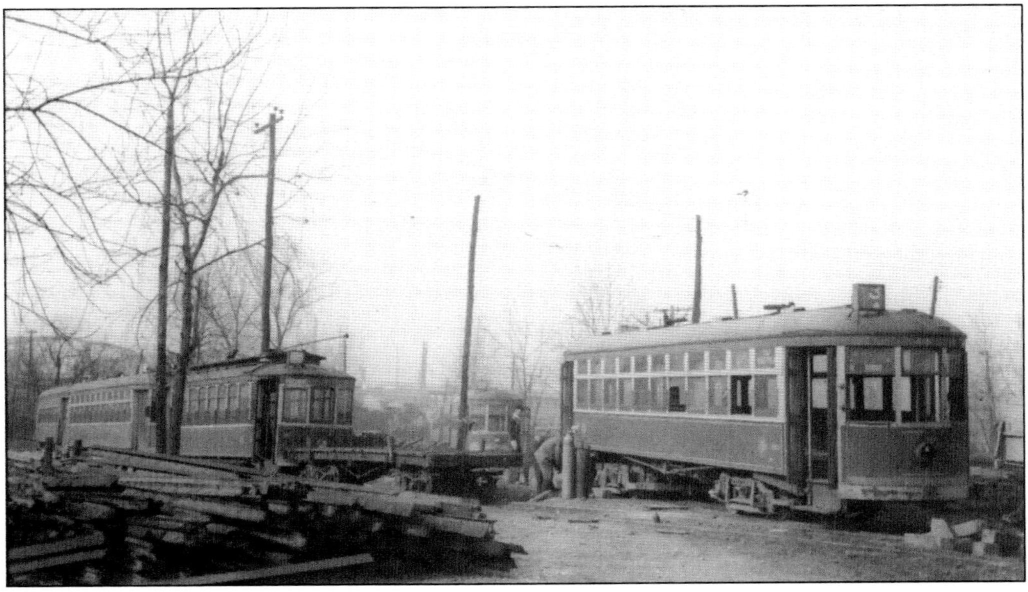

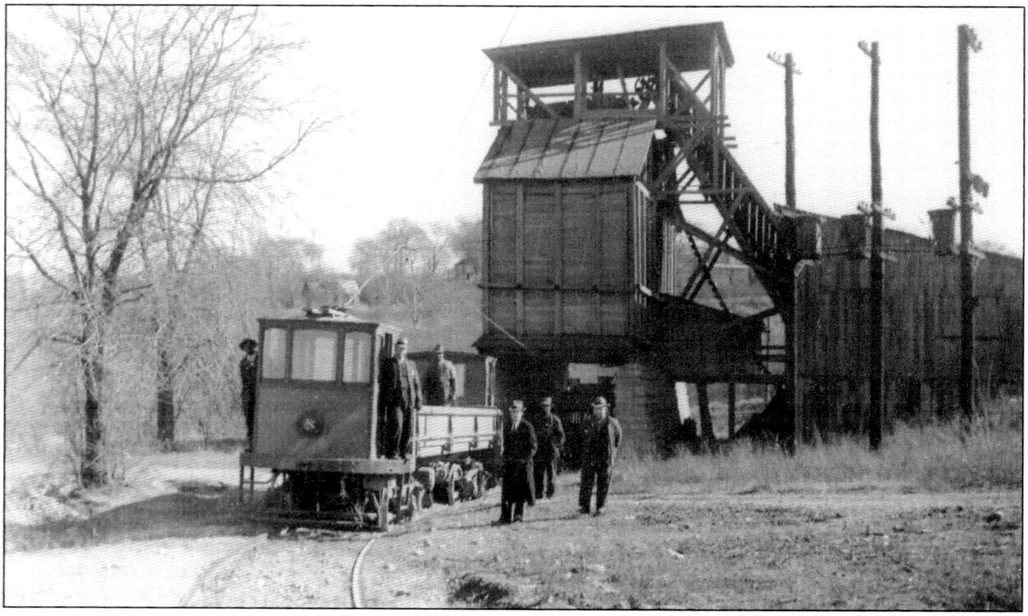

On a cold spring day in 1941, several street railway employees solemnly pose for the company photographer before preparing to dispose of former TEPCO car No. 607 at an unknown location believed to be north of downtown Nashville. Shortly, side dump car No. 100 will push several cars to the end of a spur track, where they will be set on fire. The tall structure in the background is believed to be a tipple used to load ballast into cars for maintaining tracks. (Nashville Public Library, Special Collections.)

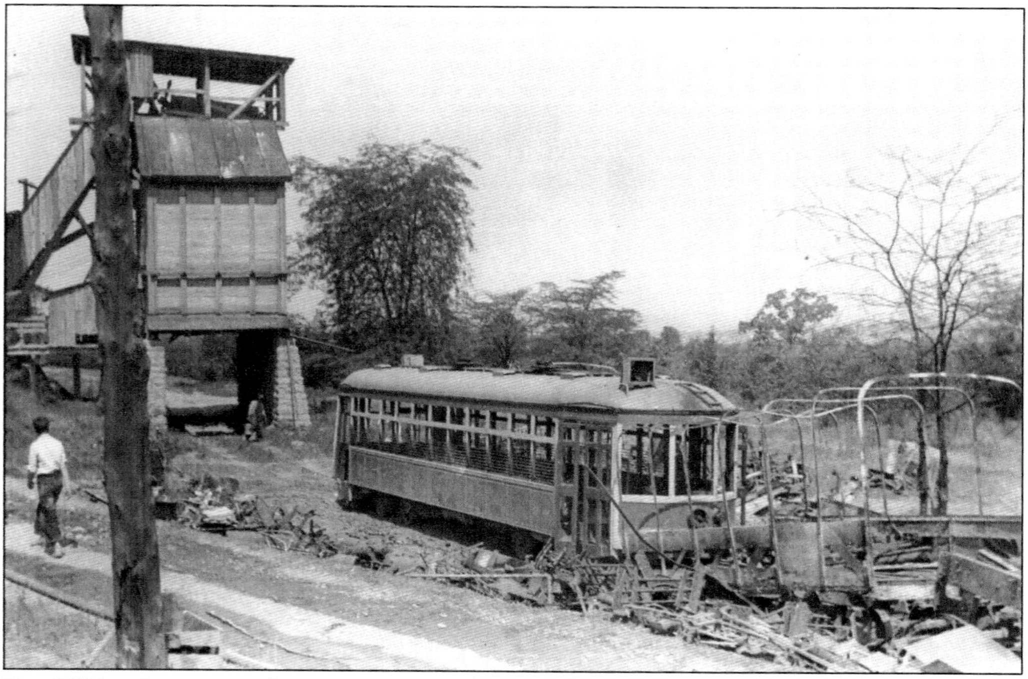

No. 607 has been moved into position, and an employee approaches from the left with a can of flammable liquid. Once the roof and interior of the car are soaked, the car will be torched. (Nashville Public Library, Special Collections.)

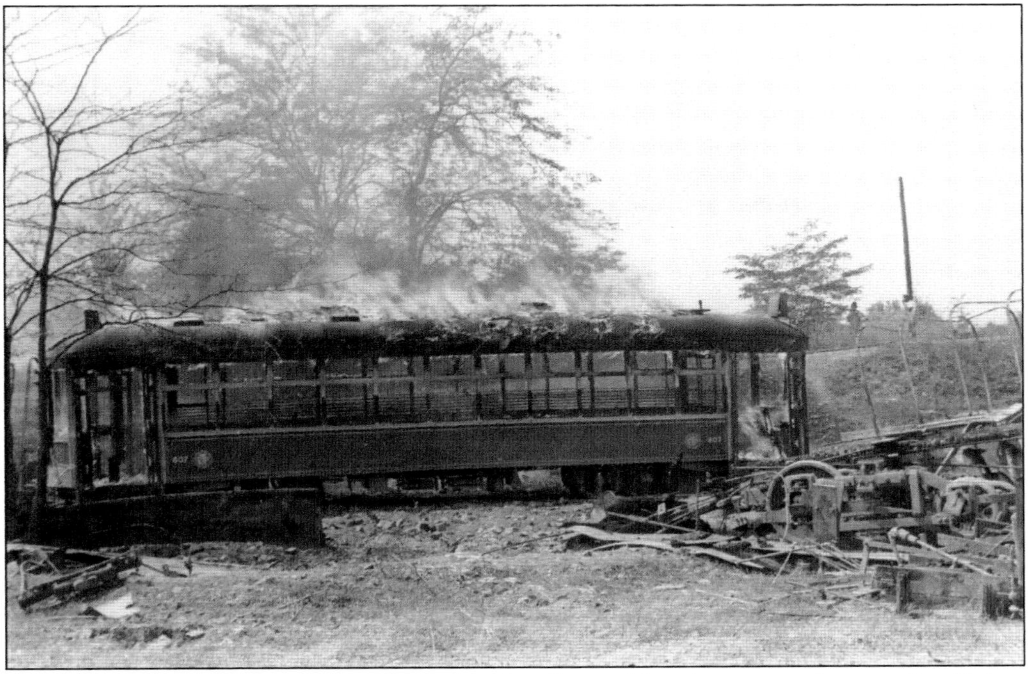

The roof of No. 607 has just been doused with a flammable substance and set on fire. Before long, the 15-year-old car will be reduced to ashes. The charred remains of other cars can be seen at right. (Nashville Public Library, Special Collections.)

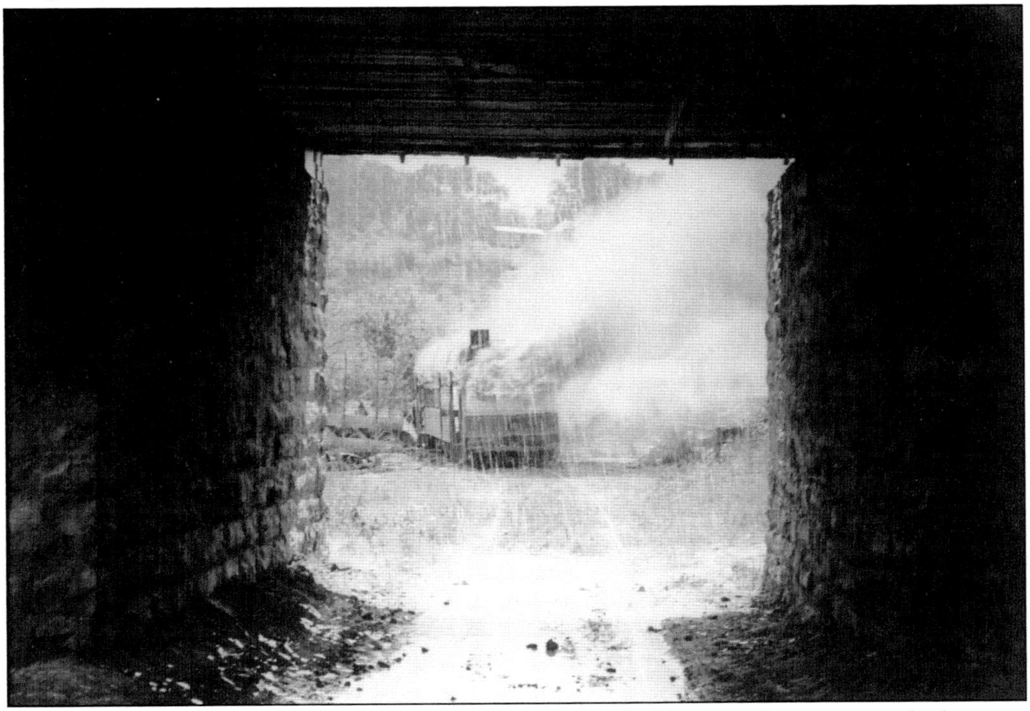

Taking refuge under the tipple from a sudden heavy rain, the photographer captures the burning car that has been partially extinguished by the unexpected downpour, using the stone foundation of the structure to frame this composition. (Nashville Public Library, Special Collections.)

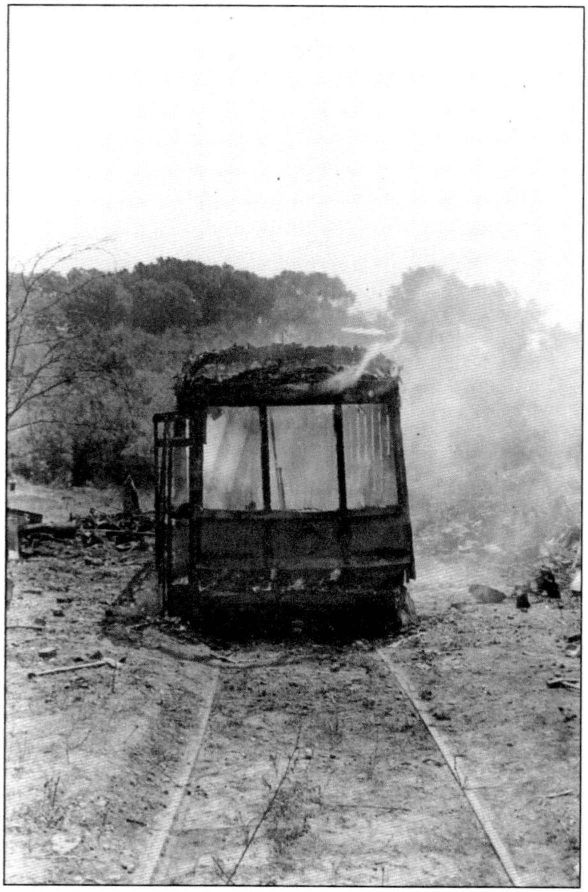

The smoldering shell of No. 607 is seen later in the day from a different angle. (Nashville Public Library, Special Collections.)

On a cold winter day in the early 1940s, a crew of workmen dismantle the tracks along the Radnor-Nolensville Road line near the Tennessee State Fairgrounds. The bridge spanning Brown's Creek has just been removed and placed in front of side dump car No. 100, at right. The men are most likely discussing how to cut up the structure. Although the tracks have been out of service for some time, the overhead trolley wire remains active—both electrically powered vehicles shown here are getting their power from the poles. (Nashville Public Library, Special Collections.)

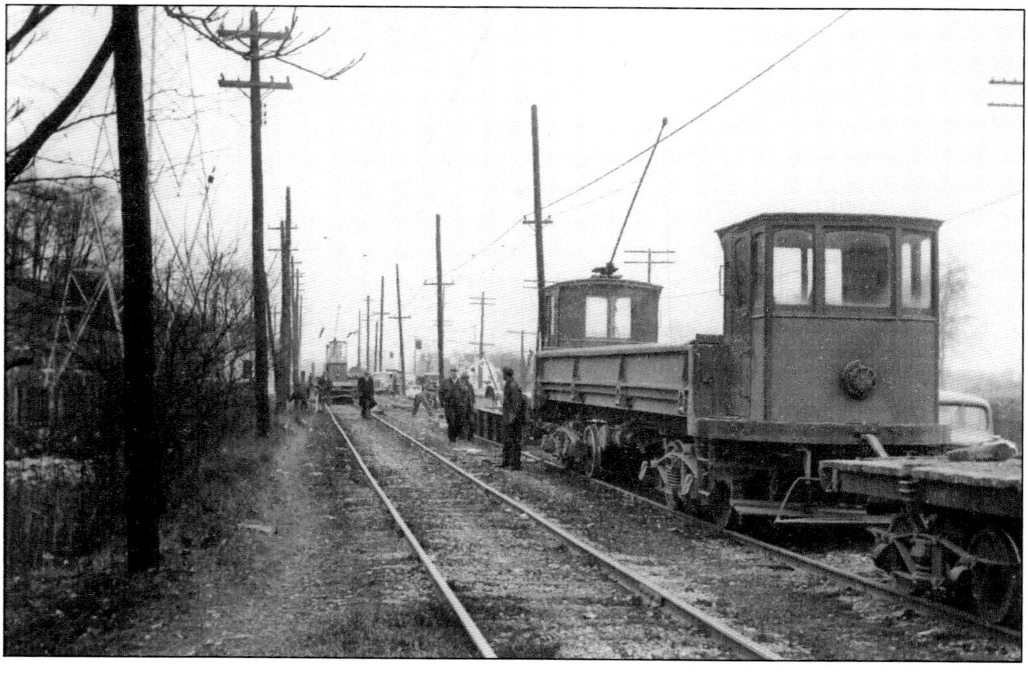

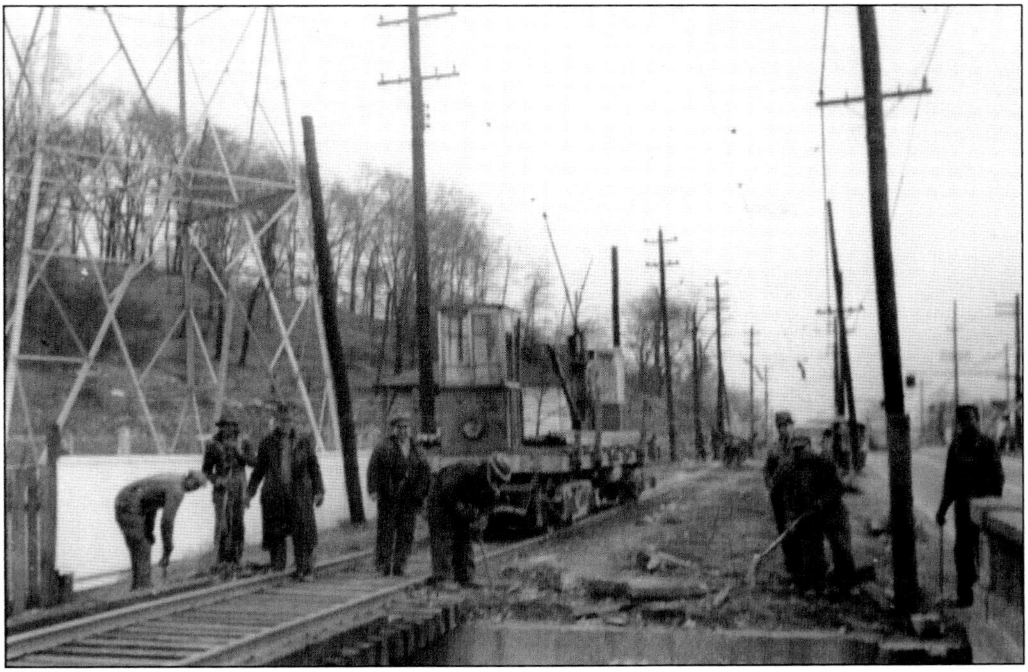

In this photograph, taken the same day as the previous scene, a demolition crew continues removing the southbound track of the Radnor line at Brown's Creek. Nolensville Road can be seen at far right. In the distance, the Tennessee Central Railway crossing is barely visible. (Nashville Public Library, Special Collections.)

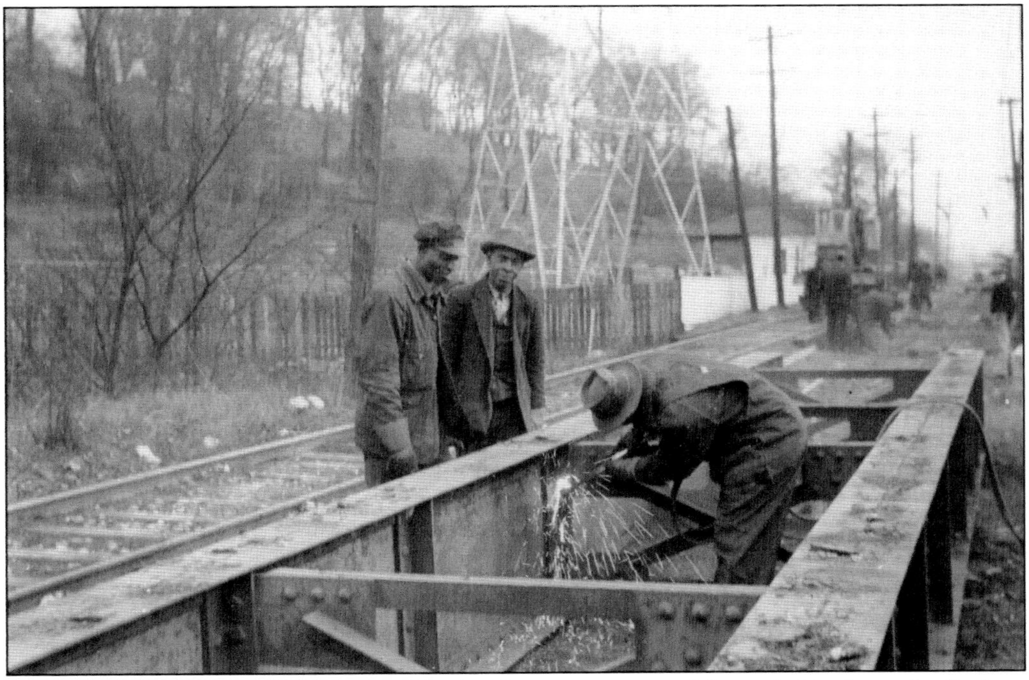

Workmen begin dismantling the steel bridge that once spanned Brown's Creek on the Radnor line near Nashville's city limits. Once work has been completed removing the southbound track, the focus will shift to the remaining track. (Nashville Public Library, Special Collections.)

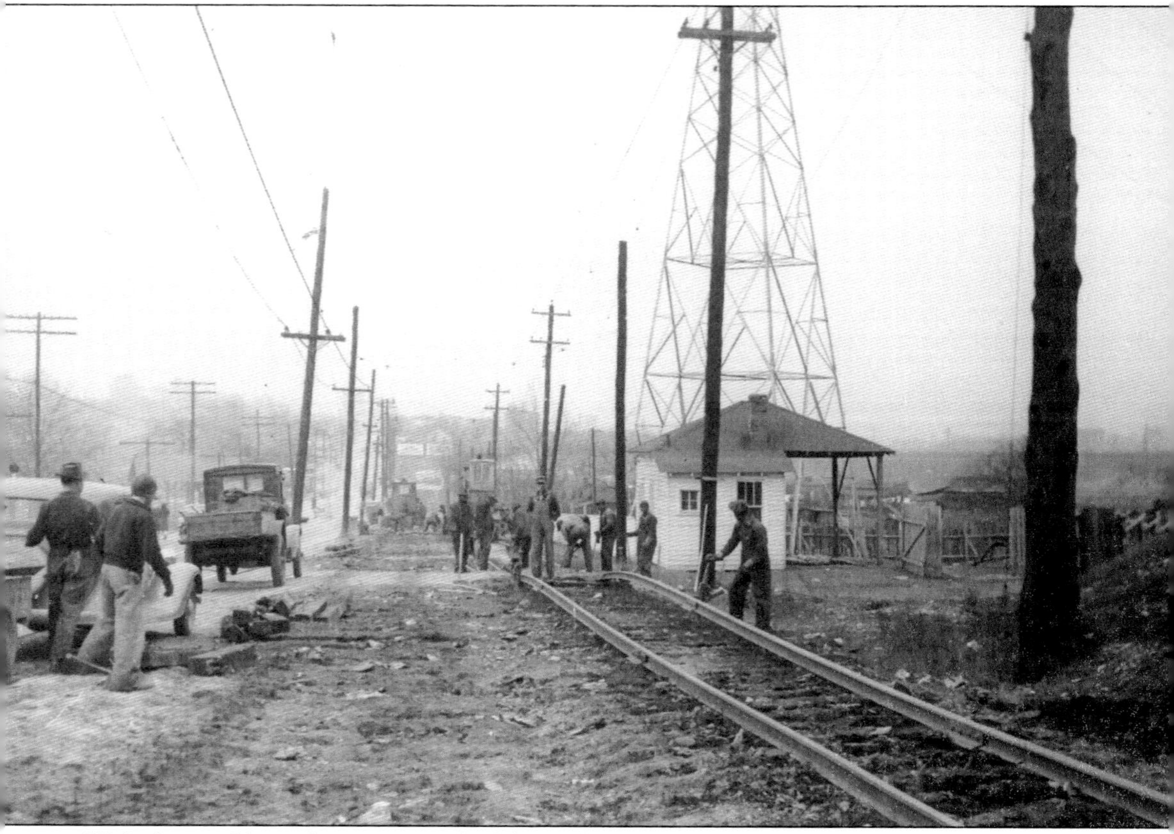

With the southbound streetcar track of the Radnor line removed, work continues on dismantling the remaining one. The double-track line ran over a dedicated right-of-way along the east side of Nolensville Road, at left, between the city limits and Wheeler Avenue. The transmission tower at right center, once owned by the Tennessee Electric Power Company, remains in use today. (Nashville Public Library, Special Collections.)

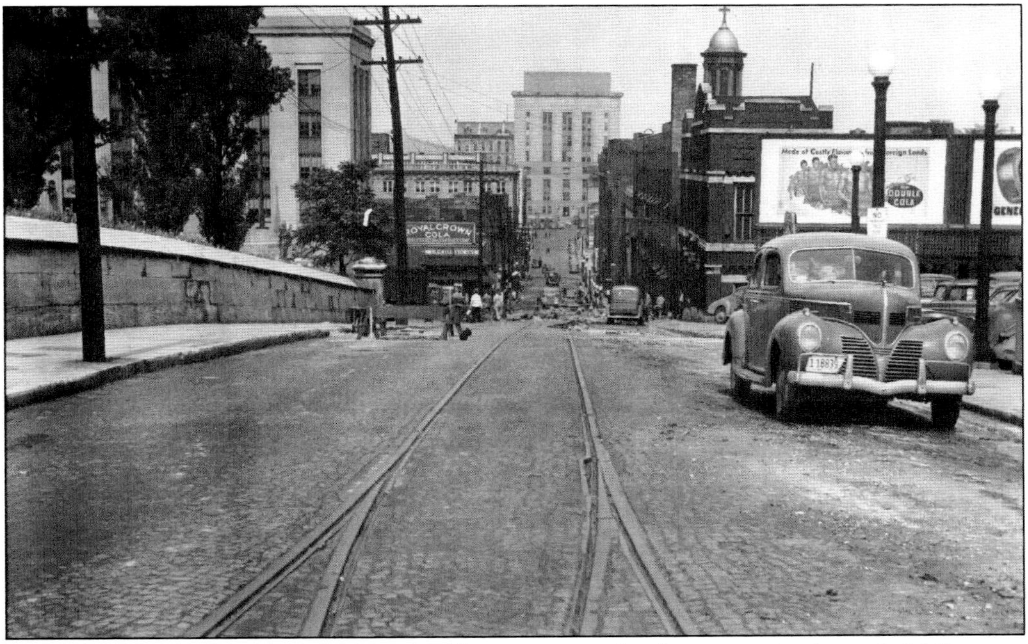

After all of Nashville's streetcar lines had been converted to bus operation by early 1941, street crews quickly worked to remove the dormant tracks across the city, considered an eyesore at the time. The rails were an important source of scrap metal during World War II. In later years, the tracks were merely paved over with asphalt to save money. Above, with the overhead trolley wire taken down months earlier, workers begin removing rails from Cedar Street before starting a repaving project. The Davidson County Courthouse can be seen at the end of the street. Below, looking in the opposite direction from the same spot, Cedar Street, renamed Charlotte Street years later, has been barricaded to vehicular traffic at Eighth Avenue for repaving. (Both, Metro Nashville Archives, MDHA Collection.)

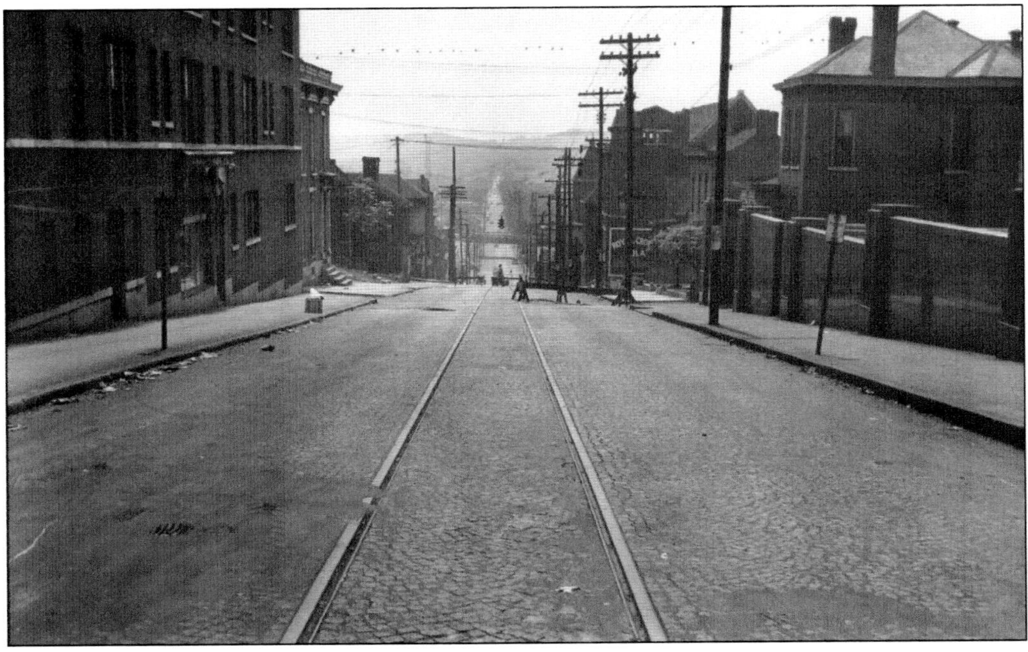

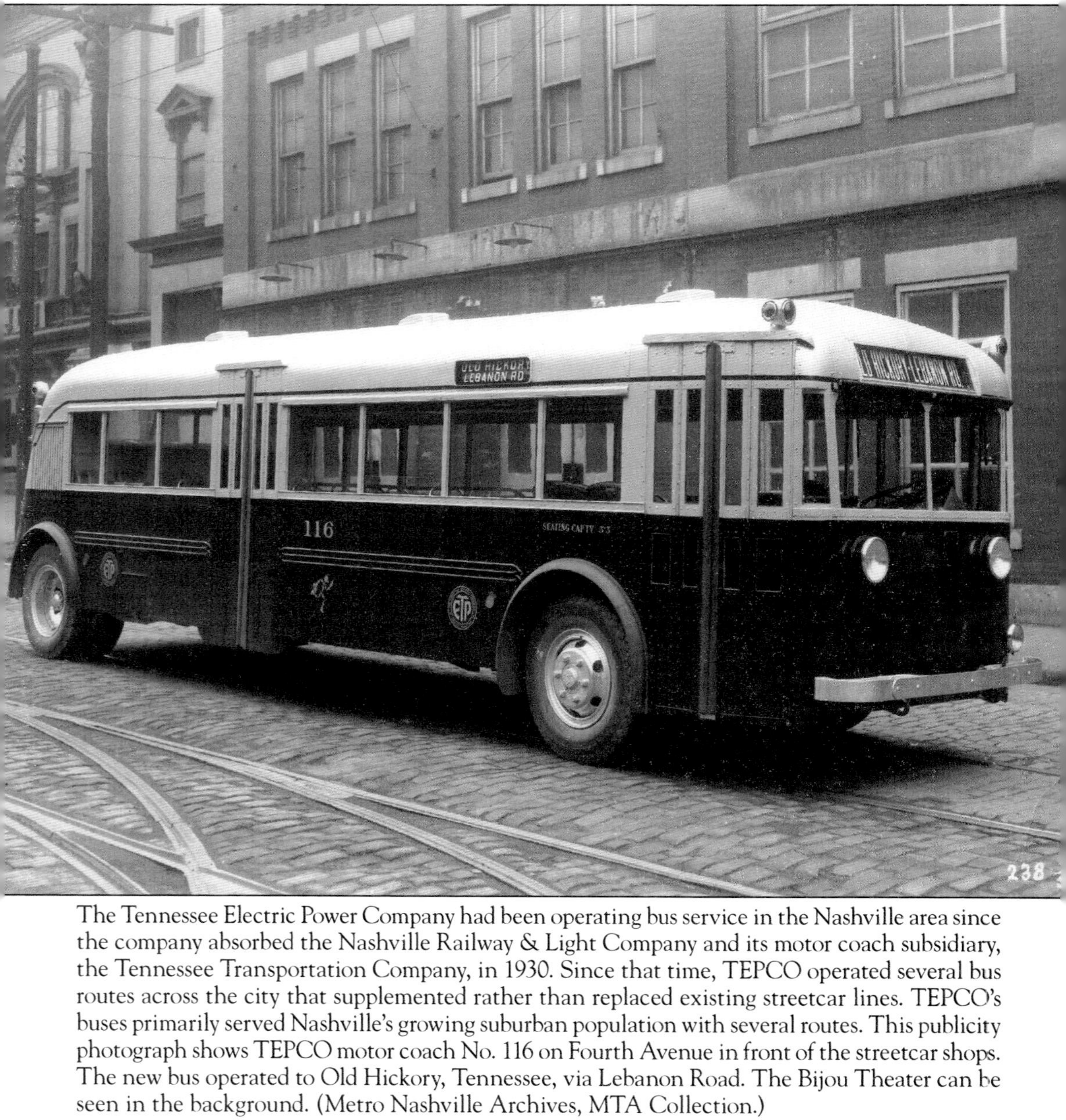

The Tennessee Electric Power Company had been operating bus service in the Nashville area since the company absorbed the Nashville Railway & Light Company and its motor coach subsidiary, the Tennessee Transportation Company, in 1930. Since that time, TEPCO operated several bus routes across the city that supplemented rather than replaced existing streetcar lines. TEPCO's buses primarily served Nashville's growing suburban population with several routes. This publicity photograph shows TEPCO motor coach No. 116 on Fourth Avenue in front of the streetcar shops. The new bus operated to Old Hickory, Tennessee, via Lebanon Road. The Bijou Theater can be seen in the background. (Metro Nashville Archives, MTA Collection.)

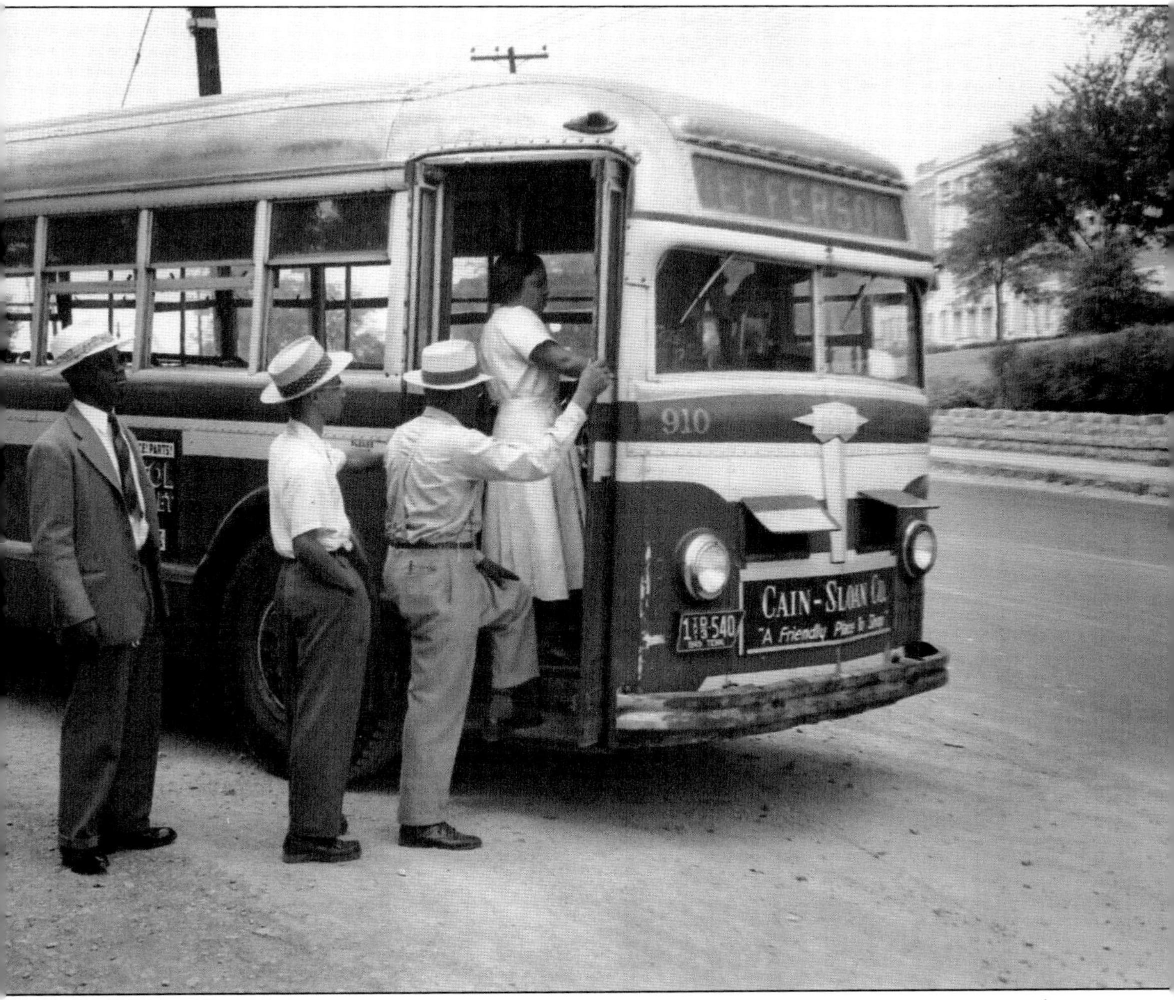

Shortly after Nashville's streetcar operation was converted to motor coaches in 1941, Southern Coach Lines assumed ownership of the transit company, and it would operate the city bus lines for more than 10 years. Having an all-bus fleet gave the carrier the flexibility to alter or extend routes with little planning or investment. In another staged publicity photograph in 1949, passengers board a Southern Coach Lines Jefferson Street bus at an unknown location. Travel on city buses was increasing in popularity. (Metro Nashville Archives, MTA Collection.)

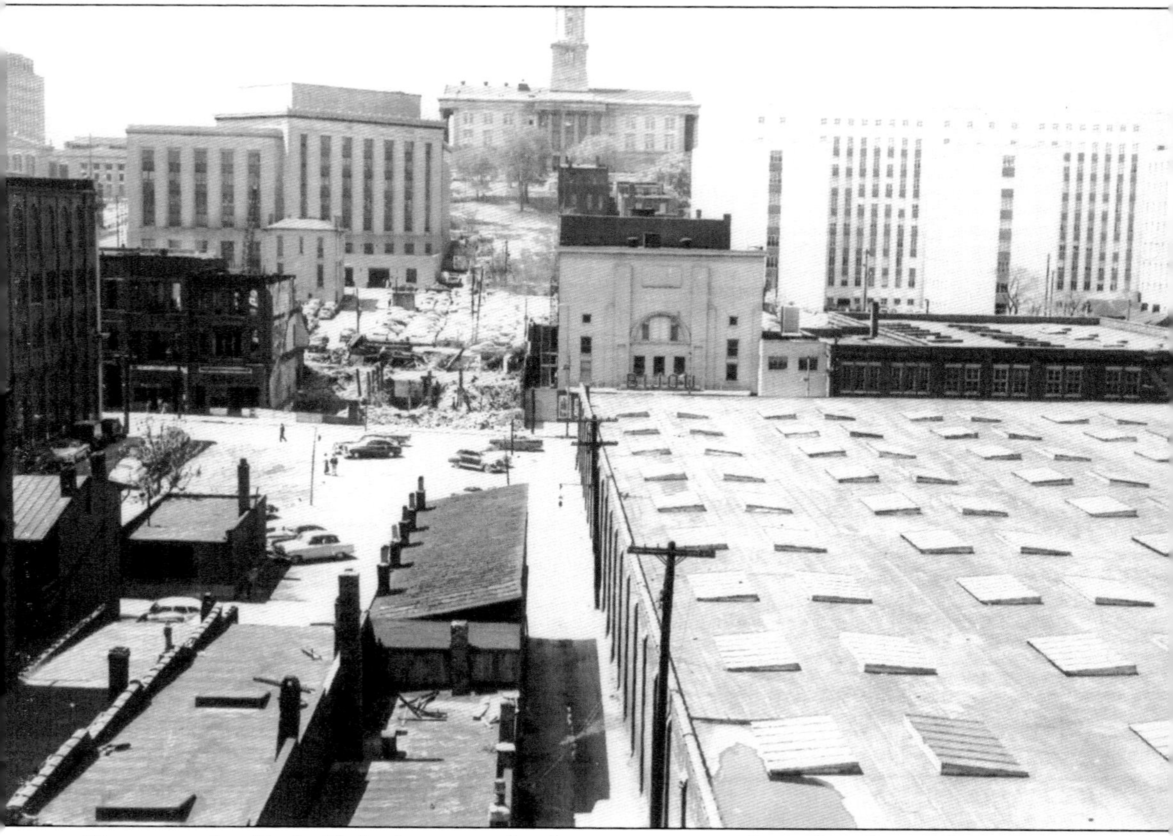

Ten years after Nashville had converted to bus transit, most physical evidence of streetcars had all but disappeared. During the mid-1950s, the last remaining physical landmarks, such as the Transfer Station, Watkins Institute Building, carbarn, and maintenance shops were obliterated as well. At this time, the city embarked on a massive urban renewal program resulting in the demolition of hundreds of buildings around the Capitol Hill area north of downtown. In this 1955 view, demolition is well under way. The roofs of both the former carbarn and the maintenance shops can be seen at right, and the venerable Bijou Theater is at center. The Morris Memorial Building, the Tennessee State Capitol, and other government buildings at the top are the only structures that remain today. (Metro Nashville Archives, MDHA Collection.)

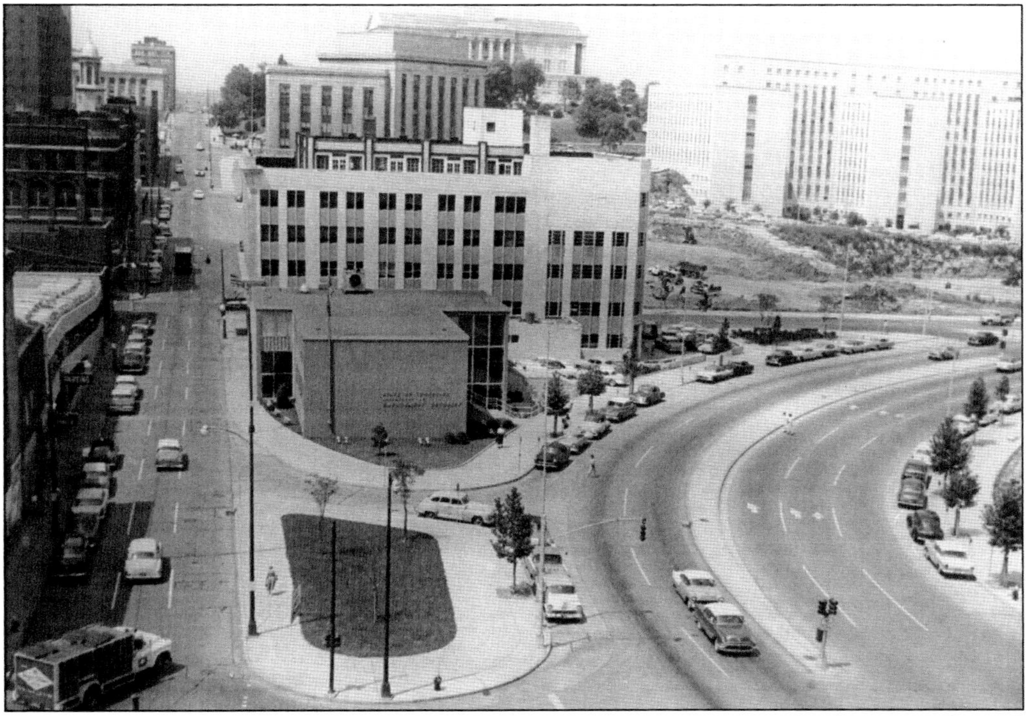

In just two years, the same block seen in the photograph on the previous page has been transformed. The new James Robertson Parkway has replaced the site of the former carbarn. The maintenance shops and Bijou Theater are now history; preparation has already begun for the foundation of Nashville's future Municipal Auditorium, which will open on the same site three years later. (Metro Nashville Archives, MDHA Collection.)

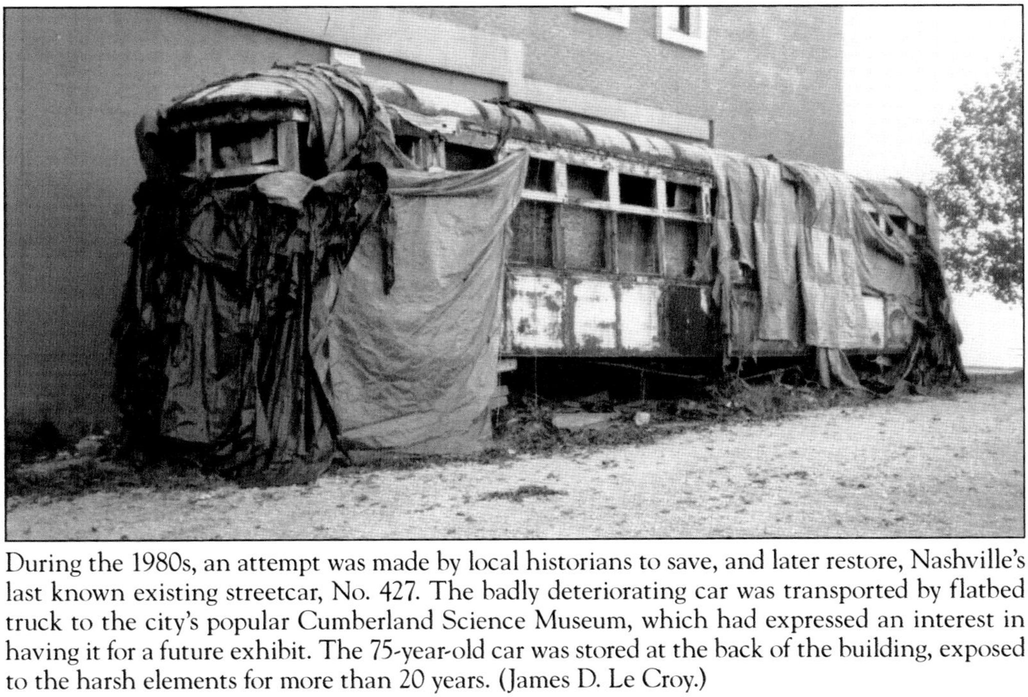

During the 1980s, an attempt was made by local historians to save, and later restore, Nashville's last known existing streetcar, No. 427. The badly deteriorating car was transported by flatbed truck to the city's popular Cumberland Science Museum, which had expressed an interest in having it for a future exhibit. The 75-year-old car was stored at the back of the building, exposed to the harsh elements for more than 20 years. (James D. Le Croy.)

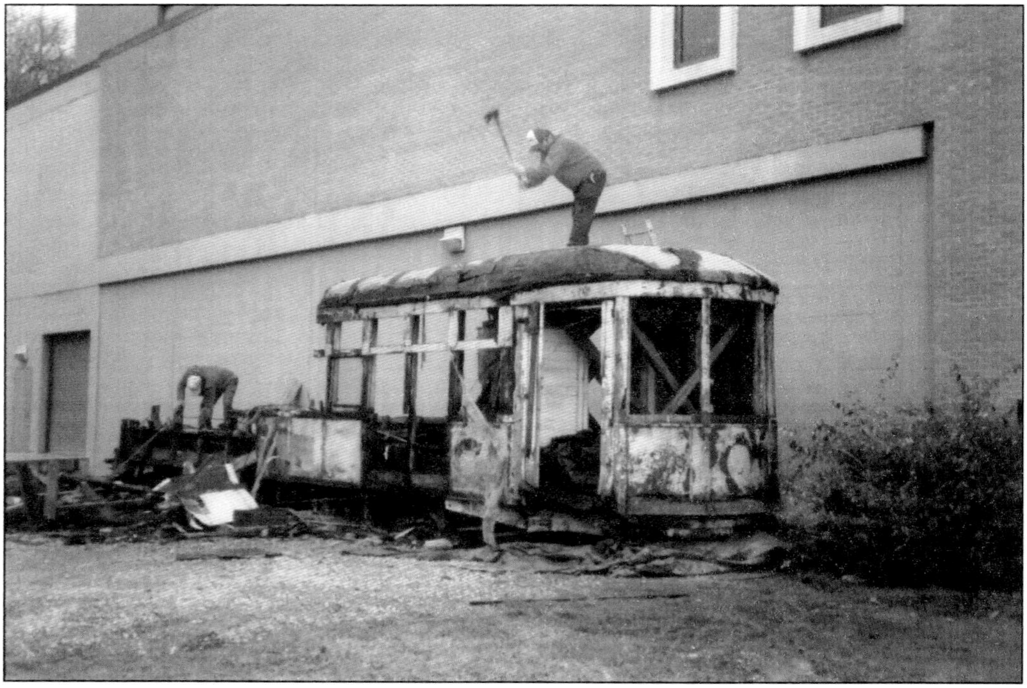

Around 2002, the museum announced a major expansion, placing more emphasis on science and technology. Sadly, the rotting wooden car, No. 427, was beyond repair, with few volunteers or the needed resources to restore it to its original glory. With heavy construction on the museum addition ready to begin and no future home for the car, there was no choice but to scrap it in place. (Both, James D. Le Croy.)

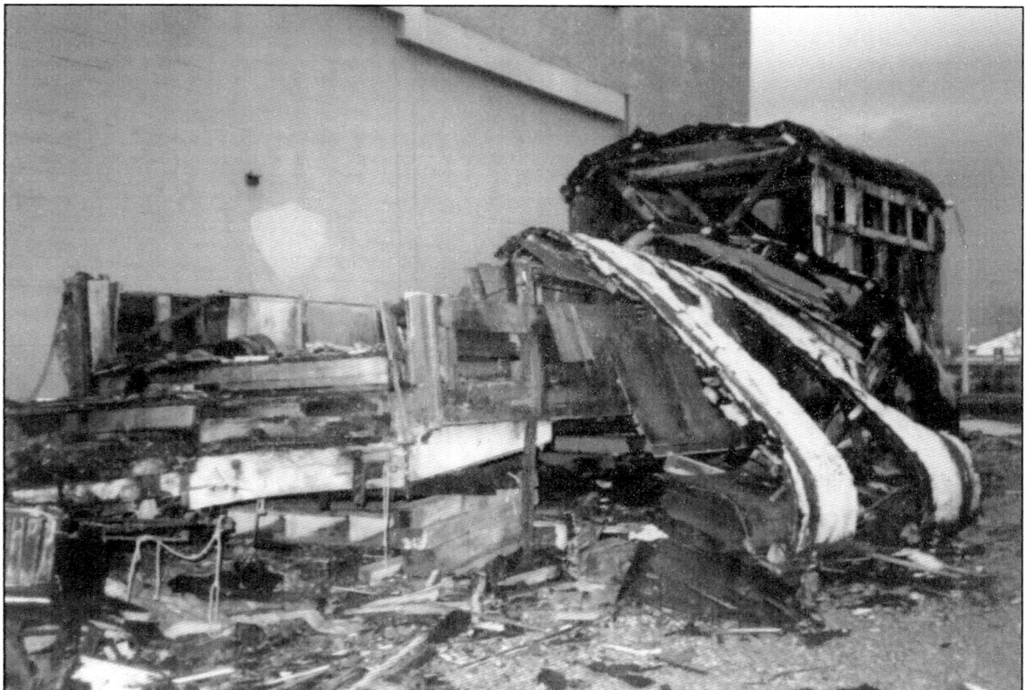

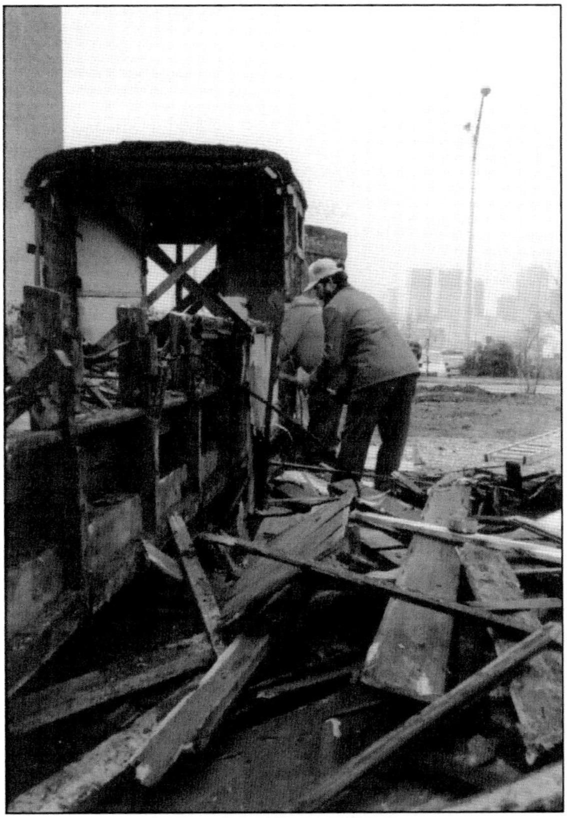

On a cold and dreary day, workmen reduce the deteriorated car to a pile of lumber. Nashville's skyline can be seen in the background. (Both, James D. Le Croy.)

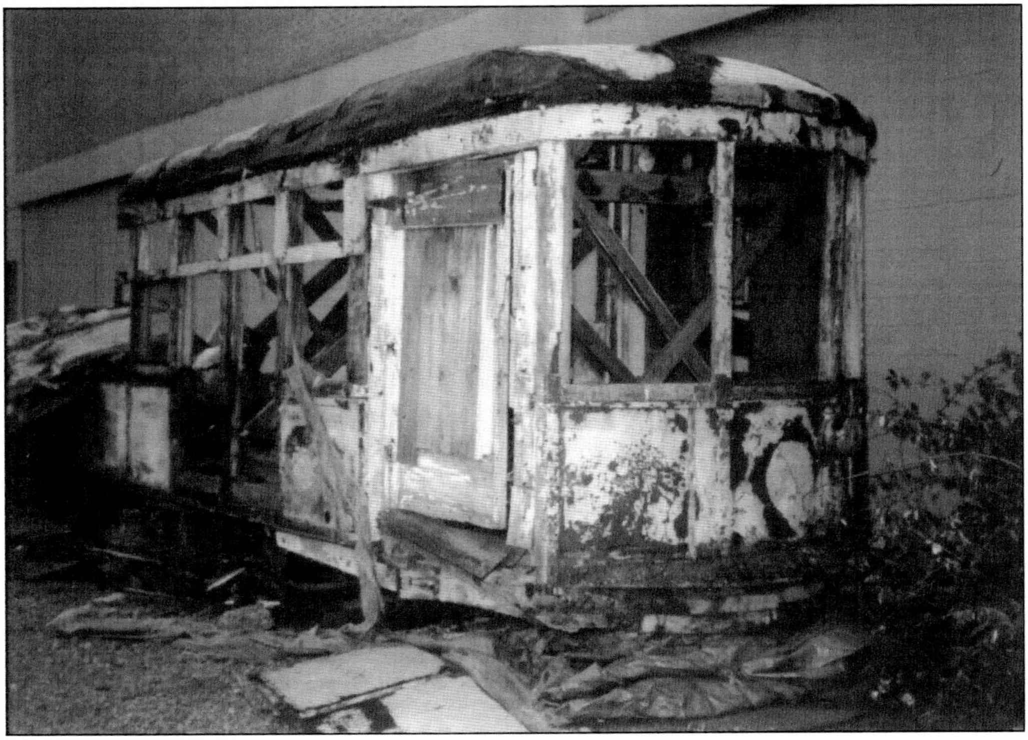

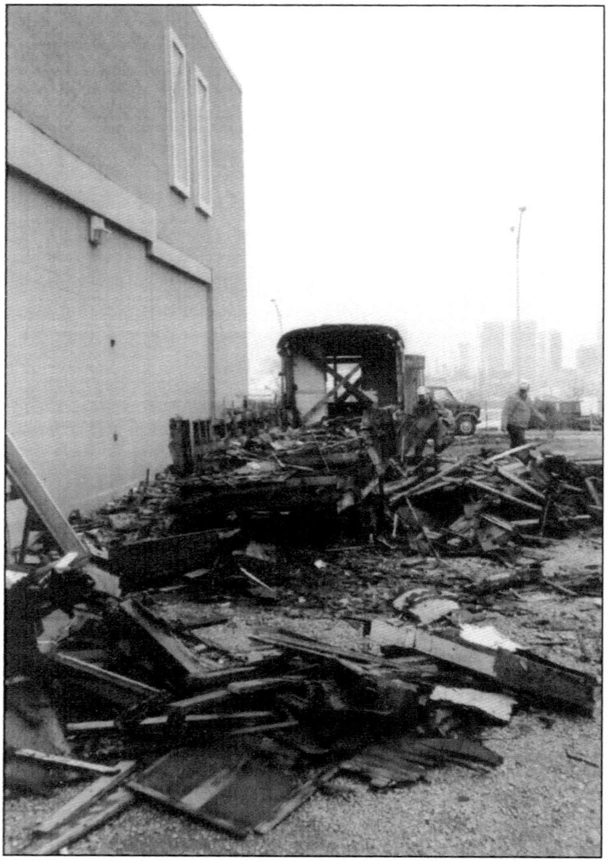

Soon, trucks will haul the wood and steel to a landfill, bringing down the curtain on the last of Nashville's streetcar history. (James D. Le Croy collection.)

Today, little remains of Nashville's street railway system. The last known remaining streetcar was scrapped in 2002. However, around that same time, a small section of streetcar track was unearthed during a sewer repair project on First Avenue; it was later donated to the Nashville-based Tennessee Central Railway Museum. The rails are preserved in concrete on the museum grounds. (Bryan Turner.)

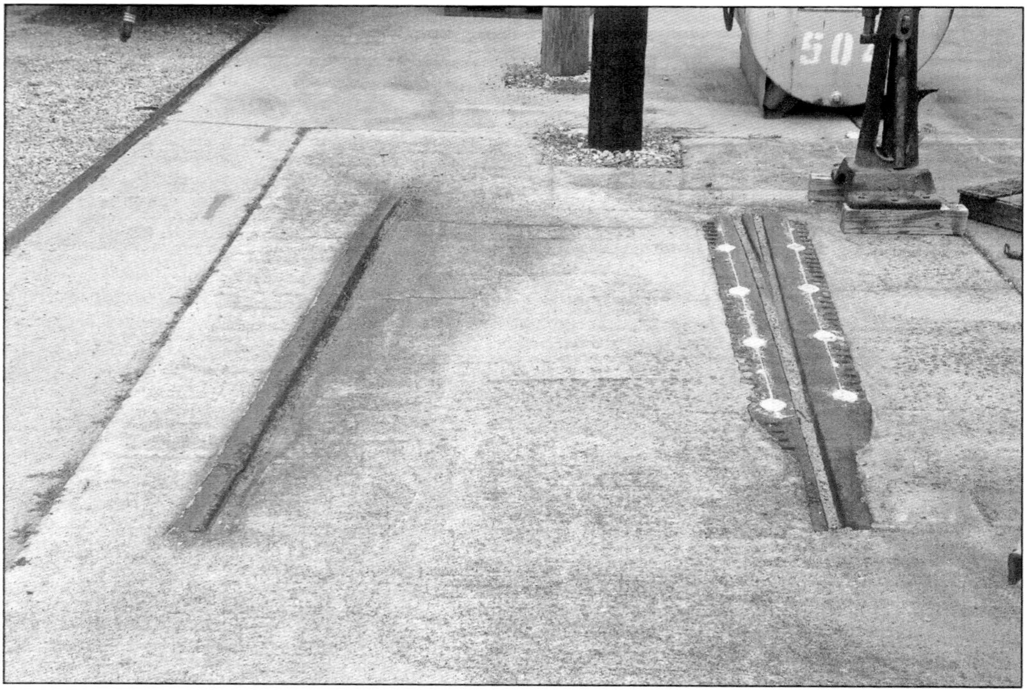

BIBLIOGRAPHY

Centennial Commission Board of Directors. *Nashville City Guide Book*. Nashville, TN: 1880.

City Planning and Zoning Commission. *Nashville Transportation Survey*. Nashville, TN: 1937.

Crouch, Arthur W. *Charters, Amendments, County Grants, City Franchises and Private Rights-of-Way of the Nashville Railway & Light Company*. Nashville, TN.

Morton, M.B. "History of the Street Railway System of Nashville." *Electro Topics Magazine*. November 1930.

Various issues of the *Nashville American*, *Nashville Banner*, *Nashville Daily Gazette*, *Nashville Tennessean*, *Street Railway Journal*, *Street Railway Review*, and *Transit Journal*.